AFFECT AS CULTURAL CRITIQUE

Methods for Ethnographic Uncovering

Edited by Daniel White, Emma E. Cook, and Andrea De Antoni

Affect as Cultural Critique assembles leading anthropologists, affect theorists, and artist-activist scholars to ask, What if the most constructive response to moments of ethnographic puzzlement was not the formulation of an answer but the cultivation of a feeling? What if understanding the powerful effects of discourses requires somatic rather than semiotic exercises? And, where habits of academic professionalism prohibit experiencing possible worlds, what if anthropology as a discipline could leverage affect to differently connect and cultivate collaboration with others?

In line with growing movements to decolonize the academy, the essays in *Affect as Cultural Critique* feature ethnographic accounts of people actively describing, experimenting with, and otherwise exercising affect in ways that challenge the academy's inherited models for analysing emotional life. Through an experimental collection of traditional ethnographic essays and artist-activist-generated critiques, this volume explores how everyday modes of feeling function as methods of knowing. By centring non-academic and non-Western affective practices as answers to traditional theoretical problems generated primarily by Western theorists, *Affect as Cultural Critique* seeks new trajectories for the discipline through a reciprocal practice of uncovering as a guiding professional aim, as methodological inspiration, and as a source of reflexive critique of the discipline's philosophical and theory-heavy analytics.

DANIEL WHITE is an associate fellow at the Leverhulme Centre for the Future of Intelligence at the University of Cambridge.

EMMA E. COOK is a professor of modern Japanese studies at Hokkaido University.

ANDREA DE ANTONI is an associate professor in cultural anthropology at Kyoto University and research coordinator of the Italian School of East Asian Studies (ISEAS) in Kyoto.

Affect as Cultural Critique

Methods for Ethnographic Uncovering

EDITED BY DANIEL WHITE, EMMA E. COOK,
AND ANDREA DE ANTONI

UNIVERSITY OF TORONTO PRESS
Toronto Buffalo London

© University of Toronto Press 2026
Toronto Buffalo London
utppublishing.com
Printed and bound by CPI Group (UK) Ltd, Croydon, CR0 4YY

ISBN 978-1-4875-5979-3 (paper)   ISBN 978-1-4875-5981-6 (EPUB)
                                 ISBN 978-1-4875-5980-9 (PDF)

___

Library and Archives Canada Cataloguing in Publication

Title: Affect as cultural critique : methods for ethnographic uncovering / edited by Daniel White, Emma E. Cook, and Andrea De Antoni.
Names: White, Daniel, 1980– editor | Cook, Emma E., editor | De Antoni, Andrea, editor.
Description: Includes bibliographical references and index.
Identifiers: Canadiana (print) 20250248514 | Canadiana (ebook) 20250248557 | ISBN 9781487559793 (paper) | ISBN 9781487559816 (EPUB) | ISBN 9781487559809 (PDF)
Subjects: LCSH: Emotions – Anthropological aspects. | LCSH: Affect (Psychology) – Research – Methodology. | LCSH: Culture – Research – Methodology. | LCSH: Ethnology – Methodology.
Classification: LCC GN519 .A34 2026 | DDC 152.4072/1 – dc23

___

Cover design: Rafael Chimicatti

The manufacturer's authorised representative in the EU for product safety is Mare Nostrum Group B.V., Mauritskade 21D, 1091 GC Amsterdam, The Netherlands. Email: gpsr@mare-nostrum.co.uk

We wish to acknowledge the land on which the University of Toronto Press operates. This land is the traditional territory of the Wendat, the Anishnaabeg, the Haudenosaunee, the Métis, and the Mississaugas of the Credit First Nation.

University of Toronto Press acknowledges the financial support of the Government of Canada, the Canada Council for the Arts, and the Ontario Arts Council, an agency of the Government of Ontario, for its publishing activities.

 Canada Council for the Arts / Conseil des Arts du Canada

 ONTARIO ARTS COUNCIL
CONSEIL DES ARTS DE L'ONTARIO
an Ontario government agency
un organisme du gouvernement de l'Ontario

 Funded by the Government of Canada / Financé par le gouvernement du Canada

Contents

List of Illustrations   ix

Motivations and Map to the Book   3
DANIEL WHITE, EMMA E. COOK, AND ANDREA DE ANTONI

Preliminaries

1 Meeting Affect Halfway   13
DOMINIC BOYER AND CYMENE HOWE

2 Where to Now? Affect and Mediation in Multimodal Productions of Ethnographic Research   18
GEORGE E. MARCUS

3 Convivialities of Emotion and Affect Research   21
DANIEL WHITE AND CATHERINE LUTZ

4 Proliferation   26
KATHLEEN STEWART

Chapters

Introduction: Affect as Cultural Critique   33
DANIEL WHITE

1 Sensing the World: Intuition as a Musical and Social Orientation   61
YANA STAINOVA

2 Interiority Currency as Affective Method: Racialized Affect,
  Therapeutic Cultures, and Latin American Elites   83
  ANA Y. RAMOS-ZAYAS

3 The Devil Is in the Details: Affect and Creativity in Discerning
  Illness and Demonic Possession in Contemporary Italy   107
  ANDREA DE ANTONI

4 Serious Play and the Facilitation of Feeling in Food Allergy
  Advocacy in Japan   132
  EMMA E. COOK

5 On Moral Thresholds: Shi'i Zakirs and the Surface Tension of Public
  Affect in Pakistan   157
  TIMOTHY P.A. COOPER

6 What Sticks: Affective Scholarship in Times of Pandemic Past
  and Present   182
  THOMAS STODULKA

Commentaries

1 Recasting Affect Theory's Genealogies: Centring Feeling with
  Historicizing Approaches   215
  YAEL NAVARO

2 Kathleen Stewart Turned Me: Apprehensions of Affect   224
  WILLIAM MAZZARELLA

Practices

1 Haku: Decolonizing Intimacies   235
  JAMAICA HEOLIMELEIKALANI OSORIO

2 Adaptation: Affect, Happiness, and Sexual Inclusion
  in *Pride and Protest*   244
  NICHOLE CARELOCK

3 Listening: Sonorous Affect   252
  MARIÉ ABE

4 Meditating: Attention to Affect   259
  JOANNA COOK

5 Making: A Robot's Homecoming   268
   ELENA KNOX

Dedication   277

Acknowledgments   279

Contributors   281

Index   289

Illustrations

P1.1 Memorial to Okjökull glacier, summer 2019   16
3.1 Differential diagnostic process (general) flowchart   116
3.2 Centre stages flowchart   120
4.1 Ranran Lunch card game   138
5.1 Overlaid posters advertise upcoming majlis gatherings   165
5.2 Budding zakirs recite to a mixed assembly of men, women, and children   166
6.1 Newspaper headline: "Thousands of people under surveillance …"   185
6.2 Thermo-gun   185
6.3 Poster: "As preventive steps …"   186
6.4 Billboard: "How to prevent COVID-19"   187
6.5 Sign in elevator   188
6.6 Sticky tape   189
6.7 Sticky tape   190
6.8 Display: "Obviously, I have the better mask!"   192
6.9 Display: "There is no need for panic buying"   193
6.10 Airport sign   194
6.11 Arrival gate at the airport   195
6.12 Barrier tape   195
6.13 Sticky tape   196
6.14 Sticky tape   197
P.5.1 PARO on location shoot of *Protective Seal*   269
P.5.2 PARO and Elena Knox on location shoot of *Protective Seal*   271

AFFECT AS CULTURAL CRITIQUE

Methods for Ethnographic Uncovering

Motivations and Map to the Book

DANIEL WHITE, EMMA E. COOK,
AND ANDREA DE ANTONI

The purpose of this volume is to explore the critical value of affective practices. Its strategy is two-fold. First, it features feeling-focused practices of interlocutors as non-discursive methods of being in the world, relating with it and others well, and empirically unravelling its mysteries. Second, it leverages those practices to forms of constructive cultural critique of both the cultural contexts interlocutors call their own and, in a reflexive mode, disciplinary habits of Western academic theorizing. Simply put, the volume features ways of feeling and of cultivating feeling that can be applied to collaborative practices of *uncovering*, which we understand as a process of ethical encounter, transformational relating, reciprocal learning, and mutual enlightening.

Given its focus on practices of feeling, we felt it appropriate to open the text with an affective practice of our own: a setting of the volume's motivations. It is a practice drawn from and shared by many contemplative traditions documented in the ethnographic record, as well as by some of those featured in this volume (see in particular J. Cook). Its purpose is to align one's affective capacities – symbolized by the "heart" in many traditions but sometimes by the "gut" or "stomach" in others – with one's conscious intentions. The practice seeks to ensure that one's motivations are best placed to be of some benefit to those the practice might impact – in this case, our readers.

So with an acknowledgment of gratitude to our readers, we express our hope that this volume serves as a broad invitation to readers of various academic schools, theories, and traditions concerned with the mechanics of human and more-than-human feeling to take refuge in *feeling* itself as a diverse but shared activity worthy of continued exercise, experimentation, and examination. As we have found over many years of practising forms of critique that we inherited through our academic – mostly anthropological – training, many times our modes of inquiry have excluded rather than invited. Even more problematically, while our polished ethnographic products (monographs, articles, lectures) often featured theory-heavy language accessible most readily to similarly trained academics, the collection of data in those products was derived from explicit affective exercises of openness and connection-making between researcher and interlocutor collaboratively working to cultivate a common ground.

When it comes to affect theory in the academy, common ground can sometimes be hard to find. But deriving inspiration from our many interlocutors, and the mutual practices of connection and conviviality that generated shared understandings within contexts of difference, we seek that ground here. We endeavour to create a welcoming textual space that invites all those engaged in inquiry and critique of emotional forms of life to learn from the diverse interlocutors featured here about how feeling itself can function as a method for constructive inquiry: *affect as cultural critique*.

Drawing inspiration from creative ethnographic formats of the 1980s and more recent innovative writings in affect-focused ethnography, our book is experimental. Accordingly, the text is organized in a non-traditional way that enables the book's structure to operate affectively and constructively for readers. We offer this uncommon but carefully considered organization for the book – and outline a map of that organization here – to demonstrate one way to shift from more conventional practices of scholarly engagements with emotion, affect, and affect theory towards increasingly non-traditional and socially engaged modes of scholarship. The volume consists of what we call *Preliminaries* (short context-setting essays), *Chapters* (traditional-length ethnographic essays), *Commentaries* (direct challenges to and suggested innovations upon established trends in affect theory), and, most importantly, *Practices* (demonstrations of how non-traditional academic practices at the intersections of anthropology, art, and activism can push affective practices into new terrain for cultural analysis and critique). We close the book with a *Dedication* that seeks to ensure our contributors' collective academic effort is charged with a form of affect that is inviting, constructive, and open to mutual discovery and collaborative forms of critique.

We find inspiration for this textual organization in practice-based contemplative traditions that are not often incorporated into Western academic analytics but are increasingly inspiring affect-based approaches around the world to public health, mental well-being, education, community building, environmental engagement, and non-materialist forms of research.[1] For example, in certain Buddhist traditions that some of our contributors study (J. Cook, De Antoni, White), particular texts or portions of texts are categorized as "preliminary practices," such as in *ngöndro* practices of Tibetan Vajrayana. These consist of practices (thematic contemplations, meditations, bodily movements, ethical reflections, commitments) that require proficiency to generate benefits from the "core practices" that follow. In this regard, preliminaries are often said to be as important as the core practices. Accordingly, in this volume our Preliminaries are not prefaces of secondary importance to the chapters that follow but rather important context-setting pieces that sequentially lay the groundwork to support and internalize what follows. Similarly, like certain commentarial collections from the Tibetan tradition (e.g., Tengyur), or collections of treatises canonical to early Buddhist traditions (e.g., Abhidharma), which incorporate scholarly insights on doctrinal texts, our own Commentaries acknowledge the tradition of affect scholarship informing our work.[2] Specifically, our Commentaries add direct interpretations of, challenges to, and innovations on currents of affect theory rather than commenting on specific chapters in the volume. From this point of view, our Commentaries facilitate a transition from the volume's more traditional academic chapters to its more unconventional *Practices*, which are not addenda to the book but rather its culminating components. Practices essays further demonstrate the book's purpose to model reparative forms of convivial critique within affect studies, which we hope will add to ongoing creative experiments taking place on the borders of and outside the academy. In this regard, the volume's structural organization, its method, and its practice-based approach to affect and the social engagement it models in its *Practices* essays constitute intentional strategies to decolonize some of the academy's traditional analytics and forms of scholarly production.

Although we recommend readers follow in sequential order the map for the book we outline above and in the Contents, we acknowledge there are alternative ways to read and teach the book – such as by drawing one essay from each section to highlight certain themes like *the sensory, politics/ethics,* or *environmental engagement*. Towards that end, in the following section, we offer a more detailed summary of the book's contents and invite our readers to explore different approaches to reading, teaching, and indeed critiquing the book.

Organization and Description of Contents

The book opens with four *Preliminary* essays offered by formative anthropological thinkers on emotion, affect, and cultural critique.

Dominic Boyer and Cymene Howe begin the volume by describing a turning point in affect studies and how and why they commissioned a series in *Cultural Anthropology* – which inspired this volume – to document it. George Marcus, who, along with Michael Fischer, authored *Anthropology as Cultural Critique* in 1986 and whose title inspires our own, situates concerns with affect within a longer history of anthropological reflexivity. Daniel White and Catherine Lutz's Preliminary essay situates affect theory within ethnographic studies of emotion, reconnecting lines of thought between the two approaches that have sometimes been unnecessarily cut. Finally, Kathleen Stewart addresses aspects of "proliferation" tied to both styles of critique and shared predicaments, demonstrating in typical eloquence what alternatives to critique's more "paranoid" habits of thought might look like.

The book then proceeds to an introductory chapter called "Affect as Cultural Critique," which lays out in detail the central argument and purpose of the volume. Following this introduction are six core chapters that take on different engagements with affect as experimental exercises in critique. Each chapter follows a similar strategy of undoing and reworking established anthropological theory towards productively diverse ends. They do so in three principal ways, albeit not necessarily in this order. First, each essay identifies a problematization familiar to both anthropological and interlocutor theorists, such as the boundary between reason and intuition (Stainova), the anxiety inspired by potentially dangerous food (Cook), or the fear of individuals possessed by dangerous spirits (De Antoni). Next, each chapter describes how anthropological theory has faced limitations by treating this problematization as an analytical puzzle in need of a logical resolution. Finally, in response, each chapter explores – sometimes experimentally – how an affective encounter generates ways of acting and feeling that do not resolve in an explanatory framework of traditional anthropological analytics but nonetheless powerfully hold cultural, ethical, political, and technological worlds together *affectively* in ways that seem impossible *discursively*. In privileging a description of what affect does over an explanation of what it is and how it works, each of the authors leverages the affective methods of interlocutors to uncover experiences, stories, and knowledge that have, until now, been marginalized by anthropology's dominant styles of theorization and knowledge production. In this, the volume presents the affective methods of our interlocutors' engagements with the world as resources for the constructive critique of anthropology's own disciplinary culture.

In chapter 1, Yana Stainova builds off her previous work on enchantment as an anthropological method. Grounded in long-term ethnographic fieldwork with classical musicians in Venezuela, she engages with the social production of *intuición*, or intuition, as a force in people's lives in the realm of the aesthetic and in the everyday. Through intimate stories surrounding the growth of a community music school, she shows how sensations of *intuición* can radically interrupt the logics of racial and gender violence deeply rooted in Venezuelan society.

In chapter 2, Ana Y. Ramos-Zayas develops her previous work on "racialized affect" (Berg and Ramos-Zayas 2015) and applies it to the everyday lives of upper-class parents in the neighbourhoods of Ipanema (Brazil) and El Condado (Puerto Rico). By documenting the ubiquity of therapeutic cultures and public feelings in intimate conversations between ethnographer and interlocutor, she breaks down the surfaces that enclose the "interiority" of feelings and instead posits affect as a shared problem that risks certain racist and classist complicities.

In chapter 3, Andrea De Antoni analyses processes of doing mental illnesses and demonic possession through "differential diagnosis" among Roman Catholic exorcists and the medical doctors who collaborate with them in contemporary Italy. By shedding light on how affects can shift the distribution of authority and responsibility in diagnostic practices in ways that challenge dominant scientific analytics, he argues that affective methods can uncover novel understandings of both demonic possession and illness.

Chapter 4 takes up sensitivities to food allergens in Japan. By "playing and thinking seriously" about a food allergy card game organized by a non-profit organization that supports people with allergic diseases, Emma E. Cook communicates what it might be like to eat out while navigating the anxious practicalities of asking about allergens. Challenging anthropological accounts that suggest that empathy is a quality that individuals possess or need to cultivate more of to understand others, Cook argues that empathy can be made productive to trace how feelings are mobilized in efforts to increase cooperation and collaboration to affectively empathic ends.

In chapter 5, Timothy Cooper takes up the question of moral limits as a sensation rather than as a code or set of prescriptions. The problem of how to cohabit affective thresholds is one that animates the lives of Shi'i Muslim *zakirs* and their audiences in Pakistan. Zakirs are responsible for cultivating the affective and emotional atmosphere at Shi'i mourning and celebratory assemblies. Based on ethnographic encounters with Shi'i media, mediators, and categories of mediation, the chapter follows a single Shi'i zakir's navigation of the moral thresholds implicit in his craft and the ways in which these thresholds are redrawn in collaboration with Shi'i and non-Shi'i audiences.

Chapter 6 offers a retrospective on anxiety over COVID-19, its aftermath, related states of global crisis, and the transformative impacts on anthropological research contexts. As Thomas Stodulka observes, the COVID-19 pandemic compelled anthropologists to reflect on the strengths of their intimate in-person methods, the limits of those methods under states of crisis, and the advantages of collaborating with interlocutors through digital forms of online conversation and the analysis of mediatized artefacts. Through part photo-essay, part emotion-diary, and part travelogue from COVID-19-sensitive Indonesia to Germany, Stodulka explores the affects that stick in difficult situations, as well as affects that stick situations and people together in spaces of collaborative body-based theorizing.

Next, the text turns to Yael Navaro and William Mazzarella, who answered our invitations to offer a critique of this volume itself. In the form of *Commentaries*, each essay exercises ways of writing affect as cultural critique. While also anticipating limits to this mode, each author opens possibilities for affect as cultural critique beyond the volume. Navaro seeks specific ways to decolonize affect theory, pointing to dominant theoretical trends in the field as well as to alternatives. Mazzarella, drawing direct inspiration from Kathleen Stewart, performs a personal undoing of his own inherited modes of critique, demonstrating what affective alternatives might arise as a consequence.

Finally, while affective methods of ethnographic uncovering feature throughout the volume, the last section turns more explicitly to *practice*. These essays respond to Boyer and Howe's call in their Preliminary essay to this volume to "meet affect halfway" by diversifying the mediums through which scholars engage with affect. The Practices section features colleagues who work in but also actively beyond the academy in ways that challenge conventional depictions of affect. Through poetry, fiction, music, meditation, and performative art, the closing and culminating *Practices* essays offer examples of the many creative projects by which people respond – responsively and responsibly – to the world first and foremost through affect. We hope these essays might contribute to similar projects of engaged anthropology and activism already in action around the globe.

NOTES

1 In the last two decades, the concept of the *contemplative* has globalized, in large part due to increasing intersections between Western academic scholars/scientists and Asian Buddhist practitioners, and formal

discussions among these groups facilitated by organizations such as the Mind and Life Institute. The term has also been incorporated into an emerging academic field called *contemplative science*. Informed heavily by the work of B. Alan Wallace, former scholar of religious studies at the University of California, Santa Barbara and Director of the Center for Contemplative Research (CCR) in Crestone, Colorado, the CCR (2025) defines *contemplative science* as "a discipline of first-person, subjective inquiry into the nature of the mind and its role in Nature, which utilizes methods for developing refined attention, mindfulness, and introspection to directly observe states of consciousness and mental functions in their relationship with the body and the physical world at large" ("Contemplative Science"). We find this a good definition of contemplative traditions more broadly, inclusive of diverse philosophical and religious traditions that emphasize first-person inquiry and affective experiences that often feel to practitioners as more legitimate and truer than can be captured in discursive descriptions of those experiences.

2 See Baums (2015) for a brief history of Buddhist commentarial traditions.

REFERENCES

Baums, Stefan. "Commentary: Overview." In *Brill's Encyclopedia of Buddhism online*, 409–18. Brill, 2015.

Berg, Ulla D., and Ana Y. Ramos-Zayas. 2015. "Racializing Affect: A Theoretical Proposition." *Current Anthropology* 56 (5): 654–77. https://doi.org/10.1086/683053.

Center for Contemplative Research (CCR). 2025. "Terms and Definitions: Contemplative Science." Accessed 15 August 2025. https://centerforcontemplativeresearch.org/terms-definitionst/.

Preliminaries

Preliminary 1

Meeting Affect Halfway

DOMINIC BOYER AND CYMENE HOWE

We wish to thank the editors of *Affect as Cultural Critique* for their kind invitation to join the ranks of this volume's talented preliminarians. We have been asked to write a few words about how an earlier edition of this project first took shape during our editorship (2015–8), together with James Faubion, of the journal *Cultural Anthropology* (*CA*). The story begins with the design process that went into our editorial mission. In addition to managing the ongoing processes of the journal's open-access transition and online publishing expansion, we added two new features to the legacy journal during our editorship.

The first feature, *Sound + Vision*, sought to advance the multimodal transformation of anthropological publication. It did so for reasons that tap deeply into the affective attentions and ambitions of this volume. Academic writing has a fairly narrow affective bandwidth (and, pen to table, perhaps 90 per cent of that bandwidth seems to be occupied by anxiety). We wondered if adding new mediational capacities could create new kinds of creative and communicative experiences. We asked authors about how they thought the anthropological research article of the future should look (and sound and feel). What features and affordances could it offer? Should embedded video and moving images play a role? How about soundtracks and sound clips? What if you were able to connect an article to a three-dimensional printer to materialize certain objects of ethnographic narrative? We hoped to create an epistemic infrastructure rather than a series of one-offs; that is, reinventing the platform for each individual article was not tenable in terms of time, labour, and expense. Our objective was instead to serially develop an infrastructure that would, nonetheless, be potentially transformative in how anthropological knowledge could be expressed and circulated. The desire was to find new ways to capture and mobilize the unique intimacy and multisensory character of anthropological research.

Sound + Vision had some genuine experimental successes – perhaps most notably "Golden Snail Opera," a magnificent fusion of film and research article, undertaken by Anna Tsing and her collaborators (2016). But on the whole, our sense in retrospect is that *Sound + Vision*'s exploratory adventure was either ahead of its time or too illegible to the genre and publishing conventions of academic anthropological writing. Surprisingly few authors seemed interested in animating their articles with new mediational capacities.

The second feature, *Openings and Retrospectives*, was much more popular with authors and readers alike. *Openings and Retrospectives* was meant as *CA*'s take on the special issue collection. Most of our articles were ethnographically driven, but we wanted to create space for more conceptually driven interventions as well. Still, we knew that less was generally more when it came to theoretical articles. The audience's patience with extensive theoretical commentary was low. Ditto with circuitous argument-building as authors froggered their way forward from log to log across a fast-moving river of concepts. So we sought clusters of shorter essays, maximum four thousand words, putting forth tight arguments around contemporary thematics of interest. We borrowed the language of the art world to organize a distinction between two kinds of clusters. *Openings* focused on emergent thematics, imagining what anthropologists ought to be talking about next. *Retrospectives* intervened in already mature thematic conversations, not only looking backwards to take stock but also seeking to spin them in new directions. Both kinds of clusters were encouraged to be contemporary in their orientation, providing commentary on where anthropological thinking and writing were at that moment. Interestingly, the vast majority of proposed collections were *Openings*, as authors seemed much more eager to advise where anthropological conversation ought to move next than to probe, for example, why a thematic or analytic like affect already seemed so diversely compelling.

This is why we were so delighted when Daniel White developed a *Retrospective* on affect, which was published in the May 2017 issue. White did an excellent job of pulling the many philosophical, psychological, and anthropological threads of the "affective turn" together while showing how affect's capacity to evade epistemic "capture" created unique challenges and opportunities for anthropology to pursue affect's various intensities, "arisings, and appropriations." In the same collection, Catherine Lutz (2017) analysed the rise of affect theory with a view to its precursors, arguing that anthropological studies of emotion yielded equally keen insight into relational personhood and the capillary politics of sociality. Kathleen Stewart (2017) mused that affect "forms part of a renewed search for modes of ethnographic theory and critique divested from the distanced, sheerly evaluative plane of academic conversation based on the stability of academic terms" (195) inciting us to attend instead to the "labors of living" (195) and how things move in and out of existence in states of emergence and precarity. William Mazzarella (2017) highlighted the interfolding of the intimate and impersonal in affect theory and suggested the "affect/ethics impasse necessarily triggered by the existential predicament of mass-mediated subjectivity" (204) as fertile ground for further anthropological inquiry. Finally, Yael Navaro (2017) encouraged readers to seek out non-Western genealogies of affect, surfacing three cross-communitarian forms – the remnant, the serendipitous, and the transcendent – that arose out of her fieldwork in Turkey.

Eight years later, affect theory remains a nourishing aquifer for anthropological reflection and conversation. Unsurprisingly, White's *Retrospective* became one of the most widely read and cited collections that we published at *CA*. It seems fitting that the project continues to develop and to acquire new shapes and intensities in the present volume.

Circling back to where we started, we do wonder, however, what might have happened had *Affect as Cultural Critique* begun its life in the *Sound + Vision* incubator rather than as a *Retrospective*. Writing is a marvellous medium for corporeal imagination; it can stir the heart and move the hands. But what critical capacities might have been unlocked had the pursuit of affective intensities been opened to a wider sensorium via sound, image, touch, and taste? This is not meant as criticism of the present volume but rather as an invitation, perhaps in future project iterations, to eventually exceed it.

Although neither of us is an affect scholar per se, we are certainly "affect-curious" and have in the past few years come to feel the substantial gap between the affective capacities of academic writing and other media. This feeling, itself a restless intensity, has prompted us to lean ever more heavily into creative approaches to forming and sharing anthropological knowledge. We have a long-running podcast (https://cenhs.libsyn.com); we made a documentary film (www.notokmovie.com) and an experiential game and are currently developing a television series. We work on climate change, and the existential stakes of this struggle, combined with widespread political inaction, make us twitchily hungry for modes of intervention capable of affecting thought and action. Katie Stewart (2008) has written that there are moments when a new sensibility "snaps into place" (77). We are eager to do what we can with our anthropological skills to prompt these moments to inspire

16   Dominic Boyer and Cymene Howe

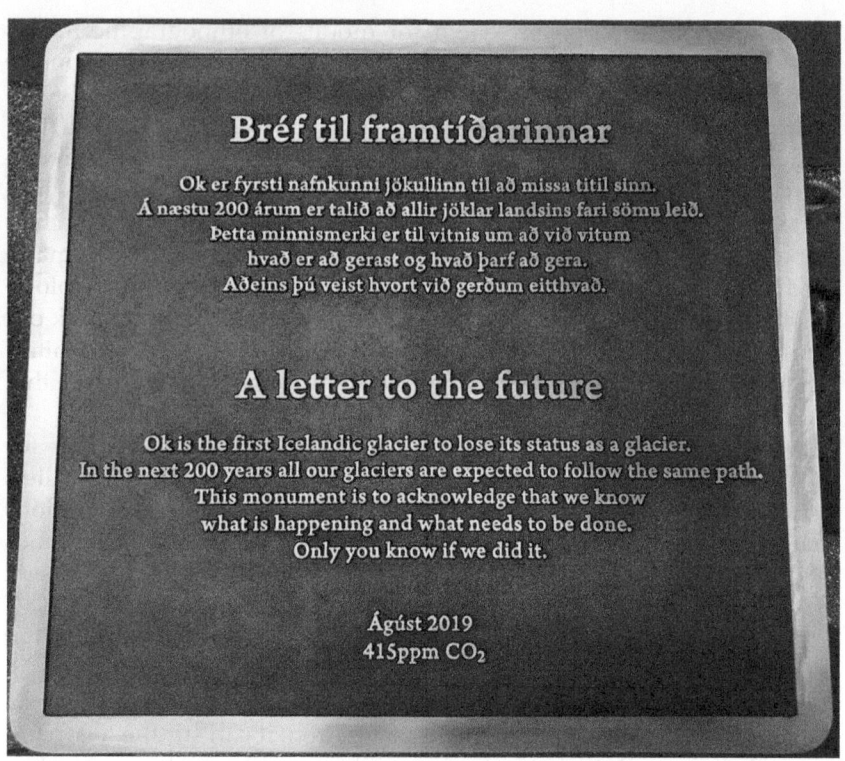

Figure P1.1. Memorial to Okjökull glacier, summer 2019.
Photo by Dominic Boyer.

climate awareness and action; we are also acutely aware of the limits of conventional academic writing to prompt snapping into place beyond specialized academic sub-publics.

Our concern, to be clear, comes from a place of love. During our four years of editing *CA*, we read and produced editorial commentary on over one thousand manuscripts, some of them several times over. What kept us going through those long hours of editorial care work was a bottomless affection for anthropological knowledge. It is academia at its best. But we also feel that it is fair to recognize that the sum total of the affective impact of our years of editorial engagement at *CA* will be far smaller than the sixty words we commissioned from Icelandic writer Andri Snær Magnason (and reshaped ever so slightly) for the memorial to Okjökull glacier that we created in the summer of 2019 (Figure P1.1).

Within days of the first publication of this image, the story of the world's first memorial to a glacier fallen to climate change circulated in thousands of news media outlets across the world. It found lift from the usual stalwarts of environmental journalism like *The Guardian*, but it also wormed itself into strange places like *Elle* magazine and even *Popular Mechanics*, hardly a pillar of the environmental movement. The glacier memorial brought tears to many, and it angered some. But its intensity was conveyed to millions; it *moved* people. We mention it only to say that we agree wholeheartedly that anthropology should engage affect as a mode of cultural critique. This is long overdue. But to make the most of that intervention, we would urge anthropologists to exceed their own publishing conventions and encourage themselves to take their remarkable capacities into new narratives, media, and even materialities. If the true objective is cultural critique on a wider scale, we have to ask how anthropology can better move people, either on its own or in collaboration. We need to meet affect halfway.

REFERENCES

Lutz, Catherine. 2017. "What Matters." *Cultural Anthropology* 32 (2): 181–91. https://doi.org/10.14506/ca32.2.02.
Mazzarella, William. 2017. "Sense Out of Sense: Notes on the Affect/Ethics Impasse." *Cultural Anthropology* 32 (2): 199–208. https://doi.org/10.14506/ca32.2.04.
Navaro, Yael. 2017. "Diversifying Affect." *Cultural Anthropology* 32 (2): 209–14. https://doi.org/10.14506/ca32.2.05.
Stewart, Kathleen. 2008. "Weak Theory in an Unfinished World." *Journal of Folklore Research* 45 (1): 71–82. muse.jhu.edu/article/239801.
Stewart, Kathleen. 2017. "In the World that Affect Proposed." *Cultural Anthropology* 32 (2): 192–8. https://doi.org/10.14506/ca32.2.03.
Tsai, Yen-Ling, Isabelle Carbonell, Joelle Chevrier, and Anna Lowenhaupt Tsing. 2016. "Golden Snail Opera: The More-Than-Human Performance of Friendly Farming on Taiwan's Lanyang Plain." *Cultural Anthropology* 31 (4): 520–44. https://doi.org/10.14506/ca31.4.04.
White, Daniel. 2017. "Affect: An Introduction." *Cultural Anthropology* 32 (2): 175–80. https://doi.org/10.14506/ca32.2.01.

Preliminary 2

Where to Now? Affect and Mediation in Multimodal Productions of Ethnographic Research

GEORGE E. MARCUS

Adopting *affect as method* means using feeling as a means for generating insight, guiding fieldwork choices and practice, and, above all, understanding interlocutors when they are suggesting that neither their own nor the anthropologists' terms are quite adequate.
– Daniel White, Introduction to this volume

I very much appreciate the opportunity to join others in writing one of the brief *Preliminaries* to this collection, an earlier version of which I first read and was stimulated by in the journal *Cultural Anthropology* in 2017. The contributors to this volume have expanded and richly elaborated that issue.

About that time, "multimodality" was also gaining ground and legitimation in US anthropology, increasing immensely the possibilities of new collaborations between ethnography and an array of performing and graphic arts, design disciplines, and information and engineering sciences, moving by different degrees and leaps of the imagination in similar directions. The ethnographic study of affect as both a mode and a subject of representation during the heady late twentieth-century years of cultural critique (including intense interest in cultural constructs of the self and personhood), and the critical theories and writing styles which it inspired, is a notable outgrowth of that period, which sustains vitality because it suits the new media and conditions of experimentation and collaboration that are not only encouraged but also required by them.

For anthropology, it is not unlike the moment that Nietzsche evoked in "The Gay Science" of his time. Current projects of ethnography are determined to come to terms with phenomena of the contemporary, some through the study of affect as it ignites – as argued for and realized in various papers of this collection – subsequent research projects or performative collaborations. The latter are contemporary projects concocted out of fieldwork, or newly expanded dimensions of fieldwork that begin more conventionally. The attention to affect immediately expands collaborative possibilities and strategies, with partners both within and brought into the field of study.

The greatest challenge in furthering ethnography based on explorations of affect as primary data is how to work with and produce alternative modes of experimentation and performance, how to relate these with the authoritative texts and visual media that are well recognized and have been emblematic of anthropology until now while also continuing novel multimodal experiments in the affectual.

Affectual understanding and nuance are at the heart of designing ethnographically appropriate projects that depend on much more sophisticated approaches to collaborative work with those who are also ethnography's subjects, and who, these days, share in the ethnographer's perplexities, puzzles, and strains regarding the degrees of immersion in constantly changing technologies of all sorts that persistently challenge and raise both new and old questions.

What a focus on affect or the affectual (a good thing, I believe) requires in many, if not most, arenas of contemporary ethnographic research is an adaptation of all we have known and favoured as ways of thinking in sociocultural anthropology to present conditions. The study of affect in this ever-revising endeavour is the critical feeling out of what anthropology has long sought (at least since the critical theory transformations of the late twentieth century) in producing deeply descriptive understandings of the present as it rapidly evolves. This is the niche or opportunity anthropology has historically been reserved for itself but has sometimes been ambivalently occupied. The query into affect – into the often unsaid with and to the limits of signs, signals, and expressions that excite and challenge ethnographic observation and question-asking – invites new partners and collaborators into sites of inquiry. It is a key entrée into new research and a core driver for continuing the intensive reflection on and attempt to articulate the closely observed, the intently listened to, and the artful articulation of the sensed or felt.[1]

NOTE

1 My own somewhat bittersweet but thrilling experience of affective wayfinding in an ethnographic project was an art/anthropology installation of mixed success at the headquarters of the World Trade

Organization in Geneva (see Cantarella, Hegel, and Marcus 2019). It was for me an education in how the introduction of a deeply affective artistic practice of contact improvisation (the form that our installations following ethnographic fieldwork took) might galvanize the latent potency of otherwise unnoted potential in ethnographic fieldnotes – the often submerged or neglected affective in the keenly observed.

REFERENCE

Cantarella, Luke, Christine Hegel, and George E. Marcus. 2019. *Ethnography by Design: Scenographic Experiments in Fieldwork*. London: Routledge.

Preliminary 3

Convivialities of Emotion and Affect Research

DANIEL WHITE AND CATHERINE LUTZ

There are many convivialities of emotion and affect research in anthropology, as well as in its allied disciplines. These come not only from the shared family resemblances between the terms *emotion* and *affect* but also from the collegial affinities of anthropologists who study them. That a conviviality in analytics overlaps with a collegiality in disciplinary culture – although we admit *contestations* are also at play – is a social fact of theory not always acknowledged. For this reason, and because we think it of value to highlight what anthropologists of emotion in the 1970s, 1980s, and 1990s share with affect theorists who came after, we reflect in this short preliminary on how such convivialities might contribute to what this volume calls *affect as cultural critique*.

We imagine that many readers at the outset might question the notion of affect as critique. This is because, for better or worse, the term *affect* is often used today in shorthand to reference that which happens outside the explicit terms of discourse. This particular use of the term is dependent on a definition of *affect* as an intensity flowing through and between multiple bodies (both human and otherwise), which is distinct from *emotion*, understood as a conceptual capture of those intensities in human minds. Even if many affect theorists might reference this distinction, often by acknowledging Brian Massumi's (1995, 2002) work, neither Massumi nor many of his advocates or critics ever saw this distinction as so starkly drawn. While acknowledging the prominence of this distinction between affect and emotion in affect literature, we think it might also be helpful to place the distinction itself – what one of us has called the "affect-emotion gap" (White 2017) – in historical context by reflecting briefly on how emotion theorists grappled with this puzzle. We do so to convivially leverage the work of both emotion and affect researchers toward a more collaborative form of exploration and critique.

Although anthropologists writing on emotion, primarily through the 1980s and 1990s, often focused on the linguistic and discursive differences between how certain cultural groups approached expressions of sentiment, such questions were never so starkly disambiguated from those of affective impact. In their edited volume *Language and the Politics of Emotion*, Catherine Lutz and Lila Abu-Lughod (1990) wrote:

> To take language as more than a transparent medium for the communication of inner thoughts or experience, and to view speech as something essentially bound up with local power relations that is capable of socially constructing and contesting realities, even subjectivity, is not to deny non-linguistic "realities." It is simply to assert that things that are social, political, historically contingent, emergent, or constructed are both real and can have force in the world. (13)

Similarly, in a description that retrospectively captures what a 1980s' anthropology of emotion shares with today's affect studies, Catherine Lutz (1988) wrote in her work on the Ifaluk that "emotion" can refer to what is "culturally *defined* and *experienced* as '*intensely meaningful*'" (8, emphasis added). This emphasis on the puzzling imbrication of language and force, emotion and affect, highlights how the multiple dimensions of feeling operate synergistically in cultural worlds. From this perspective, those writing on emotion in the 1980s and 1990s and on affect thereafter have at times mutually laboured to communicate, as one of us put it in a previous essay, "presubjective and asocial intensity that is nonetheless not presocial" (Lutz 2017, 186).

The question of how social arrangements take on a force that is felt before it is conceived is a classic one in social theory, as William Mazzarella has comprehensively documented (2017). It is also one that was taken up directly by embodiment theorists. Maryon McDonald notes how early anthropological works on embodiment, and in particular those of Thomas Csordas (1990, 1993), had sought to challenge hard body-mind dichotomies that resemble those of affect and emotion. McDonald (2018) writes:

> For Csordas and others, "embodiment" meant changing gear analytically to take up phenomenological notions of being-in the-world as prior … In this approach, dualities such as subject and object or meaning and the material world (evoking mind/body) can be collapsed. They are collapsed in the world of analysis – but may take on an ethnographic reality instead, as the experiential realities of those whom we study. (187)

Additionally, in a volume on the body and embodiment, Frances Mascia-Lees (2011) collects a wide variety of ethnographic examples for how bodies know by feeling. With important contributions that addressed aspects of race, gender, and ethnicity where it was argued these had sometimes been left out of affect theory, Mascia-Lees's volume serves as a powerful testament to the value of collaboratively assembling as many diverse voices as possible – those before, during, and after the formal "affective turn" (Clough 2007) – for better documenting affect.

By referencing these convivialities of emotion studies in the past with affect research today, we hope that others might find inspiration in multiple theoretical trajectories for rethinking what critique might newly do. In other words, and in affective terms, while adversarial dispositions have often structured dominant forms of critique in anthropology and resulted in the building of artificial boundaries between so-called anthropologies of emotion and affect, more convivial approaches may unearth constructive intersections we have overlooked. This is not an effort to puzzle over and fix the boundaries between concepts like emotion and affect once and for all. Rather, it is an attempt to acknowledge the diverse contributions of multiple voices so that we might continually expand who does critique and how. As White emphasizes in his introduction, the many bodily practices found across the ethnographic record serve as resources for affective critique, so long as we begin to accept affect as a legitimate response to problematizations that anthropologists and interlocutors share. Because these shared problematizations are today as political and existential as they are theoretical, they require pushing the limits of what affect and embodied practices can add to analytical forms of critique.

In a 2017 essay, part of which we reproduce here, Lutz alluded to the importance of engaging with the bodily in ways that can advance affect theory while also acknowledging its genealogical precursors – a convivial gesture. She did this by writing about how emerging work in affect theory has taught anthropology ways of talking about personhood as genuinely relational or transpersonal, beyond even what psychoanalytic theory offered. She noted that affect theory has helped track the ways that power is capillary in more aspects of sociality and object worlds than formerly recognized. It has produced a more consistent way to see the politics and moralities of everyday life as powerfully organized (and disorganized) through emotion discourses. It has given new insight into the ways the institutions of knowledge production have reinforced a bifurcated self divided between reason and emotion along gender lines. Furthermore, Lutz noted how affect theory has led us to think more about fieldwork itself as a complex emotional activity, in an extended relational and political sense. Finally, says Lutz (2017, 189), an orientation towards the affective has directed us to focus more intensely on what matters to the communities we study, what moves them through the day, and thus what makes the emergent material and social worlds in which we are immersed.

We think that this latter direction in particular is constructive for inviting and leveraging new voices, as well as bodily practices, to continually and convivially expand what affect theory and affect writing in ethnography can do. As Lutz (2017) has previously remarked, "We can take from affect theory the healthy reminder that human life is messier and more resistant to our efforts to make sense of it as social analysts than we might think, and we might consider returning to the strengths of earlier moments by writing rich narratives based in field conversation, observation, and reflexive self-critique" (188). Building on this, we also emphasize the value of continually experimenting with ways of casting critique not in the usual voices and analytics of anthropologists themselves but rather in those of our interlocutors, letting their own forms of critique undo and remake our own. In this spirit of conviviality, the contributors to this volume have at times drawn as much on the anthropology of emotion, embodiment, feminism, and race as they have on affect theory. In doing so, they set constructive precedents for leveraging multiple traditions of anthropology toward the multiplication of styles of critique for the future.

REFERENCES

Clough, Patricia Ticineto. 2007. "Introduction." In *The Affective Turn: Theorizing the Social*, edited by Patricia Ticineto Clough and Jean Halley, 1–33. Durham, NC: Duke University Press.

Csordas, Thomas J. 1990. "Embodiment as a Paradigm for Anthropology." *Ethos* 18 (1): 5–47. https://doi.org/10.1525/eth.1990.18.1.02a00010.

Csordas, Thomas J. 1993. "Somatic Modes of Attention." *Cultural Anthropology* 8 (2): 135–56. https://doi.org/10.1525/can.1993.8.2.02a00010.

Lutz, Catherine. 1988. *Unnatural Emotions: Everyday Sentiments on a Micronesian Atoll and Their Challenge to Western Theory*. Chicago: University of Chicago Press.

Lutz, Catherine. 2017. "What Matters." *Cultural Anthropology* 32 (2): 181–91. https://doi.org/10.14506/ca32.2.02.

Lutz, Catherine, and Lila Abu-Lughod, eds. 1990. *Language and the Politics of Emotion (Studies in Emotion and Social Interaction)*. Cambridge; New York: Cambridge University Press.

Mascia-Lees, Frances E., ed. 2011. *A Companion to the Anthropology of the Body and Embodiment*. Oxford: Wiley-Blackwell.
Massumi, Brian. 1995. "The Autonomy of Affect." *Cultural Critique* 31: 83–109. https://doi.org/10.2307/1354446.
Massumi, Brian. 2002. *Parables for the Virtual: Movement, Affect, Sensation*. Durham, NC: Duke University Press.
Mazzarella, William. 2017. *The Mana of Mass Society*. Chicago; London: The University of Chicago Press.
McDonald, Maryon. 2018. "From 'the Body' to 'Embodiment,' with Help from Phenomenology." In *Schools and Styles of Anthropological Theory*, edited by Matei Candea, 185–94. Oxon: Routledge.
White, Daniel. 2017. "Affect: An Introduction." *Cultural Anthropology* 32 (2): 175–80. https://doi.org/10.14506/ca32.2.01.

Preliminary 4

Proliferation

KATHLEEN STEWART

Every practice is a mode of thought. ... To dance: a thinking in movement. To paint: a thinking in color. To perceive in the everyday: a thinking of the world's varied ways of affording itself.
– Manning and Massumi (2014, vii)

We're all *differently feeling our way through the* transitional immediacy of a present unstable, damaging, and made durable in the suggestion of a coherence. Drop the mimetic ambitions of a thinking subject trying to represent a world *per se* and it matters how things happen. Think, then, of critique as a method of following the activist occurrent arts of everyday life (Massumi 2002). As when a bouncer in a strip club watches for pockets of possible trouble in which

> you can feel in the details of those dark human spaces in the room where something has just changed ... a man lets out an appreciative yell where before he was silent ... one of the dancers out on the floor laughs a little too hard or steps back too fast; a chair leg scrapes the carpet ... a shift of objects in the space ... [a] change in the air. (Dubus 2008, 38)

Or in Ta-Nehisi Coates (2015) feeling out the racial fear transmogrifying into rage on the streets he grew up in "in the music that pumped from boom boxes full of grand boast and bluster ... in the girls, their loud laughter ... how they squared off like boxers, vaselined up, earrings off, Reeboks on, and lunged at each other" (15). An affect touching matter, an agitation finding its mark, is a vivid pragmatics (Stengers, Massumi, and Manning 2009). Mis-recognized, it can also be deadly.

Critique as a rigid conscription of abstracted thought that judges its objects is not enough, and too much, in a world where minor keys roost beyond critique's rough handling not as reason's leftovers, the marginal, or micro, but as all the meanwhiles of what happens, the fake fundaments of what hardens up, an energetic entrapment or release. In the broken realism of morphing forces and ongoing histories of dehumanization and foreclosure, words and "big" forces compose worlds, but so does swimming or an odd encounter on a city street.

Every worlding has its imperatives (Lingis 1998): jazz musicians are supposed to smoke pot, graduate students learn how to please their professors, Camden in 1971 was the present-future of storefronts permanently closed, houses vanishing "first behind the telltale of wood and neighborhood tags, then in fire, smoke or wrecking ball" (Romero 2021, 2).

Being-in-a-world is a tunnelling, an unsettling, that has somehow become primary and generative (Wylie 2007). A real saturates for some; bodies hold tight in a worldly ambit. A subject, already multiplied and amplified by its own strange and continuous efforts to emerge (Lepselter 2016), leans into the existing knowledge in a shrug, a medium becoming phenomenal, like a prism throwing colour "before the infinite play of the world ... is traversed, intersected, stopped, plasticized by some singular system" (Barthes 1992, 7).

The contingencies of infrastructures of living are not a flat sum game but an ongoing multiplication embedded in the mode of the possible (Muñoz 2009) or as-if. The I is not the beginning or hero of such a story but itself a tensile, shape-shifting infra-world unfolding in a field of *metamorphic, interstitial, intensive, and expressive intensities*.

***

None of this is innocent. In the US, the sensation of being in a world is the afterlife of settler colonialism, slavery, the culture wars built into the original and ongoing fractious hegemony of a protestant–secular state, the virulent battle of a one-world fantasy and its proper subject, the decompositional bloat of violent inequality and racial criminalization, the infrastructures of an official world (Seltzer 2016) that incite an orchestra of minor keys, the countless speculative patches twisting off from the paranoid to the queer utopian (Berlant 2023). The claim to one world-as-a-given is a claim to whiteness, or class, or some other normativity now grown as arcane and bizarre as the practices of a cult wearing out under pressure. *Critique as a blanketing worldly diagnosis can't hold the* fabulations of literally millions of worlds (Cavitch 2022), a thousand plateaus (Deleuze and Guattari 1987), a billion Black anthropocenes (Yusoff 2018).

In the new ordinary, we wake up wondering what's happened. The wake (Sharpe 2016) of slavery, gender, genocide, environmental destruction, and capitalism is palpable with rot and collateral damage. Reals, infinitely divisible in built environments, sequesterings, and contact points now scatter, decay, and aspire in rickety masses of matter, aesthetics, biomes, and politics. The subject *transes and skews across what's still verging or languishing*.

Something in the world makes us think. Resonances, labours, and compositions built out of worldly decomp present in the long-standing stories of abused women who one day just step out the back window, with or without their kids. In Texas women become welders and build an underground railroad to abortion. Seekers everywhere serially immerse in religion, then pyramid schemes, then Bitcoin, then nightly self-care blogging. LARPers with money plunge into Disney's latest experiment of world-immersion on steroids. Anti-vaxxers pick up steam. Your daily Wordle! practice is a distraction that becomes a dull grind. Play is work. Being in this world costs.

To approach such a world takes modes of critique like black shoals offshore that slow and obstruct claims of mastery (King 2019), the gappy angles, inclines and echoes of a critical fabulation (Hartman 2019), or queering suggestions of non-human becomings to foster new modes of being affected.

Fred Moten (2003) writes thought as a sounding. For Steven Feld (2015, 2021), worlds and thoughts are multi-modal compositions that lay down tracks. Raymond Williams (1973) thought with the particular quality or sense of a period through the tilt of his father's hat – where that tilt came from, what heads it rested on, how it became a character actor in a world of its own. LeFebvre (2013) attuned to the city by abstracting its sheer rhythms. A wide range of experimental writing in autoethnography, post-phenomenology, non-representational theory, new materialism, fictocriticism, autotheory, sensory studies, affect studies, flash fiction, multi-modal and cross-modal work, and queer, gendered, and anti-racist work aims to re-pair composition and critique to provoke maximal perspective. This is a work of proliferating concepts used to approach what's happening rather than represent a generality.

Modes of worldly approach work not for the sake of critique or clarity but for the impersonal music of what's at hand, the feeling of a question, moving in fits and starts or slowing on an arc across the surface of a plane. The method, if you can call it that, is to be in the middle (what else is there?) of what just doesn't add up. Believing in reals, it has to wonder what they are. It tries to sidle up to what's starting up or falling away in a present fractious with difference and indifference and sedimented with horrors and the unrelenting creativity of desperation, calculated opportunism, and all the ways of being in between or left behind.

This is thought as an exposure that does not return to itself (Latour 2010) but lingers "as long as necessary on narratives, examples, singularities – the things in themselves" (Serres 2016, 42–3). If it had a slogan, it might be "World First!"

REFERENCES

Barthes, Roland. 1992. *Incidents*. Berkeley: University of California Press.
Berlant, Lauren. 2023. *On the Inconvenience of Other People*. Durham, NC: Duke University Press.
Cavitch, Max. 2022. "Everybody's Autotheory." *Modern Language Quarterly* 83 (1): 81–116. https://doi.org/10.1215/00267929-9475043.
Coates, Ta-Nehisi. 2015. *Between the World and Me*. New York: One World.
Deleuze, Gilles, and Felix Guattari. 1987. *A Thousand Plateaus*. Minneapolis: University of Minnesota Press.
Dubus, Andre. 2008. *The Garden of Last Days*. New York and London: W. W. Norton.
Feld, Steven. 2015. "Acoustemology." In *Keywords in Sound*, edited by David Novak and Matt Sakakeeny, 12–21. Durham, NC: Duke University Press.
Feld, Steven. 2021. *Acoustemology: Four Lectures*. DVD. Santa Fe, NM: VoxLox.
Hartman, Saidiya. 2019. *Wayward Lives, Beautiful Experiments: Intimate Histories of Social Upheaval*. London: Serpent's Tail.
King, Tiffany Lethabo. 2019. *The Black Shoals: Offshore Formations of Black and Native Studies*. Durham, NC: Duke University Press.
Latour, Bruno. 2010. *On the Modern Cult of the Factish Gods*. Durham, NC, and London: Duke University Press.
LeFebvre, Henri. 2013. *Rythmanalysis*. Translated by Stuart Elden and Gerald Moore. London: Bloomsbury.
Lepselter, Susan. 2016. *The Resonance of Unseen Things: Poetics, Power, Captivity and UFOs in the American Uncanny*. Ann Arbor: University of Michigan Press.
Lingis, Alphonso. 1998. *The Imperative*. Bloomington and Indianapolis: Indiana University Press.
Manning, Erin, and Brian Massumi. 2014. *Thought in the Act: Passages in the Ecology of Experience*. Minneapolis: University of Minnesota Press.
Massumi, Brian. 2002. *Parables for the Virtual: Movement, Affect, Sensation*. Durham, NC: Duke University Press.
Moten, Fred. 2003. *In the Break: The Aesthetics of the Black Radical Tradition*. Minneapolis: University of Minnesota Press.

Muñoz, José. 2009. *Cruising Utopia: The Then and There of Queer Futurity*. New York and London: New York University Press.
Romero, Mercy. 2021. *Toward Camden*. Durham, NC, and London: Duke University Press.
Seltzer, Mark. 2016. *The Official World*. Durham, NC, and London: Duke University Press.
Serres, Michel. 2016. *The Five Senses: A Philosophy of Mingled Bodies*. Translated by Margaret Sankey and Peter Cowley. London: Bloomsbury.
Sharpe, Christina. 2016. *In the Wake: On Blackness and Being*. Durham, NC, and London: Duke University Press.
Stengers, Isabelle, Brian Massumi, and Erin Manning. 2009 "History Through the Middle: Between Macro and Mesopolitics – An Interview with Isabella Stengers." *INFLeXions* 3. www.inflexions.org/n3_stengershtml.html.
Williams, Raymond. 1973. *The Country and the City*. New York: Oxford University Press.
Wylie, John. 2007. "The Spectral Geographies of W.G. Sebald." *Cultural Geographies* 14 (2): 171–88. https://doi.org/10.1177/1474474007075353.
Yusoff, Kathryn. 2018. *A Billion Black Anthropocenes or None*. Minneapolis: University of Minnesota Press.

Chapters

Introduction: Affect as Cultural Critique

DANIEL WHITE

There are certain engineers in Japan who are adamant that the robots they build have heart (*kokoro*). In fact, this idea that robots *feel* is not limited to professional roboticists but can be found among amateur robot builders, computer coders, Buddhist priests, and robot fans at large. Over several years of collaborative research on emotional robotics in Japan, a colleague and I spent countless hours with people who felt this way. After many months of multiple conversations, we gradually began to grasp what they meant. They did not mean that robots are living beings that have, for example, spirit or a soul (*tamashii*). (We are certain of this because when we asked one Buddhist priest who conducts memorial services for broken robots if they *did* have souls, he replied only partly in jest, "Are you idiots?") Neither did our interlocutors mean that they simply *imagine* that robots can feel. Indeed, no one was quite happy with explanations of *anthropomorphic projection*, although they understood the term perfectly well. Rather, what they mean is actually quite simple: they *feel* that robots feel. This volume explores this simple but understudied alternative often offered by interlocutors: affect as answer.

The pervasive experience of intense but not easily qualifiable sensations, such as those evoked in human–robot encounters, points to the power of affect in social life. Theorists have been making this point most publicly since what has been called the "affective turn" (Clough 2007) in the social sciences. To be fair, anthropologists, sociologists, and feminist geographers of emotion writing before this official turn had been making it as well (see Boler and Zembylas 2016; Liljeström 2016). And philosophers like Gilles Deleuze, Henri Bergson, William James, and Baruch Spinoza, as well as others not often canonized in traditions of Western thought, had theorized affect long before them.

However, the problem this book addresses is not nearly that everything has already been said about affect. Rather, drawing from Yael

Navaro (2017), it is that, in spite of our many critiques of emotional life, "[o]ur toolboxes for the study and imagination of affect still remain predominantly Western in their crafting" (109). Increasingly troubled by this point, recent ethnographic accounts of affect are more deliberately pointing to the fact that academics are not nearly the only ones who theorize affect. Like our interlocutor Buddhist priest from Japan mentioned above, who conducts ceremonies for broken-down robots to cultivate a sense of the non-duality between living and non-living things (see White and Katsuno 2021), many people deliberately model, exercise, modulate, manipulate, and otherwise do things with affect in ways that can expand the imagination beyond what anthropological theories circumscribe. Additionally, like the robot engineers who install in those same robots "affective engines" (see Fujita and Kitano 1998) or like their computer science colleagues who build taste recommendation algorithms for social media feeds (Seaver 2021), many in the hard sciences are currently operationalizing their own theories of affect in the wild to much greater publicity and impact than anthropologists. These many ongoing experiments with affect and affective methods deserve broader attention.

The point of doing anthropology, of course, is not to simply become more imaginative or impactful producers of theory – even if disciplinary trends often push professional anthropologists in that direction. However, neither is imagination nor impact irrelevant to doing anthropological theory well. This point is especially relevant when it comes to anthropological engagements with affect, where certain theoretical critiques of it have calcified into hard positions that are easily summarized and cited but do not necessarily facilitate the documentation of affective differences in the field. Continuing the line of argument introduced above, Yael Navaro (2017) says, "Many recent engagements with affect theory have therefore inadvertently been repetitive, reiterating by now well-rehearsed analyses about the distinction between affect and the emotions, referring to the particularly nondiscursive qualities of the former and the linguistic embedment of the latter" (209). Highlighting both the power and danger of this trend, she notes, "It is worrisome when evocations of a theoretical notion close down on themselves" (209).

Navaro points to how with the rise of affect theory and certain forms of philosophical puzzling over a distinction (Massumi 1995, 2002; Thrift 2008) between the somatic experience of *affect* and the semiotic representation of *emotion*, diverse accounts of affective life have sometimes been lost in old and overly certain habits of academic theorizing and philosophical problem-solving. Consequently, while anthropologists have offered ample analytical answers to problematizations of feelings that mystify, enchant, illuminate, depress, excite, enrage, or otherwise stoke and stimulate the human imagination, they have not always effectively engaged with affect as a social fact that operates outside the boundaries of the discipline's established modes of geographically Western theory.[1] Nor have they fully allowed affect to challenge anthropology's own modernist explanatory drive and – in Kathleen Stewart's (2017) articulate phrasing – "unfortunate affective habits of snapping at the world as if the whole point of being and thinking is just to catch it in a lie" (196). This volume seeks an alternative.

The essays in this collection ask, What if the most constructive response to moments of ethnographic puzzlement and problematization was not the formulation of an answer but the cultivation of an affect? What if understanding the powerful and unanticipated effects of collective life required somatic rather than semiotic exercises? Furthermore, when speaking from habituated perspectives of anthropological professionalism prohibits experiencing possible worlds, What if anthropology as a discipline could leverage affect to differently connect and cultivate collaboration with others? Finally, What if the affect of others could serve as a critique not merely of cultural formations one calls one's own, in Marcus and Fischer's (1986) classic rendering, but rather of a certain culture of anthropological theorizing itself? In other words, what new methods, exercises, and experiments might affect generate towards ethnographic discovery – or, what we call in this volume, *uncovering*?[2]

Each of the main chapters in this volume describes encounters in fieldwork in which typical theorizations, problematizations, and other conceptual frameworks brought to the field are contested not only through discursive tactics but also through *affective practices* – ways of feeling and cultivating feeling – drawn from and in collaboration with interlocutors. Such practices can disrupt the anthropologist's frames of reference in productive ways that invite critique of the discipline's dominant analytics. Most importantly, the chapters in this volume expand the space for ethnographic uncovering both within and beyond anthropology. They do so by not only attending to researchers' feelings (Stodulka et al. 2019) but also documenting how interlocutors' engagements with affect do critical work. Terms like *theory* and *critique* in this volume's framing correspond not to an established and largely Western philosophical heritage of recognizable problems or exclusively to a disciplinary "theory-ethnography relation" (Boyer and Marcus 2015, 3) but, rather, to the material and embodied methods that people employ to transform a postulated problem into an alternative for action. In short, the purpose of this volume is not to explain affect but to describe what affect does through its embodied exercises by others – to expand, in other words, what affect "is good for" (Mazzarella 2009).

Genealogies of Affect

Because *affect* in its theoretical ambiguity and flexibility is a term that infuriates some readers as much as it inspires, it is worth setting out what we editors mean by the concept and offering some genealogical context. However, we do this summarily, only for the sake of clarifying our terms, and with sensitivity to the dangers of this exercise. As famously noted by Yael Navaro-Yashin (2009), the genealogical work that establishes certain traditions of theory can also lead to the "ruination" of others. Indeed, there exists no "monoaffective imaginary," in the words of Lauren Berlant, nor is one recommended (Seigworth and Pedwell 2023b, 4). Heeding this warning, at the start of our genealogical discussion, we believe offering some historical context is helpful to connect what is now called the "anthropology of affect" with an "anthropology of emotion" that came before it to draw on the various contributions of these and related scholarly traditions (also see White and Lutz, this volume).

Anthropologists, particularly in North America, have long attended to how "culture" shapes emotion. Early works that addressed this most directly were later categorized together under what was called culture and personality studies, represented most prominently by US anthropologists Ruth Benedict and Margaret Mead in the early to mid-twentieth century. However, emotion as a focused object of ethnographic observation and theoretical discussion most crystallized in the 1970s and 1980s. For example, in the application of psychodynamic analyses to cultural worlds, Robert Levy (1973) aimed to capture the "interior" experiences or "ethnopsychology" of the "Tahitians." Writing a few years later, Michelle (1980) and Renato Rosaldo (1989) analysed emotional experiences of the Ilongot in the northern Philippines, with the latter provocatively describing a feeling called *liget* that, although not having an exact equivalent in anglophone cultures, could be conveyed when Ilongot spoke of it as the "source of their desire to cut off human heads" (R. Rosaldo 1989, 3; Spiegel 2017). Catherine Lutz (1982, 1988), in her study of the Ifaluk in Micronesia, analysed local words that combined moral reflection and sentiment, such as *fago* (loneliness/sadness) and *song* (justified anger), to build a critique of the highly contextual and gendered division between reason and emotion in Western cultures. Other important works on emotion from this period followed a similar approach (Abu-Lughod 1986; Levy 1984; Lutz and Abu-Lughod 1990; Lutz and White 1986; Myers 1991; Schieffelin 1976; Schieffelin and Ochs 1986; Wikan 1990).

These works found evidence for different arrangements of affective experiences in emotion words that did not neatly map onto words in other languages and the cultures in which they were presumably bound. In this sense, anthropologists of emotion added important cultural and discursive context to classic sociological debates on how collective life engenders sentiments, or what Émile Durkheim ([1912] 2008) called "collective effervescence." As processes of global movement and capital exchange rendered these culture-bound emotional words less distinct, and a 1980s' critique of the production of anthropological knowledge challenged an "us–them" model of culture on both epistemological and ethical grounds (Clifford and Marcus 1986; Marcus and Fischer 1986), a culture- and language-based approach to emotion faced limitations. According to some reflecting on the period, who would later label a shift away from this perspective the "affective turn" (Clough 2007), missing in these approaches to emotion were aspects of sensorial intensity that never quite contracted into language and that often exceeded and confounded it.

Although many anthropologists of emotion writing in the 1980s and 1990s had considered aspects of emotive life that scholars would later call "affect" (see White and Lutz, this volume), affect theorists also sought to address more explicitly what linguistic approaches to emotion sometimes implicitly left out. Two genealogical forerunners of affect theory are commonly cited in scholarly literature, although they do not nearly determine or encompass the diversity of affect theories taken up by the contributors to this volume. Accordingly, and keeping in mind Navaro-Yashin's (2009) point on ruination introduced above, we also add to these what we think is an important third body of literature.

The first of these genealogies is psychological. Its earliest references often include Darwin's ([1872] 2018) *The Expression of the Emotions in Man and Animals*; then pass through a critical debate focused on William James's (1884), "What is an Emotion"; and land with forceful – some might say devastating (Anderson, Jenson, and Keller 2011; Khanna 2003) effect in Freudian theory and its subsequent globalized discourses on the instincts, id, and the unconscious. A more recent addition to this genealogy is the work of Silvan Tomkins (2008) and his momentous *Affect Imagery Consciousness*. This study received renewed interest among critical theorists, most notably with Sedgwick and Frank's 1995 reader on Tomkins, *Shame and its* Sisters (1995a), and its introductory essay, "Shame in the Cybernetic Fold" (1995b). These essays connected a history of psychology with one of critical theory, paving the way for a critical affect theory.

The second often-cited genealogy of affect theory is philosophical, beginning with Baruch Spinoza's *Ethics* in 1677, rekindled in Deleuze's materialism, and most popularized today in the work of Brian Massumi (2002). Recent literature in this tradition treats affect as a product of nature that, at the same time, does not exclude social dimensions. It draws attention to sensations and intensities between subjects, objects, and environments, and to "arrangements" of affect (Slaby et al. 2017) that exert a force that is often conceived as prior to affect's conceptual capture in human minds. The abundance of scholars within the humanities and social sciences engaging with affect today often acknowledge this tradition, even if also sometimes critical of it (Berlant 2011; Berlant and Stewart 2019; Brennan 2004; Clough 2007; DeLanda 2016; Gregg and Seigworth 2010; Stewart 2007; Terada 2003; Thrift 2004, 2008).

To these two bodies of literature we add a third that includes a wide variety of studies from geography, literature, feminist studies, critical race studies, Black and ethnic studies, religious studies, cultural studies, and art and that have sometimes reproduced and sometimes criticized the citational politics and practices that have emphasized the importance of the Spinoza–Deleuze–Massumi nexus cited above. Many debates within these literatures focus on a representation of Brian Massumi's definition of "affect" as something that relies on a hard distinction with "emotion." In this particularly dominant reading of Massumi (1995), *affect* refers to nonconscious modulations of "intensity" moving through and between bodies. Emotion, on the other hand, is "qualified intensity," the "socio-linguistic fixing of the quality of an experience which is from that point onward defined as personal" (88). Although Massumi's model of affect and emotion is arguably more dynamic than has been portrayed (see White 2018; White and De Antoni 2025), some critics (Leys 2011, 2017; Martin 2013) have worried that Massumi's approach treated affect as grounded exclusively in the body's biological triggers that take place outside spheres of social conditioning. Writing against such views of biological determinism, however, studies from the fields mentioned above situate affect not in universalizing figures of the body and biology but, rather, in historical and cultural contexts that are as material as they are social. Examples of these works include Ahmed (2004a, 2004b), Berg and Ramos-Zayas (2015), Boler and Zembylas (2016), Kasmani (2022), Muehlebach (2011), Muñoz (2006), Navaro-Yashin (2009, 2012), Newell (2018), Ngai (2005), Thien (2005), and the several essays collected by Seigworth and Pedwell (2023a) in *The Affect Theory Reader 2*.[3]

In their emphasis on the simultaneously material and socially conditioned aspects of affect, there is a helpful framing in the above-mentioned works that allows for the acknowledgment of how previous anthropological and allied disciplines' studies of the emotions in the 1970s and 1980s both laid important groundwork and still contribute to affect studies today. This acknowledgment might help scholars see what studies of emotion and of affect share towards exploring new forms of critique that are less polemical and that better foreground how interlocutors themselves theorize, model, and otherwise do things with affect.

Towards this end, the preceding genealogical mapping offers introductory context for outlining how *Affect as Cultural Critique*'s contributors approach definitions of affect. In its limitations and diversity, this mapping should also help clarify why our contributors at times purposefully *avoid* defining affect, lest they risk the suggestion that taking up one thread of affect might cut them off from another. Although many of the contributors to this volume find it helpful to distinguish between the somatics of affect and the semiotics of emotion, others, for the previously mentioned reasons, treat them as a dynamic relation, a continuum, or even as one and the same. What the contributors share, however, is a commitment to the idea that affect is of most benefit to us today not as an abstract model of an ontological reality of physio-psychic dynamics; rather, affect can point us to the variety of *methods* by which people relate to intimately felt experiences as tools for literally *making sense* of worlds. From this point of view, the purpose of the above genealogies is not to canonize affect but, rather, to make it better available for experimental projects of diversification (Navaro 2017).

Affect as Experimental Method

As suggested above in relation to fans and engineers of robots described as having heart, there is something deceptively simple in the phrase "I *feel*" that this volume seeks to draw out. For Western engineers of artificial emotional intelligence in particular, to take one example (White and Katsuno 2021, 2022), this is not necessarily the case. Following dominant theories of emotion, especially those of psychologist Paul Ekman (1999) and his theory of "basic emotions," some engineers of the latest emotional artificial intelligence (AI) technologies argue that feelings are universal across cultures, are visible in the face, can be coded by humans, and can thus be reliably automated in machines (see White 2019). Both despite and because of its simplicity, the basic emotions model of feeling has enormous public impact. For anthropologists, social psychologists, and many other socially inclined scholars, however, "emotions" is far more complex. To list only a few of the objections to the basic emotion paradigm, an emotion indicates not a uniform expression of a universal experience but rather a dynamic process; it incorporates physiological sensations and stages triggered by causes, internal and external, but also degrees of conscious recognition and the labelling of those states; it can express differently externally from how it feels internally (such as pain expressed variably as a grimace or a suppressive smile); moreover, it involves reverberation and socially dynamic feedback loops (Wetherell 2012, 153), whereby conscious identifications of feelings affect a body's somatic responses. Given the complexity of this process, adding words like *affect* to a conceptual repertoire of related terms like *sensation*, *sentiment*, and *emotion* can increase precision in describing interactive processes that often get lumped under a broad category of "feeling."[4] It is important to note, however, that these affective processes are likely too complex to ever document comprehensively. That is, although for some engineers of artificial emotional intelligence a smile is simply a coded meaning (e.g., "happiness"), for the anthropologist of affect, a smile is the surface expression of an intergenerational history of connections, traces, proclivities, capacities, experiences, traumas, celebrations, and so much more. From this perspective, the seemingly simple phrase "I feel" encapsulates not just a momentary somatic signal but rather a cosmically interwoven history of relations.

It is for this reason that the practice of proposing affect as a theoretical model of how emotional processes "really work" may have reached a productive impasse – a critical mass of reflection that requires a shift to the methodological.[5] Although affect theory has helpfully pointed to the complex processual dimensions of feeling outlined above and demonstrated limitations of approaches to *emotion* that preceded it, it is clear that within traditional practices of critical theory *affect* as a concept can never be officially confirmed or consecrated. Given affect's inextricability from the diverse socio-material relations that condition it, its possibilities are endless. This is not exactly how Spinoza seemed to originally conceive of it. In a line from his *Ethics* cited widely by affect theorists, Spinoza ([1677] 1996, 72–3) writes, "No one has yet determined what the body can do. … For no one has yet come to know the structure of the body so accurately that he could explain all its functions." One wonders if many of the AI engineers referred to above might be enticed by a (mis)reading of Spinoza that suggests the possibility of an end to the body's meaning with the ascendance of technologies that can comprehensively code and communicate it. However, an anthropological perspective on Spinoza's claim, informed by the diversity of the ethnographic record, would take a different view. It would reason that the future of affect, however desirable to document in detail, will always be unfinished inasmuch as affect is a consequence of evolving material and social arrangements.

Consequently, and in the spirit of the formative 1986 text *Anthropology as Cultural Critique* from which this volume's title draws inspiration, the contributors to this volume offer no new theoretical model, analytic, or -ism for affect. Instead, *Affect as Cultural Critique* turns to method and experimentation. It documents moments when affect arises as a practice for generating insights inspired by interlocutors. In this regard, the practices this book features as pathways towards what we call ethnographic *uncovering* steer away from discursive and rhetorical diagnostics, such as the impressive *Methods of Discovery* by the sociologist Andrew Abbott (2004). Instead, we hope that affective practices featured here might help us chart new analytical terrain while also uncovering traditions of inquiry that have remained hidden from certain analytical biases.

As referenced above, when in the course of fieldwork a colleague's and my (White and Katsuno 2021) interlocutors claimed to feel that robots can *feel*, that they can in fact *sense* a "sense of life" (*seimeikan*) in manufactured objects, this was not mere observation on their part. Instead, it was a methodological practice of feeling that was applied to a variety of practical problems. For robotics engineers in Japan, for example, feeling into a sense of life became the method by which they improved the lifelike quality of their companion robots, such as Sony's pet robot AIBO, as well as a tool to help them understand the relational reality of intimacy they aspired to model. Alternatively, for our interlocutor Buddhist priest conducting funerary rites for broken-down AIBO, sensing the "heart," "spirit," or "Buddha-nature" (*busshō*) of robots offered a means to break down mistaken human distinctions between animate and inanimate life to communicate the means by which consciousness pervades all matter. Further still, for a group of Osaka University engineers and monks at a Zen temple in Kyoto who collaborated to build Japan's first android bodhisattva (White and Katsuno 2022), sensing the reality of the Bodhisattva of Compassion Kannon in a robot became a pedagogical tool for teaching Mahayana Buddhist principles of "emptiness" (*kū*) to temple visitors in order to facilitate self-transformation. As they reasoned to us in conversation, "[w]hat better way to express the ever-changing emptiness of the mundane world than through a robot empty of affective attachments to it!"

Adopting *affect as method* means using feeling as a means for generating insight, guiding fieldwork choices and practice, and, above all, understanding interlocutors when they are suggesting that neither their own nor the anthropologists' terms are quite adequate.[6] Applied in this way, affect as method can do several useful things. It can hold disparate propositions, possibilities, and even contradictions together – such as that of a *"living* robot"; it can modulate a researcher's body to better sense alternative points of view grounded in and guided by feeling; it can leverage common feelings of vulnerability (Behar 1997) experienced in fieldwork to constructively intimate forms of connecting with and deeply hearing interlocutors; and it can reveal how affective experiences, mutually if imperfectly shared in degrees of commensurability between researcher and interlocutor, can serve as legitimate replies to theoretical propositions.[7] In this sense, affect as method functions equally as a feeling-focused method of anthropological fieldwork, a tool for anthropological uncovering, and, finally, as a mode of both collaborative and reflexive anthropological critique.

The Decolonial: From Discovery to Uncovering

In earlier iterations of this collaborative project, we had discussed repurposing the word *discovery* for decolonial ends. We wanted to acknowledge and, in any way and degree possible, work to repair such a loaded signifier of anthropology's complicity with colonial histories of violence, disappearance, and destruction. Furthermore, we recognized what many Indigenous scholars, including especially scholars of Polynesian oral histories, have argued about Indigenous people long playing the role of "active agents of global exploration" as much as "passive objects" (Chang 2016, vii). Ultimately, with so much pain and trauma still associated with European histories of "discovery," and with so much work still needed to unveil what European histories and accompanying styles of critique had covered over, we felt an alternative was needed. As Kanaka Maoli (Native Hawaiian) scholar David A. Chang (2016) describes of James Cook's first encounters with the peoples of the Hawaiian Islands, "[h]e could not see the Kānaka at Kaua'i clearly, as Western fantasies of discovery and superiority obscured his vision" (27). Drawing from the work of Chang and others engaged in decolonial scholarship (Harrison 1991; Osorio 2021; Tuhiwai 1999), we propose that today we may need to methodologically *feel* differently to see more clearly – a process requiring not a repurposing of discovery but rather a reciprocal process of *uncovering*.

Many of the contributions to this volume seek to uncover certain affective dimensions of race, ethnicity, gender, colonialism, and violence that have sometimes been left out of affect scholarship (see, in particular,

Stainova, Ramos-Zayas, Navaro, Carelock, and Osorio in this volume). As both affect theory proponents and critics have noted, literature on affect can, in its most theoretically ambitious and abstract articulations, feel socially disconnected. They point to "occlusions" of race, indigeneity, and decoloniality (Seigworth and Pedwell 2023b, 4); to a "curious silence" on "Black affect" and disproportionately "affirmationist" logics emphasizing "the generative, the possible, the new" (Palmer 2023, 122, 124); to theoretical trending of #affectsowhite;[8] and to the many racially and colonially inscribed conflicts around the world generating both affectively sudden traumas and slow "titration[s] of life" (Abu-Sittah cited in Puar 2023, 412). In face of these critiques, some advocate for "unlearning affect" and some of its "enlightenment/en*whiten*ment" legacies (Hamner 2023, 234).[9] In this regard, we are reminded again of Kathleen Stewart's (2017) description of affect theory's potential for undoing and "sidestepping" certain "dualist dead ends of modernist, humanist social science" and some of "its unfortunate affective habits" of overly strong critique (196; more on this below). We are also reminded of important early efforts to decolonize anthropology that challenged certain affective academic styles of critique before "affect theory" became so named, such as Faye V. Harrison's volume *Decolonizing Anthropology*, which emerged out of an invited session under the same name at the 1987 meeting of the American Anthropological Association, organized with the Association of Black Anthropologists.

In these critiques of affect theory, there is a strong drive to uncover what has remained hidden or not seen clearly. In fact, it is often the uncomfortable affect generated by critiques that feel narrow or too disciplinarily contrived that pushes ethnographic work to unveil something stirring beneath theoretically hard surfaces. To learn from affect may therefore require some theoretical unlearning, a process of uncovering that inevitably entails change and experimentation, along with possible failures along the way. It is in this spirit of experimentation, and for the purpose of leveraging the forms of uncovering and self-examination it engenders, that we revisit a classic text and trope of interpretive anthropology, along with some considerations of its limitations.

In the introduction to the second edition of their *Anthropology as Cultural Critique*, in conceding some shortcomings of the original volume (1986), Marcus and Fischer (1999) write that "no longer, then, is the project of anthropology the simple discovery of new worlds, and the translation of the exotic into the familiar, or the defamiliarization of the exotic. It is increasingly the discovery of worlds that are familiar or fully understood by no one, and that all are in search of *puzzling out*" (xvii, emphasis added). Marcus and Fischer go on to suggest alternatives to the "discovery" paradigm, advocating that anthropologists pay more attention to the "stream of already existing representations produced by journalists, prior anthropologists, historians, creative writers, and of course the subjects of study themselves" (xx). Building on these reflexive critiques in times of increasing alignment between social sciences and decolonial practices, we propose the term *uncovering* as an alternative framework that foregrounds decolonial views on the history of social scientific methods, and that serves as a useful description of collaborative experiments for reciprocally "puzzling out" contemporary cultural predicaments.

As Faye Harrison (1991, 2) and her collaborators point out in *Decolonizing Anthropology*, experimental and reflexive practices were as much a part of early decolonial critiques as they were of the *Writing Culture* and *Anthropology as Cultural Critique* movement, with which those practices are more often associated. And decolonial perspectives often pushed self-reflexive critique of dominant disciplinary tropes much further. For example, Harrison cites the limitations of certain postmodern-inspired critiques that treated ethnographic tropes like "dialogic relationships" as only "textual strategies" rather than pushing towards "concrete collaborations (e.g., co-authorship and co-editorship) between ethnographers and informants" (5). Harrison adds, "A decolonizing and decolonized anthropology can indeed benefit from an 'experimental moment,' but one directed towards the empowerment of its studied populations" (5). We suggest that processes of uncovering – referring to practices of uncovering things unseen, unfelt, or unbelieved because of inherited academic predispositions – can serve as one additional way of decolonizing ethnographic production.

One reason to keep tropes of "discovery" under scrutiny, and propose alternatives such as uncovering in their place, is to avoid leaving discovery solely in the hands of so-called professional and technocratic classes who are historically habituated to speaking for it in exclusive terms. For example, as we alluded to above in our description of AI engineers, today's anthropological problems, such as the puzzling over affect and emotion, are not nearly the exclusive domain of anthropologists. From mass media content producers to financial analysts to engineers of recommendation algorithms and artificial emotional intelligence, many specialists today are theorizing and exercising affect to powerful ends. Moreover, many of those professionals most financially aligned with capital accumulation are building tools that embed, amplify, and powerfully operationalize those theories. Engaging with these shared problems requires – much as Marcus and Fischer's original volume called for – collaboration. It requires tackling problems that are, as Marcus and Fischer (1999, xvii) articulate, "fully understood by no one." However, a critical caveat here is that even in an age of digitally facilitated and enhanced connection, where problems, solutions, and the often black-boxed technological modes of their mediation are fully understood by only a few, claims to knowledge – as well as to ignorance – are unevenly distributed. Although Meta and Google may not actively seek to deliver increasingly polemical content via recommendation algorithms on Facebook or YouTube, they nonetheless have the most powerful and public claims to explaining how those algorithms work, defending their public value, and denying blame when things go wrong. This exemplifies one reason why affect as method might be leveraged not only to innovative forms of uncovering but also to critique.

To revisit another reason for leveraging affect as method to both uncovering and critique, where tropes of discovery in the academy have been historically tied to mostly European agents and methods of research, the affective consequences have often been painful. Reconciling with that pain will require more than just reworking uncomfortable tropes but also collaborating with others to reformulate problematic terms for more equitable applications. We wonder if processes of mutual *discovery* might thus be recast as processes of *uncovering* to better fit what Anand Pandian (2019) calls in dramatic understatement "uneasy times" – times when continued violences of colonialism, racism, patriarchy, economic inequity, and resulting social precarity challenge the existential legitimacy of academic anthropology. Despite an affective "buoyancy" (12) that Pandian notes underlies anthropological repurposing projects for research, for many of those not white and male in anthropology, the work of academic anthropology can, paraphrasing Indigenous Métis scholar Zoe Todd referenced by Pandian, wear away at one's bones (1). Not only does doing research according to dominant analytical modes of anthropology not always feel safe or supportive, it can also feel downright harmful. As Māori scholar Linda Tuhiwai Smith (1999) says, among many Indigenous communities, the word *research* remains "one of the dirtiest words in the indigenous world's vocabulary" (1). To the degree *discovery* connotes colonial legacies of knowledge extraction and exclusion, only appearing in Indigenous scholarship in incriminating quotes, it may not seem like a trope worth recuperating for Pandian's uneasy times; however, to the degree *uncovering* can repurpose discovery as a domain of mutual curiosity and reciprocal relationship building (with people, ancestors, knowledge, earth, spirits) to which many different people's traditional affective methods have long been applied, affective practices of critique in the form of *uncovering* may hold power within collaborative modes of research as reconciliation.[10]

Affect as and after Cultural Critique

But what kind of critique are we talking about? Critique of what? And for whom? In their original volume *Anthropology as Cultural Critique*, Marcus and Fischer (1986) noted some of the ends to which they hoped to apply anthropology as "critique": "to offer worthwhile and interesting critiques of our own society; to enlighten us about other human possibilities, engendering an awareness that we are merely one pattern among many; to make accessible the normally unexamined assumptions by which we operate and through which we encounter members of other cultures" (ix). This comparative framing, they argued, "plays off other cultural realities against our own in order to gain a more adequate knowledge of them all" (x). There is obviously a strong us-them dynamic here. In the introduction to the second edition of their text (Marcus and Fischer 1999, xviii), the authors admit that this dialectic by which anthropology was to "repatriate" itself was "too simple and binary." Their concession points to the fact that then, as well as now, the most interesting social and cultural formations facing anthropologists could neither be studied nor sustained within a framework of cultural boundaries, even if a kind of comparison could endure in diverse and experimental forms (see Candea 2019).

Furthermore, as they write in a reflective footnote, Marcus and Fischer (1999) began composing this second introduction in 1997 while visiting the University of Cape Town's Business School, "housed in an interesting renovation of a prison that had once been occupied by 'Bushmen' (San) convicts who had provided the labor to build Cape Town's picturesque harbor" (xv). With this note they allude to the unreconciled racial and post-colonial conditions that many would argue today demand far more of anthropological "critique" than what was imagined in their original volume. Thus, the second edition of the text, published in 1999, marks an important moment when anthropology faced two limit points: one of cultural comparison and one of the irreconcilable interdependences of analysis and politics. Still confronting the discipline today, such challenges beg the questions of what new methods may better account for the *cultural* in theory and, relatedly, for whom *critique* most matters.

By now many anthropologists are familiar with, if not exhausted by, critiques of *critique*. Bruno Latour's (2004), for example, is particularly scathing, accusing social scientists of attacking the fetishization of facts on one hand while appealing to social determinism in challenging anyone who would assert untasteful degrees of agency on the other. Matters of fact could never withstand such brutal attacks, Latour suggests. Yet this game of critique still seems to many the only one in town. In Latour's (2004, 227) observation, "entire Ph.D. programs are still running to make sure that good American kids are learning the hard way that facts are made up, that there is no such thing as natural, unmediated, unbiased access to truth." In an age of largely North American–driven post-truth, one wonders if they learned too well. In fact, according to the kind of repatriation Marcus and Fischer imagined, it is precisely the kind of analytical critique Latour laments to which an *ethnography as cultural critique* could be applied, so long as it targeted anthropology's own theoretical apparatuses. This is precisely the target of our expression *affect as cultural critique:* anthropology's dominant disciplinary analytics. However, whereas Marcus and Fischer (1999, 119–28) advocated drawing on the best of German (the Frankfurt school), French (surrealism), and American (documentary criticism) traditions for reinvigorating critique, they would likely concede that more diverse sources are needed today.

Affect as Cultural Critique explicitly targets those conceptual apparatuses – German, French, American, and others – that, whether out of tradition or of disciplinary pedagogy and practice, still implicitly limit what is understandable through ethnography. The point here is not to tear down the last bastions of "Western" theory, to finally, out of justifiable theoretical or political concerns, "[let] anthropology burn" (Jobson 2020). The point is to expand what anthropology can know, feel, and experience; broaden who it collaborates with and includes in its practices; and render critique into a shared enterprise whose purposes and ends are mutually determined. From this point of view, critique moves from an analytical skill taught, measured, and evaluated within academically guarded institutions and becomes a set of diverse practices for actively expanding one's capacity to connect with others and collaboratively share what they experience, evaluate, and offer to teach us all. In this regard, the volume follows a recent anthropological turn to focusing not on critique as the content of knowledge but rather as an orientation to knowledge, of which affect is always one formative component (Felski 2015, 3–4; Morningstar 2024, 608, 610).[11]

The contributors to this volume propose that attention to affect can help cultivate this more capacious approach to critique. This approach may be especially important today given the ways academics have embodied certain analytical styles of critique that divide and disconnect them from interlocutors and colleagues with whom they work.

Kathleen Stewart has demonstrated this perhaps most clearly and eloquently. Drawing on the work of Eve Sedgwick (2003), she writes:

> What is often called critical thinking and enacted as strong theory plowing through data on the strength of its independent logic is a paranoid approach to the world. Its repetitive resting point is the conviction that something is *wrong* with other people, and it dreams of finding some bad fixative of state power or normative fantasy as if these might be the only problem. (Stewart 2017, 196)

This inherited style of what Sedgwick calls "paranoid" forms of academic critique, drawing on Paul Ricoeur's "hermeneutics of suspicion" (Sedgwick 2003, 124), is characterized by a scepticism that can easily run out of road – right past the possibilities of learning anything new. How would we better, and more collaboratively, open ourselves to learning otherwise? How might we find methods for doing thought differently? And why not, as Stewart (2018) again asks, "utter the amazingly still unuttered question of whether *our* thought could be anything other than critique" (17)?

One place to turn for alternative modes to paranoid critique are feminist, Black, queer, Indigenous, and other critical scholars who have long identified the limits and exclusionary politics of the academy's dominant forms of problem-solving (Ahmed 2004a; Behar 1997; Berg and Ramos-Zayas 2015; Felski 2015; Kasmani 2022; Muñoz 2006; Osorio 2021; Pandian 2019; Sedgwick 2003; Sedgwick and Frank 1995b). Among the many alternatives proposed, Sedgwick's proposal of "reparative reading" is one compelling response to the negative affective disposition of "paranoid reading" (Sedgwick 2003). Paranoid reading breaks objects of research into parts, anticipating contradictions therein and exposing them to the selective ordering of a prefigured theoretical trend (of which some affect theory is admittedly guilty). It is a "thought style," in Rita Felski's (2015, 2) terms, that relates suspiciously with knowledge and others. Reparative reading assembles or "repair[s] ... part-objects into something like a whole," with an affective inclination towards connection and integration. "Whole," here, suggests not a complete or pre-existing figure but rather a capacious orientation to expansive and reciprocal vision: like reading affect theory not as a "turn" away but a facing towards one's theoretical ancestors.[12] As Heather Love (2010, 237) writes of reparative reading, it is on the side of "multiplicity, surprise, rich divergence, consolation, creativity, and love." But this does not make it "*un*critical" (Felski 2015, 2). Importantly for both Love and the contributors to this volume, one can ultimately refuse to choose between the paranoid and reparative, recognizing that different affects afford different insights. And hard times often require thought styles that *feel* hard: "Sedgwick taught me to let the affect in, but it's clear that by doing so I won't only be letting the sunshine in" (Love 2010, 239).

Reparative readings teach and inspire our contributors. But adopting one proposition of critical theory over another does not necessarily break strong and straight habits of thought.[13] Therefore, a more fundamental place to turn is anthropology's interlocutors. This is where a refocusing of affect theory on method and ethnography can help. Because a style of suspicious critique is still so broadly embodied in academic habits, it may take time and practice to constructively undo it towards alternative modes of ethnographic listening and connection. When, again, my colleague and I did not quite understand what our interlocutors meant when they referred to robots as *living*, this was not a matter of perspective. Nor was it one of belief. It was more a matter of *feeling* what they meant – or of what Andrea De Antoni and Paul Dumouchel (2017) call "feeling with the world." In fact, this is precisely the reason that the Buddhist priest with whom we most spoke conducted rituals for robots. It is, in fact, one of the reasons why many rituals are done: to deliver an affective charge that makes somatic sense in a way semiotic reasoning never could (although, as Sasha Newell [2018] has argued, the former is always inextricably part of the latter).[14] Adopting not the perspectives but the *practices* of others offers ways to undo one's theoretical attachments in ways that bring forth previously unrecognized realities.

When with furrowed brows my fieldwork collaborator and I kept prodding our robot-fan interlocutors for clear answers on whether robots were alive or not, we noticed that answers were often returned with smiles. In fact, it was only after many conversations, rituals, and a form of deep listening that unwound our analytical fixations that we finally started to get it. It was only after time and practice that we "finally learned to relax – to enjoy the conversation rather than answer the conceptual riddles, and to experiment with what it feels like to marvel at what perplexes us rather than target it for attack" (White and Katsuno 2021, 243). This mode of relating has the power to render practice into a mode that critiques *affectively* – that unwinds, expands, or deconstructs one's analytical positions towards new possibilities. In our fieldwork, we had limited our approach by treating the question of animacy in Japan as a puzzle to be solved. Our interlocutors, however, treated it as a game whose tensions, challenges, and contradictions brought delight. Importantly, it was only in sharing in the delight of our interlocutors that their perspective on robots made sense. It was only in the practised pleasure of interacting with robots and robot fans over time that we finally opened to the possibility that robots were not artificial or alive but could, in fact, through a pleasure of deeply serious play, be both.

This is how affect can serve as cultural critique, whereby *cultural* refers primarily to those disciplinary theories, concepts, and habits of Euro-American anthropological training that inhibit processes of uncovering something new or something unseen or unfelt. From this basis, we then propose that many other and broader forms of critique of the cultural might productively follow, so long as they are framed not as a tradition from "elsewhere" that are borrowed to solve a problem "at home" but rather as a practice cultivated collaboratively to engage problems of mutual concern. In fact, many ethnographic trends are pushing anthropology in this direction. Many recent ethnographies are showing how alternative possibilities for life on, with, and even beyond (Olson 2018) Earth require feeling them personally to understand them effectively. They are showing us not that affect operates exclusively outside symbols and representation but that it expands them (Newell 2018), making them into far more dynamic entities than we had previously conceived. Key ethnographic studies are now demonstrating, for example, that "forests" (Kohn 2013) and "climates" (Knox 2020) *think*, that robots *feel* (Katsuno 2011; White and Katsuno 2021), that mountains *live* and are thus deserving of rights and respect (De la Cadena 2015), that the world is, at large, *animate* (Chen 2012; Weston 2017). By focusing on the social facts of affect, these works show how affect speaks through dynamic systems of its own. Where affect can be used today as a tool for cracking open previously unrecognized possibilities within the academy, for both connecting to others and reinventing ways of collaborative flourishing, it serves as an important method for cultural critique.

***

The following chapters in this volume propose that by centring alternative modes of feeling encountered in fieldwork as methods of knowing, and accordingly "diversifying affect" (Navaro 2017), those modes can productively undo some of anthropology's limited, biased, and otherwise problematically inherited modes of analytical (i.e., overly paranoid) – thought. The various essays show in different ways how taking on the affective methods of interlocutors as modes for inquiry might lead to a form of ethnographic uncovering that was always central to the best contributions of anthropology but not always open enough to incorporate views that challenged dominant styles of theorizing. Drawing from the many currents of emotional (Lutz and Abu-Lughod

1990), affective (Clough 2007; Stewart 2007), embodied (Csordas 1994), and sensorial (Howes 2005; Pink 2015) thought that inspire us, and that have taught us to listen more carefully and corporeally to our interlocutors, *Affect as Cultural Critique* seeks reinvigoration for the discipline through a mode of reciprocal uncovering as a guiding professional aim, as methodological inspiration, as a community and interlocutor-driven research ethos, and as a source of reflexive critique of the discipline's philosophical and theory-heavy analytics.

NOTES

1 Comparing what he sees as similarly limiting "geopolitics and analytical habits" of affect theory and queer studies, anthropologist Omar Kasmani cites Anjali Arondekar and Geeta Patel's (2016, 152) observation that "non-Euro-American sources, settings, and epistemes, if and when invoked, appear only as exemplars, never as sites of theory making" (Kasmani 2022, 28).
2 For other discussions on the relation between ethnographic method, feelings, and affect from which we draw, see Faubion and Marcus (2009), Henare, Holbraad, and Wastell (2007), Hickey-Moody (2013), Holbraad and Pedersen (2017), Knudsen and Stage (2015), Miyazaki (2004), Stodulka et al. (2019), and Walkerdine (2010).
3 For other genealogical summaries of affect theory, see De Antoni (2019), Rutherford (2016), and, especially for what has been criticized as missing from it from feminist theory, Liljeström (2016).
4 Adding to this complexity is the fact that some researchers in cognitive neuroscience and psychology (Barrett 2017; Damasio 1994) refer to "emotion" in much the way that anthropologists refer to "affect."
5 We acknowledge, again, that we are not the first to make this call for more methodological attention to affect. Our work builds on important precursors such as Coleman and Ringrose (2013), Hickey-Moody (2013), Knudsen and Stage (2015), and Walkerdine (2010).
6 In adopting the phrase "affect as method," we also acknowledge the work of Thomas Csordas (1990, 1993), Hirokazu Miyazaki (2004), Yana Stainova (2019), and others similarly taking up experiments with affect as method.
7 In this specific application of affect as method, we acknowledge intersecting aims with that of Britta Timm Knudsen and Carsten Stage, who in the introduction to their volume, *Affective Methodologies* (2015, 5), write, "Research questions about affect become increasingly more answerable if they are concretely linked to specific bodies (for instance, the researcher's own body) in specific (and empirically approachable)

social contexts, as this makes it more likely that the researcher can actually collect/produce material that allows for empirically based argumentation." We keep Knudsen and Stage's guidance close to heart as we experiment with ethnographic ways of bringing particular experiences of affect to bear on anthropological uncovering and critique.

8 Greig Seigworth and Carollyn Pedwell have described "#AffectSoWhite" critiques as a collection of direct confrontations to "the ongoing historical persistence of Eurocentric blind spots in affect inquiry and the lived deracinated equivalences between the capacities to affect and to be affected" (Seigworth and Pedwell 2023b, 5). As one part of a response to grapple with these critiques, as well as with certain "pretentious positionings" toward "nonsubscribers" of affect theory, Seigworth helped organize the #AffectWTF conference in 2015 which reportedly received seven hundred submissions (Seigworth 2022).

9 Hamner (2023) attributes the phrase "en*whiten*ment to Ashley Cake (Hamner 2023, 234), noting also a key point on the difficulty of "unlearning affect because when it happens – if it happens – it does so at scales of temporality and spatiality that do not register as an event" (250).

10 I draw this language not only from decolonial scholars (Harrison 1991; Smith 1999) and advocates of reparative writing (Love 2010; Sedgwick 2003) but also from mentors and community advocates in Kalihi, Hawai'i among whom I worked as a grant writer in 2023–2024. (See in particular the work of Hoʻoulu ʻĀina [hoouluaina.org], Odom et al. (2019), and Kōkua Kalihi Valley [kkv.net]).

11 Drawing on critical reflections of critique, such as of Fassin (2017) Felski (2015), Yurchak (2003), and Zerilli (2019), anthropologist Natalie Morningstar argues that a Western legacy of critical theory has habituated theorists to think in terms of critique as either detached empiricism, on one hand, or critical engagement, on the other (Morningstar 2024, 614). As demonstrated by her artist-activist interlocutors in Dublin, who see both their art and activism as political, detachment can be an affect that yields constructive empirical critique that is at the same time a critical engagement. While detachment and engagement are seemingly contradictory within the genealogies of Western theory, they are regularly operationalized in art-as-activist practice. Morningstar therefore effectively leverages her ethnographic findings towards the proposition of an alternative analytic: an "anthropology of critique *as* critique" (622). For more on detachment as analytic, see Yarrow et al. (2015).

12 As James Laidlaw and Paolo Heywood (2013) allude to in their discussion of the ontological turn in anthropology, in their article "One More Turn and You're There," the idea that one might arrive at the truth of a theoretical problem with one more analytical turn is both a dominant rhetorical strategy and core fallacy of strong theory.

13 For another affectively rich critical alternative to straight theory, see Omar Kasmani's (2022, 2) discussion of "unstraight affordances" in his ethnography of Islamic saints in Pakistan, who are read as "queer companions" to queer and affect studies.

14 The deep connection between ritual and what Schaefer (2015) calls "religious affects" points to religion, healing, the mystical, and related queer intimacies as, in Kasmani's (2022, 28) assessment, underacknowledged resources for affect studies. Accordingly, religious studies is also another major contributing field to genealogies of affect theory that a full literary review of affect theory would need to account for.

REFERENCES

Abbott, Andrew. 2004. *Methods of Discovery: Heuristics for the Social Sciences*. New York: W.W. Norton & Company.

Abu-Lughod, Lila. 1986. *Veiled Sentiments: Honor and Poetry in a Bedouin Society*. Berkeley: University of California Press.

Ahmed, Sara. 2004a. "Collective Feelings: Or, the Impressions Left by Others." *Theory, Culture & Society* 21 (2): 25–42. https://doi.org/10.1177/0263276404042133.

Ahmed, Sara. 2004b. *The Cultural Politics of Emotion*. New York: Routledge.

Anderson, Warwick, Deborah Jenson, and Richard C. Keller, eds. 2011. *Unconscious Dominions: Psychoanalysis, Colonial Trauma, and Global Sovereignties*. Durham, NC: Duke University Press.

Arondekar, Anjali, and Geeta Patel. 2016. "Area Impossible: Notes Toward an Introduction." *GLQ: A Journal of Lesbian and Gay Studies* 22 (2): 151–71. https://doi.org/10.1215/10642684-3428687.

Barrett, Lisa Feldman. 2017. *How Emotions Are Made: The Secret Life of the Brain*. Boston: Houghton Mifflin Harcourt.

Behar, Ruth. 1997. *The Vulnerable Observer: Anthropology That Breaks Your Heart*. Boston: Beacon Press.

Berg, Ulla D., and Ana Y. Ramos-Zayas. 2015. "Racializing Affect: A Theoretical Proposition." *Current Anthropology* 56 (5): 654–77. https://doi.org/10.1086/683053.

Berlant, Lauren Gail. 2011. *Cruel Optimism*. Durham, NC: Duke University Press.

Berlant, Lauren Gail, and Kathleen Stewart. 2019. *The Hundreds*. Durham, NC: Duke University Press.

Boler, Megan, and Michalinos Zembylas. 2016. "Interview with Megan Boler: From 'Feminist Politics of Emotions' to the 'Affective Turn'." In *Methodological Advances in Research on Emotion and Education*, edited by Michalinos Zembylas and Paul A. Schutz, 17–30. Cham, Switzerland: Springer.

Boyer, Dominic, and George E. Marcus. 2015. "New Methodologies for a Transformed Discipline." In *Theory Can Be More Than It Used to Be: Learning Anthropology's Method in a Time of Transition*, edited by Dominic Boyer, James D. Faubion, and George E. Marcus. Ithaca, NY: Cornell University Press.

Brennan, Teresa. 2004. *The Transmission of Affect*. Ithaca, NY: Cornell University Press.

Candea, Matei. 2019. *Comparison in Anthropology: The Impossible Method*. Cambridge, UK: Cambridge University Press.

Chang, David A. 2016. *The World and All the Things Upon It: Native Hawaiian Geographies of Exploration*. Minneapolis and London: University of Minnesota Press.

Chen, Mel Y. 2012. *Animacies*. Durham, NC: Duke University Press.

Clifford, James, and George E. Marcus, eds. 1986. *Writing Culture: The Poetics and Politics of Ethnography*. Berkeley: University of California Press.

Clough, Patricia Ticineto. 2007. "Introduction." In *The Affective Turn: Theorizing the Social*, edited by Patricia Ticineto Clough and Jean Halley, 1–33. Durham, NC: Duke University Press.

Coleman, Rebecca, and Jessica Ringrose, eds. 2013. *Deleuze and Research Methodologies*. Edinburgh: Edinburgh University Press.

Csordas, Thomas J. 1990. "Embodiment as a Paradigm for Anthropology." *Ethos* 18 (1): 5–47. https://doi.org/10.1525/eth.1990.18.1.02a00010.

Csordas, Thomas J. 1993. "Somatic Modes of Attention." *Cultural Anthropology* 8 (2): 135–56.

Csordas, Thomas J., ed. 1994. *Embodiment and Experience: The Existential Ground of Culture and Self*. Cambridge, UK: University of Cambridge Press.

Damasio, Antonio R. 1994. *Descartes' Error: Emotion, Reason, and the Human Brain*. New York: Putnam.

Darwin, Charles. [1872] 2018. *The Expression of the Emotions in Man and Animal*. Mineola, NY: Dover Publications, Inc.

De Antoni, Andrea. 2019. "Affect." In *The International Encyclopedia of Anthropology*, edited by Hilary Callan, 1–8. Hoboken, NJ: John Wiley & Sons.

De Antoni, Andrea, and Paul Dumouchel. 2017. "The Practices of Feeling with the World: Towards an Anthropology of Affect, the Senses and Materiality – Introduction." *Japanese Review of Cultural Anthropology* 18 (1): 91–8. https://doi.org/10.14890/jrca.18.1_99.

De la Cadena, Marisol. 2015. *Earth Beings*. Durham, NC: Duke University Press.

DeLanda, Manuel. 2016. *Assemblage Theory*. Edinburgh: Edinburgh University Press.

Durkheim, Émile. [1912] 2008. *The Elementary Forms of the Religious Life*. Translated by Joseph Ward Swain. Mineola, NY: Dover Publications, Inc.

Ekman, Paul. 1999. "Basic Emotions." In *Handbook of Cognition and Emotion*, edited by Tim Dalgleish and Mick Power, 45–60. Chichester: John Wiley & Sons.

Fassin, Didier. 2017. "The Endurance of Critique." *Anthropological Theory* 17 (1): 4–29. https://doi.org/10.1177/1463499616688157.

Faubion, James D., and George E. Marcus. 2009. *Fieldwork Is Not What It Used to Be: Learning Anthropology's Method in a Time of Transition*. Ithaca, NY: Cornell University Press.

Felski, Rita. 2015. *The Limits of Critique*. Chicago and London: University of Chicago Press.

Fujita, Masahiro, and Kitano Hiroaki. 1998. "Development of an Autonomous Quadruped Robot for Robot Entertainment." *Autonomous Robots* 5: 7–18. https://doi.org/10.1023/A:1008856824126.

Gregg, Melissa, and Gregory J. Seigworth. 2010. *The Affect Theory Reader*. Durham, NC: Duke University Press.

Hamner, M. Gail. 2023. "Unlearning Affect." In *The Affect Theory Reader 2: Worldings, Tensions, Futures*, edited by Gregory J. Seigworth and Carolyn Pedwell, 233–54. Durham, NC, and London: Duke University Press.

Harrison, Faye V. 1991a. "Anthropology as an Agent of Transformation: Introductory Comments and Queries." In *Decolonizing Anthropology: Moving Further Toward an Anthropology of Liberation*, edited by Faye V. Harrison, 1–15. Arlington, VA: Association of Black Anthropologists, American Anthropological Association.

Harrison, Faye V., ed. 1991b. *Decolonizing Anthropology: Moving Further Toward an Anthropology of Liberation*. Arlington, VA: Association of Black Anthropologists, American Anthropological Association.

Henare, Amiria, Martin Holbraad, and Sari Wastell, eds. 2007. *Thinking through Things: Theorising Artefacts Ethnographically*. Abingdon, UK: Routledge.

Hickey-Moody, Anna. 2013. "Affect as Method: Feelings, Aesthetics and Affective Pedagogy." In *Deleuze and Research Methodologies*, edited by Rebecca Coleman and Jessica Ringrose, 79–95. Edinburgh: Edinburgh University Press.

Holbraad, Martin, and Morten Axel Pedersen. 2017. *The Ontological Turn: An Anthropological Exposition*. Cambridge, UK: Cambridge University Press.

Howes, David. 2005. *Empire of the Senses*. Oxford: Berg Publishers.

James, William. 1884. "What Is an Emotion?" *Mind* 9 (34): 188–205.

Jobson, Ryan Cecil. 2020. "The Case for Letting Anthropology Burn: Sociocultural Anthropology in 2019." *American Anthropologist* 122 (2): 259–71. https://doi.org/10.1111/aman.13398.

Kasmani, Omar. 2022. *Queer Companions: Religion, Public Intimacy, and Saintly Affects in Pakistan*. Durham, NC, and London: Duke University Press.

Katsuno, Hirofumi. 2011. "The Robot's Heart: Tinkering with Humanity and Intimacy in Robot-Building." *Japanese Studies* 31 (1): 93–109. https://doi.org/10.1080/10371397.2011.560259.

Khanna, Ranjana. 2003. *Dark Continents: Psychoanalysis and Colonialism.* Durham, NC: Duke University Press.

Knox, Hannah. 2020. *Thinking Like a Climate.* Durham, NC: Duke University Press.

Knudsen, Britta Timm, and Carsten Stage. 2015. *Affective Methodologies: Developing Cultural Research Strategies for the Study of Affect.* Basingstoke, UK: Palgrave Macmillan.

Kohn, Eduardo. 2013. *How Forests Think: Toward an Anthropology Beyond the Human.* Berkeley: University of California Press.

Laidlaw, James, and Paolo Heywood. 2013. "One More Turn and You're There." *Anthropology of This Century* 7. http://aotcpress.com/articles/turn/.

Latour, Bruno. 2004. "Why Has Critique Run Out of Steam? From Matters of Fact to Matters of Concern." *Critical Inquiry* 30 (2): 225–48. https://doi.org/10.1086/421123.

Levy, Robert I. 1973. *Tahitians: Mind and Experience in the Society Islands.* Chicago: University of Chicago Press.

Levy, Robert I. 1984. "The Emotions in Comparative Perspective." In *Approaches to Emotion*, edited by Klaus R. Scherer and Paul Ekman, 397–412. Mahwah, NJ: Lawrence Erlbaum Associates.

Leys, Ruth. 2011. "The Turn to Affect: A Critique." *Critical inquiry* 37 (3): 434–72. https://doi.org/10.1086/659353.

Leys, Ruth. 2017. *The Ascent of Affect: Genealogy and Critique.* Chicago: University of Chicago Press.

Liljestrom, Marianne. 2016. "Affect." In *Oxford Handbook of Feminist Theory*, edited by Lisa Disch and Mary Hawkesworth, 16–38. New York: Oxford University Press.

Love, Heather. 2010. "Truth and Consequences: On Paranoid Reading and Reparative Reading." *Criticism* 52 (2): 235–41. https://doi.org/10.1353/crt.2010.0022.

Lutz, Catherine. 1982. "The Domain of Emotion Words on Ifaluk." *American Ethnologist* 9 (1): 113–28.

Lutz, Catherine. 1988. *Unnatural Emotions: Everyday Sentiments on a Micronesian Atoll & Their Challenge to Western Theory.* Chicago: University of Chicago Press.

Lutz, Catherine, and Lila Abu-Lughod. 1990. *Language and the Politics of Emotion, Studies in Emotion and Social Interaction.* Cambridge, UK: Cambridge University Press.

Lutz, Catherine, and Geoffrey M. White. 1986. "The Anthropology of Emotions." *Annual Review of Anthropology* 15 (1): 405–36. https://doi.org/10.1146/annurev.an.15.100186.002201.

Marcus, George E., and Michael M.J. Fischer, eds. 1986. *Anthropology as Cultural Critique: An Experimental Moment in the Human Sciences*. Chicago: University of Chicago Press.

Marcus, George E., and Michael M.J. Fischer. 1999. *Anthropology as Cultural Critique: An Experimental Moment in the Human Sciences*. 2nd ed. Chicago: University of Chicago Press.

Martin, Emily. 2013. "The Potentiality of Ethnography and the Limits of Affect Theory." *Current Anthropology* 54 (S7): S149–58. https://doi.org/10.1086/670388.

Massumi, Brian. 1995. "The Autonomy of Affect." *Cultural Critique* 31: 83–109. https://doi.org/10.2307/1354446.

Massumi, Brian. 2002. *Parables for the Virtual: Movement, Affect, Sensation*. Durham, NC: Duke University Press.

Mazzarella, William. 2009. "Affect: What Is It Good For?" In *Enchantments of Modernity: Empire, Nation, Globalization*, edited by Saurabh Dube, 291–309. London: Routledge.

Miyazaki, Hirokazu. 2004. *The Method of Hope: Anthropology, Philosophy, and Fijian Knowledge*. Stanford, CA: Stanford University Press.

Morningstar, Natalie. 2024. "Critique Refigured: Art, Activism, and Politics in Post-Recession Dublin." *Journal of the Royal Anthropological Institute* 30 (3): 606–26. https://doi.org/10.1111/1467-9655.14097.

Muehlebach, Andrea. 2011. "On Affective Labor in Post-Fordist Italy." *Cultural Anthropology* 26 (1): 59–82. https://doi.org/10.1111/j.1548-1360.2010.01080.x.

Muñoz, José Esteban. 2006. "Feeling Brown, Feeling Down: Latina Affect, the Performativity of Race, and the Depressive Position." *Signs: Journal of Women in Culture and Society* 31 (3): 675–88. https://doi.org/10.1086/499080.

Myers, Fred R. 1991. *Pintupi Country, Pintupi Self: Sentiment, Place, and Politics Among Western Desert Aborigines*. Berkeley: University of California Press.

Navaro, Yael. 2017. "Diversifying Affect." *Cultural Anthropology* 32 (2): 209–14. https://doi.org/10.14506/ca32.2.05.

Navaro-Yashin, Yael. 2009. "Affective Spaces, Melancholic Objects: Ruination and the Production of Anthropological Knowledge." *Journal of the Royal Anthropological Institute* 15 (1): 1–18. https://doi.org/10.1111/j.1467-9655.2008.01527.x.

Navaro-Yashin, Yael. 2012. *The Make-Believe Space: Affective Geography in a Postwar Polity*. Durham, NC: Duke University Press.

Newell, Sasha. 2018. "The Affectiveness of Symbols: Materiality, Magicality, and the Limits of the Antisemiotic Turn." *Current Anthropology* 59 (1): 1–22. https://doi.org/10.1086/696071.

Ngai, Sianne. 2005. *Ugly Feelings*. Cambridge, MA: Harvard University Press.

Odom, Sharon Kaʻiulani, Puni Jackson, David Derauf, Megan Kiyomi Inada, and Andrew H. Aoki. 2019. "Pilinahā: An Indigenous Framework for

Health." *Current Developments in Nutrition* 3: 32–8. https://doi.org/10.1093/cdn/nzz001.

Olson, Valerie. 2018. *Into the Extreme: U.S. Environmental Systems and Politics Beyond Earth*. Minneapolis: University of Minnesota Press.

Osorio, Jamaica Heolimeleikalani. 2021. *Remembering Our Intimacies: Moʻolelo, Aloha ʻĀina, and Ea*. Minneapolis: University of Minnesota Press.

Palmer, Tyrone S. 2023. "Affect and Affirmation." In *The Affect Theory Reader 2: Worldings, Tensions, Futures*, edited by Gregory J. Seigworth and Carolyn Pedwell, 122–40. Durham, NC, and London: Duke University Press.

Pandian, Anand. 2019. *A Possible Anthropology: Methods for Uneasy Times*. Durham, NC, and London. Duke University Press.

Pink, Sarah. 2015. *Doing Sensory Ethnography*. London: Sage.

Puar, Jasbir K. 2023. "Dividual Economies, of Data, of Flesh." In *The Affect Theory Reader 2: Worldings, Tensions, Futures*, edited by Gregory J. Seigworth and Carolyn Pedwell, 406–22. Durham, NC, and London: Duke University Press.

Rosaldo, Michelle Zimbalist. 1980. *Knowledge and Passion: Ilongot Notions of Self and Social Life*. Cambridge, UK; New York: Cambridge University Press.

Rosaldo, Renato. 1989. "Grief and a Headhunter's Rage." In *Culture and Truth: The Remaking of Social Analysis*, 1–21. Boston: Beacon Press.

Rutherford, Danilyn. 2016. "Affect Theory and the Empirical." *Annual Review of Anthropology* 45 (1): 285–300. https://doi.org/10.1146/annurev-anthro-102215-095843.

Schaefer, Donovan. 2015. *Religious Affects: Animality, Evolution, and Power*. Durham, NC, and London: Duke University Press.

Schieffelin, Bambi, and Elinor Ochs, eds. 1986. *Language Socialization Across Cultures*. Cambridge, UK: Cambridge University Press.

Schieffelin, Edward L. 1976. *The Sorrow of the Lonely and the Burning of the Dancers*. New York: St. Martin's Press.

Seaver, Nick. 2021. "Care and Scale: Decorrelative Ethics in Algorithmic Recommendation." *Cultural Anthropology* 36 (3): 509–37. https://doi.org/10.14506/ca36.3.11.

Sedgwick, Eve Kosofsky. 2003. "Paranoid Reading and Reparative Reading; or, You're So Paranoid, You Probably Think This Essay is About You." In *Touching Feeling: Affect, Pedagogy Performativity*, edited by Michèle Aina Barale, Jonathan Goldberg, Michael Moon, and Eve Kosofsky Sedgwick, 123–52. Durham, NC, and London: Duke University Press.

Sedgwick, Eve Kosofsky, and Adam Frank. 1995a. *Shame and Its Sisters: A Silvan Tomkins Reader*. Durham, NC: Duke University Press.

Sedgwick, Eve Kosofsky, and Adam Frank. 1995b. "Shame in the Cybernetic Fold: Reading Silvan Tomkins." In *Shame and Its Sisters; A Silvan Tomkins Reader*, edited by Eve Kosofsky Sedgwick and Adam Frank, 1–28. Durham, NC: Duke University Press.

Seigworth, Gregory J. "AffectWTF Conference Introduction."*YouTube Video*, 8:22. Uploaded 12 April 2022. www.youtube.com/watch?v=kSe1my1x1qo.

Seigworth, Gregory J., and Carolyn Pedwell, eds. 2023a. *The Affect Theory Reader 2: Worldings, Tensions, Futures*. Durham, NC, and London: Duke University Press.

Seigworth, Gregory J., and Carolyn Pedwell. 2023b. "Introduction: A Shimer of Inventories." In *The Affect Theory Reader 2: Worldings, Tensions, Futures*, edited by Gregory J. Seigworth and Carolyn Pedwell, 1–59. Durham, NC, and London: Duke University Press.

Slaby, Jan, Rainer Mühlhoff, and Philipp Wüschner. 2017. "Affective Arrangements." *Emotion Review* 11 (1): 3–12. https://doi.org/10.1177/1754073917722214.

Smith, Linda Tuhiwai. 1999. *Decolonizing Methodologies: Research and Indigenous Peoples*. London and New York: Zed Books.

Spiegel, Alix. 2017. "Invisibilia: A Man Finds an Explosive Emotion Locked in a Word." *NPR*, 1 June. www.npr.org/sections/health-shots/2017/06/01/529876861/an-anthropologist-discovers-the-terrible-emotion-locked-in-a-word.

Spinoza, Benedictus de. [1677] 1996. *Ethics*. Translated by Edwin Curley. London: Penguin Books.

Stainova, Yana. 2019. "Enchantment as Method." *Anthropology and Humanism* 44 (2): 214–30. https://doi.org/10.1111/anhu.12251.

Stewart, Kathleen. 2007. *Ordinary Affects*. Durham, NC: Duke University Press.

Stewart, Kathleen. 2017. "In the World That Affect Proposed." *Cultural Anthropology* 32 (2): 192–8. https://doi.org/10.14506/ca32.2.03.

Stewart, Kathleen. 2018. "'Worldy Thinking.' Comment on Sasha Newell's 'The Affectiveness of Symbols: Materiality, Magicality, and the Limits of the Antisemiotic Turn.'" *Current Anthropology* 59 (1): 16–8. https://doi.org/10.1086/696071.

Stodulka, Thomas, Samia Dinkelaker, and Ferdiansyah Thajib, eds. 2019. *Affective Dimensions of Fieldwork and Ethnography*. Cham, Switzerland: Springer.

Terada, Rei. 2003. *Feeling in Theory*. Cambridge, MA: Harvard University Press.

Thien, Deborah. 2005. "After or Beyond Feeling? A Consideration of Affect and Emotion in Geography." *Area* 37 (4): 450–4. https://doi.org/10.1111/j.1475-4762.2005.00643a.x.

Thrift, Nigel. 2004. "Intensities of Feeling: Towards a Spatial Politics of Affect." *Geografiska Annaler. Series B, Human Geography* 86 (1): 57–78. https://doi.org/10.1111/j.0435-3684.2004.00154.x.

Thrift, Nigel. 2008. *Non-Representational Theory: Space, Politics, Affect*. New York: Routledge.

Tomkins, Silvan S. 2008. *Affect, Imagery, Consciousness*. New York: Springer.

Walkerdine, Valerie. 2010. "Communal Beingness and Affect: An Exploration of Trauma in an Ex-Industrial Community." *Body & Society* 16 (1): 91–116. https://doi.org/10.1177/1357034X09354127.

Weston, Kath. 2017. *Animate Planet*. Durham, NC: Duke University Press.

Wetherell, Margaret. 2012. *Affect and Emotion: A New Social Science Understanding*. Los Angeles: SAGE.

White, Daniel. 2018. "'Critique in the Gap.' Comment on Sasha Newell's 'The Affectiveness of Symbols: Materiality, Magicality, and the Limits of the Antisemiotic Turn.'" *Current Anthropology* 59 (1): 18–9. https://doi.org/10.1086/696071.

White, Daniel. 2019. "The Mechanics of Fear. Re-Envisioning Anxiety through Emerging Technologies of Affect." *TG Technikgeschichte (History of Technology)* 86 (3): 245–64. https://doi.org/10.5771/0040-117X-2019-3-245.

White, Daniel, and Andrea De Antoni. 2025. "Affect." In *The Open Encyclopedia of Anthropology*, edited by Hanna Nieber. http://doi.org/10.29164/25affect.

White, Daniel, and Hirofumi Katsuno. 2021. "Toward an Affective Sense of Life: Artificial Intelligence, Animacy, and Amusement at a Robot Pet Memorial Service in Japan." *Cultural Anthropology* 36 (2): 222–51. https://doi.org/10.14506/ca36.2.03.

White, Daniel, and Hirofumi Katsuno. 2022. "Modelling Emotion, Perfecting Heart: Disassembling Technologies of Affect with an Android Bodhisattva in Japan." *Journal of the Royal Anthropological Society*. Published ahead of print, 24 April 2022. https://doi.org/10.1111/1467-9655.13813.

Wikan, Unni. 1990. *Managing Turbulent Hearts: A Balinese Formula for Living*. Chicago: University of Chicago Press.

Yarrow, Thomas, Matei Candea, Catherine Trundle, and Jo Cook. 2015. *Detachment: Essays on the Limits of Relational Thinking*. Manchester: Manchester University Press.

Yurchak, Alexei. 2003. "Soviet Hegemony of Form: Everything Was Forever, Until It Was No More." *Comparative Studies in Society and History* 45 (3): 480–510. https://doi.org/10.1017/S0010417503000239.

Zerilli, Linda M.G. 2019. "Critique as a Political Practice of Freedom." In *A Time for Critique*, edited by Bernard E. Harcourt and Didier Fassin, 36–51. New York: Columbia University Press.

Chapter 1

Sensing the World: Intuition as a Musical and Social Orientation

YANA STAINOVA

"You have to travel to Coro to visit Las Panelas, Isandra's *núcleo* [music school]," several musicians told me while I was doing my fieldwork based in the Venezuelan classical music program El Sistema, which brings music education and instruments to children and youth on the urban margins. Founded in 1975 by economist and musician José Antonio Abreu, the program has received support from seven different Venezuelan governments and grown to include one million students over the years. Among the 423 other núcleos scattered all over Venezuela, what people told me was distinctive about this small school was that it had been founded and developed by Isandra Campos, an Afro-descendent woman who herself was a mother of four El Sistema musicians. Like most other núcleos, Las Panelas was in a Venezuelan *barrio*, a working-class neighbourhood affected by poverty and everyday violence. "You have to see the amazing work that is being done there," I kept hearing.

At the time I heard about Las Panelas, I was feeling stuck in my fieldwork. I knew for certain that I was interested in exploring the connection between music practices and social precarity that manifested along the lines of race and class. Ironically, in an attempt to protect myself from the potential impacts of precariousness in a country with one of the highest homicide rates in the world, I had decided to do short-term preliminary research in the more economically and socially stable city of Mérida. Nestled between mountains, the city has a strong intellectual and musical tradition that appealed to my scholarly self. Its strong musical tradition theoretically made it an ideal place for my research. However, as I visited the music schools there, I did not *feel* I was finding what I intuited was the heart of my research question.

I became curious about Isandra Campos, a woman who had managed to assert her place in El Sistema, an institutional space that reflected the male and white European elite that dominated Venezuelan society. Coincidentally, I had already met her daughter Julia, also a musician in one of the most prestigious El Sistema orchestras in Caracas. In what I came to understand as strong intuition, I abandoned my original fieldwork plans in Mérida and travelled to Coro to get to know Isandra and her school. There, I experienced the kind of peace that comes when I *feel* I have found something I was looking for, even when I was not sure how to articulate it in words. In my conversations with Isandra, I found that what led to the founding of her music school was a series of decisions that radically altered her life course. Serendipitous events, visions, and dedication came together to propel Isandra, a high school-educated woman who was tethered to working-class jobs her entire life, to become the director of the Las Panelas music school. Her life story radically interrupted the logics of racial and gender violence deeply rooted in Venezuelan society.

In this chapter, I study the social production of *intuición*, or intuition, as a force in people's lives in the realm of the aesthetic and in the everyday. Hand in hand with studying intuition as a category in the field, I think about the role of intuition in my own academic work as a method of fieldwork. I investigate how intuition surfaced as a force that moved me in the field and along certain intellectual currents of thought, including towards and then away from affect theory. Rather than think about intuition as a pre-social or universal affect, I investigate the social roots of intuition by focusing on how it was felt and theorized by my interlocutors in Venezuela. I argue that for racialized women living in social precariousness in Venezuela, intuition is experienced and valued as a force that momentarily interrupts, though not always consciously, predictable cycles of patriarchy, ethno-racial discrimination, and other forms of everyday violence. In the accounts of my interlocutors, intuition is a restlessness that pushes them away from the social inertia of structural violence and along frequently unexplored paths that have the potential to break social cycles. In these fissures people create themselves anew and work towards building a life that refuses the one predestined by social currents. Even as it points *to* a future, then, an investigation into the social roots of intuition also reveals it as a reaction *against* the present, the past, and the versions of the future destined by structural violence. In this sense, intuición appears as at once an affect, an emic concept, and a somatic method for navigating structural racism, challenging anthropological characterizations of affect as absent of semantic content. Accordingly, tracing the social resonances of intuition illuminates how people on the ground critique social structures not through the habits of academic discourse but through the affective experience of encountering their resistance in the world and formulating points of escape.

Intuition

Merriam Webster dictionary defines *intuition* as "a natural ability or power that makes it possible to know something without any proof or evidence: a feeling that guides a person to act a certain way without fully understanding why." The concept figures prominently in the history of Western thought. In the *Republic*, Plato defines intuition as what enables us to perceive the true nature of reality (Kemerling 2011). Descartes describes it as "the conception of a clear and attentive mind, which is so easy and distinct that there can be no room for doubt about what we are understanding" (Adam and Tannery 1964, 10: 368), highlighting the sense of certainty that frequently accompanies sensations of intuition. Romantic ideas associated intuition with religion and posited it as universal (Schleiermacher [1799] 1996, 1, in Jager 2006). In his definition of personality types, Carl Jung introduces the category of the "intuitive type," or those who do not act on the basis of rational judgment but through "instinctive apprehension" (see Pilard 2018, 19). Popular contemporary writing on intuition includes books on mysticism that evoke the concept as an inner power one can tap into to know life and self.[15]

Intuition also figures in Latin American literary and philosophical imaginaries, where it is sometimes perceived as a concept that pushes back against the intellectualism of Western thought. Rumblings of intuition can be found in the development of the magical realism literary genre, emphasizing currents of magic in everyday life and thus opposing the dominance of Western science in identifying the workings of reality. For writers in this literary tradition, intuition does justice to the worlds of the imagination that are not subject to scientific confirmation. The movement's famous representative Gabriel García Márquez (1981) calls on fiction writers to rely on intuition, "a quality that allows us to decipher what is real without recourse to scientific knowledge" (n.p.). The Mexican philosopher Antonio Caso (1883–1946) developed the concept of *intuición analógica*, or analogue intuition, to describe "a way of knowing through seeing" and "where objects appear as they are," without being analysed (Caso 1982, 27, in Vargas 2005, 172) – a way of knowing objects through the senses (Vargas 2005, 177). For Caso, intuition emerged as a way of integrating opposites in philosophy – reason-experience, subjectivity-objectivity – without subjugating one to the other (173). Argentine philosopher and anthropologist Rizieri

Frondizi, who lived and worked in the early twentieth century, thought about philosophy not as knowledge but as "the expression of a religious or poetic intuition" (Frondizi 1947, 35).

Intuition has played an important role in a variety of disciplines, from physics to education, religious studies, psychology, philosophy, math, computer science, and environmental studies (see Lufityanto et al. 2016). Intuition also figures prominently as a topic in the realm of business, specifically within strategic planning (Calabretta et al. 2017), where the emphasis is on intuition as a form of decision-making. Across fields, the concept appears as notoriously difficult to pin down, yielding dozens of interpretations and frequently defined by what it is *not*: a form of agency *without* recourse to analytical and rational reasoning (Epstein 2010). These studies paint intuition as relying on the non-conscious recognition of patterns (Dane and Pratt 2007). It is fast (Kahneman 2011), not following linear, logical reasoning processes that can be thoroughly reconstructed or explained (Barnard 1968 [1938]; Simon 1987).

From the previously mentioned definitions, intuition emerges as an act that is not entirely conscious, is outside the realm of analytical thinking, and is characterized by certainty. However, *intuitio*, the Late Latin root of the term, means "a looking at, consideration." Intuition is also related to the past participle stem of Latin *intueri*, meaning "look at, consider" (Online Etymology Dictionary). The Latin roots of the word emphasize the acts of reflection and contemplation that are frequently a part of intuitive agency. Illuminating contemplation as part of intuition challenges the binary between rationality and analysis, on one hand, and feeling and perception, on the other, a binary that seems almost integral to definitions of intuition and anthropology's philosophical genealogies underpinning how we study emotion (see Lutz 1998).

Overt discussions of intuition have not found as much traction in anthropology. Where it does appear, it is in scholarship on fieldwork methodology. "When doing fieldwork … let yourself be led by your intuition and sensibilities," Ruth Behar (2020, 51) urges. When writing on intuition, anthropologists have described it as a form of attunement to the field (Hoffman 2016). Intuition, in this strand of scholarship, is about reading a context and adapting our sensory and cognitive frame to it instead of imposing our own. Intuition means allowing ourselves to open our perception to the field (Hoffman 2016, 29) instead of inserting an "alien cognitive frame." Thomas Csordas (2007, 115) links intuition to empathy (see also Caso 1982), calling the latter "a specific case of intuition, one that has to do with feeling for and with another person." From these studies, I glean that intuition describes more than just a passive relationship to the world but rather a way we participate in sensing our environment and in "world-making" (Kondo 2018). This is in part because intuition creates the sensation that our thoughts and feelings bring certain events to be, or, inversely, that we are able to sense future events unfolding through empathy and attunement (Stewart 2011) to the field.

Affect and Intuition

"Why did you abandon affect?" a member of my dissertation committee asked in an American Anthropological Association (AAA) 2021 roundtable about my recently published book. I was slightly surprised by this observation because, while true, I did not feel like I had abandoned affect intentionally. His words made me reflect on the intellectual currents and structures I had shed since the writing of my dissertation. The invitation to participate in a volume that reimagines affect brought up memories of my days as a doctoral student who had found in affect a productive analytical lens. Thinking through the provocations in this introduction, along with intuition, a concept that fluently fits into affect theory, I am inspired to reflect on my mentor's question: "Why did you abandon affect?"

To look for clues, I went back to my preliminary exams, when I last remember being absorbed by theories of affect. I realized that, at the time, I was attracted to affect theory because it allowed me a kind of intellectual freedom from the academic constraints I encountered in trying to write about my experience in the field. For example, the El Sistema musicians would often speak about their musical experiences as going "beyond words." From a linguistic anthropology perspective dominant in my graduate studies, it was acceptable to explain *why* people would appeal to extra-linguistic experiences without venturing to believe, myself, that such experiences were possible for people born in logocentric environments. To me, however, explaining away my interlocutors' experiences into predictable frames of analysis felt condescending and reductive. Importantly, in its excess of the social and political, affect theory allowed me another kind of freedom: to write and think about my interlocutors' experiences of music as irreducible to the political impositions, aspirations, and overdeterminations by states and institutions. Finally, affect gave me the intellectual framework for describing the "capacities to affect and be affected" (Hardt 2015, 218). To be affected as a researcher was looked down upon in academic circles, perhaps most harshly articulated in an anonymous Wenner-Gren review of my (rejected) dissertation research proposal that warned that I risked being "trapped in the object of my own fascination." I experienced this comment as a form of violence, disciplining, and aggressive gatekeeping. Against this backdrop, affect theory offered me intellectual validity when, as a student, I needed to prove myself on my own terms on the academic stage.

Affirming my right to be fascinated and describing it as an intellectually valuable disposition became the impetus of my book. There, I wrote of the experience of being affected as *enchantment*, the capacity to experience wonder and fascination. I argued for enchantment as a "method" of doing ethnographic fieldwork (Stainova 2019, 2021). When transforming my dissertation into a book – in making it my own – I moved away from affect. I suspect that I did not choose to theorize enchantment as an affect because I wanted to allow the concept to hover in the ethnographic minutiae from which it had emerged. I was attempting to stick as close as possible to the ground, to the ethnographic testimonies, while protecting them from being hijacked by theoretical currents with their own force and direction. Perhaps the most important influence in this transition was the mentors who advised me to focus on writing and crafting the ethnographic material before resorting to theoretical frameworks. It was a way of applying to ethnographic writing what Veena Das (1998), when thinking about the words of her interlocutors, calls "language as a form of experience and not only message" (186). I was, in essence, putting into practice what in my exams I had theorized as "affect-imbued" writing or trying to re-create through my writing the kinds of experiences I was writing *about*. In other words, I wanted to experience and write affect without naming it as such, abstaining as much as possible from forcing it into words and, specifically, prefigured frames of analysis.

Intuition, as a heavily sensorial and embodied dimension of lived experience that is frequently hard to define in words, resonates with the classical definition of affect as escaping language (see White intro; Massumi 1995). In this chapter, I consider intuition as an ethnographically concrete instance of affect, and I trace its material reverberations at the intersection of music practice and social marginalization in Venezuela. Beyond studying the many ways in which intuition, as I encountered it in the field, intervenes in existing theoretical debates around affect, I am drawn to Daniel White's provocation in this volume's introduction to think about *affect as method*, as a methodological and conceptual capacity to inhabit contradictions along with our interlocutors and "modulate [the] researcher's body to better sense alternative points of view grounded in and guided by feeling" (42). I am cautious, however, to avoid hijacking affect as an exclusive framing of my own fieldwork journey, although this is an important part of the story. Instead, a focus on affect as method serves as an invitation to linger on the dynamic processes of theor*izing* and method-*making*. Thinking with method *as* theory reveals how theorizing and concept-building happens while we are in the field, a labour frequently carried out by our interlocutors and in collaboration, rather than an activity that is reserved for the exclusive spaces of the ivory tower.[1] I am inspired here by Laura McTighe's (2020) phrase "theory on the ground," a form of research that centres "the theory produced by people outside the academy," our interlocutors, and "considers both how our questions and the methods we use to answer them are developed in collaboration" (432). Focusing on the concept and theory building that takes place in the field has the potential to challenge the binaries between method and theory, the field and the academy, as part of a commitment to decolonial academic practice. Beyond doing justice to the inexpressible, affect as method captures the transmission of emotions (Brennan 2004), such as urgency, passion, and devotion, in a collaborative effort towards building futures otherwise – futures still in the process of being constructed.

Isandra

Intuition first came up (in a way that I can remember) when I was chatting with a mother at an El Sistema núcleo in Merida. She was waiting at the entrance of the music building for her children to finish music classes. I asked her my usual questions: Why were her kids enrolled at El Sistema? She said that "it keeps kids away from *vicios* [bad habits]" and that "musical accomplishments give students the sensation of *ser alguien* [being someone]," or being "*una persona digna* [a dignified person]." However, she said that most children's mothers, like herself, decide to enroll their children at El Sistema because they *feel* it on the level of intuición (intuition), rather than because of conscious calculation and concrete knowledge of why classical music would be a good influence on them. "*Se siente*" (one feels it), that it is a different space, that it is important," she said in reference to the music school. This conversation reflected the importance of intuition for people who were building worlds and imagining futures in precarious contexts, who lacked full knowledge and capacity to imagine what their decisions would entail. Intuition opened up ways of sensing the future and dreaming that were not concretely available through language or rational calculation, yet propelled people in a direction that felt right.

As I revisit my ethnographic material from this period, it seems fitting that this conversation was diligently recorded in my fieldnotes just a couple of weeks before I undertook the trip to Coro to visit Isandra.

Perhaps on some subconscious level the discussion of intuition had prompted me to trust and act on my own intuition when it came to my ethnographic fieldwork.

***

After a six-hour journey in a heavily air-conditioned bus, I arrived in Coro and made my way over to Isandra's house where her núcleo was housed. I arrived at Isandra's doorstep, at her house-turned-núcleo, without ever having met her. She was a short woman with dark hair, a wide smile, and eyes that look at you as if they are laughing. Immediately she made me feel at home. In the front of her living space, at the level of the sidewalk and street, were two big rooms. During the day, they were full of children playing instruments, laughing, and playing. In the back of the house were Isandra's living quarters and where she welcomed me for the duration of my stay. The living space was simple, the walls of rough cement. A dog and some chickens occupied a den in between the núcleo and the living quarters. All but one of Isandra's five children were musicians at El Sistema. At the time of my visit, the two oldest musicians had left Coro and were members of the top El Sistema orchestras in Caracas. The younger two both played the violin, and they still lived at home.

I spent my first few hours in Las Panelas listening to the orchestra rehearsals and chatting with students and teachers. When I expressed interest in hearing the story of how the núcleo was founded, Isandra pulled out a stack of newspaper cuttings that she had carefully stored. The cuttings recorded landmark moments in the history of Las Panelas. I took photos of them, creating my own digital archive. On my most recent review of those photos, I noticed at the bottom of them the tiny fingers of Paty, Isandra's youngest daughter, who had diligently held the newspaper down while I took photos with my digital camera. At the time a child of eight, Paty was excited that there was a new guest in their house.

During a recent call, as I was sifting through memories and my photographic and digital archive, I asked Isandra to tell me the story once again of how she first came to classical music. Although I had heard it before, my memories of the telling were fuzzy. When she was young, Isandra worked as a maid in the house of an upper-class family in Caracas. She loved cleaning the library room because she could read books while she did it. One day she heard music she had never heard before. "I grew up listening to the music you hear at the bar," she told me. "I never knew of the existence of Mozart or Beethoven. She called it "música de muertos" (music of dead people). "I had feelings I'd never experienced before. A sense of peace that was inciting me to fly and to want to reach the clouds and to know God." When she returned to Coro, she quickly sought a music school for her children where they could learn the classical music she liked so much. Eventually, all of her children joined the main El Sistema school in Coro. One day Isandra was walking around the city and, by pure chance, saw a long line of people waiting outside a building to audition for the choir in Coro. On the spur of the moment, she was inspired to audition herself and was successful. This chance occurrence, much like her encounter with classical music in the rich family's library, was life-altering and radically transformative of her future path.

Years later, Isandra began teaching singing to children in her neighbourhood at her own home. Soon, her students started asking to play musical instruments. Every time Isandra took her daughter Julia to Caracas for her violin classes, Isandra would buy one recorder and bring it back. Soon, she had enough recorders for a little orchestra. When her students applied for a place in the main El Sistema branch in Coro, they were turned back. "Because they did not have the right last name," she said, referring to the favouritism and elitism that permeated El Sistema. This attitude mimicked the dynamics of ethnoracial and class discrimination in wider Venezuelan society.

Daily, Isandra was reading about the homicides that affected the neighbourhood. She was motivated to found her own music school. One day she sat down with a pen and paper and wrote up a project proposal for a music school. With a video recorder that her son Ismel had given her, she made recordings of the núcleo activities already taking place. She gathered her materials, went to Caracas, and headed straight to the office of El Sistema's founder and director – Maestro José Antonio Abreu. It was 5 May 2010. Abreu listened to her and, impressed, told her: "Usted es una mujer tenaz. Cuenta con mi apoyo mi queridísima dama" (You are a tenacious woman. You can count on my support, dear lady). I was struck by how what Isandra and I had discussed as intuition was translated into tenaciousness in the language of masculinity. He gave her twenty recorders, some financial support, and legitimized Las Panelas as a núcleo within El Sistema. With the money, Isandra bought two toilets that she installed in her house for her students. When talking to Abreu, she never mentioned she was the mother of Ismel Campos, El Sistema's top violist. When Abreu found out later and called her to ask her why she had not told him, she responded: "Because one has to do things on one's own."

The carefully preserved newspaper clippings celebrated Isandra's labour, describing her, on the year that the school was opened, as the director of Las Panelas, a núcleo serving 150 children: "Ahora me corresponde sacar adelante a este grupo de niños" (Now it's my turn to bring forward this group of children), she is quoted as saying. The article features a photograph of Isandra conducting a group of young children singing and playing recorders (Valera and Unica 2010). A few months later, in October 2010, another newspaper article commemorates a joint concert between the Falcon Symphony and musicians from Las Panelas (Rodriguez and Davalillo 2010).

While most other núcleos were started by El Sistema or were housed within already-existing classical music conservatories with long musical traditions, Isandra sought and received institutional support for Las Panelas on her own. It was the only núcleo I know of that was both founded and run by a woman. El Sistema is a male-heavy institution where most positions of power – from the leadership to orchestra spots – are occupied by men (see Baker 2014; Stainova 2021). That a woman like Isandra, especially one without a formal music background, would be able to establish a *núcleo*, was impressive. Her story challenged the social inertia of structural and systemic forces. At different points in her life she had made decisions that broke with what was thought of as possible or expected.

"[Isandra] is proud of being able to crystallize a dream from which she would not like to wake up," I read in another clipping (Colina 2011). "The dream of creating a choir that would also be an orchestra came true because I was born for this," Isandra says, speaking of her job as a calling. "I became a musician at home with my children, because this was always my dream: to put them on a path to music," she recalls in the article. The portrayal of her labour as a dream pays tribute to how much Isandra desired to work with children and classical music. Certain achievements are so improbable that they border on the miraculous. *A dream from which she would not like to wake up.*

On 14 March 2011, the newspaper records El Sistema's commitment to supporting Las Panelas by sending them instruments (Rodriguez 2011). Another article from 17 April 2011 recognizes that El Sistema donated twenty instruments to Las Panelas. This article also describes the "annexation" of Las Panelas to the main Symphony Orchestra in Falcon. This change was approved by Maiolino Comte, the director of the Coro music school and one of the male figures who simultaneously supported and challenged Isandra's efforts over the years. Portrait photos of Isandra and Maiolino appear in the newspaper side by side, divided by a chasm of gender and race: he, representing the establishment; she, a radical intervention in it.

From Isandra's story I learned about intuition as the act of being guided in a given direction, as if by a larger force. She was thrust forward by her interest in music and her desire to help her barrio community by making music more widely available to them. At several watershed moments of her life, Isandra made decisions that radically broke with her previous life course. They were not all strategic, planned, or had a clearly envisioned outcome from the outset. They were a brave turning inward towards one's passions and dreams. The chaotic bureaucracy at El Sistema was, perhaps, what allowed for such an improbable institutional development. But the patriarchal institution presented her with equally strong challenges.

"They are all men"

The initial encouragement and support Isandra received from Abreu would not go uncontested over the next few years. "It was hard," Isandra said, "because so many men see a woman and they say, 'She can't do it because she is a woman and because she does not have musical training.'" Núcleo directors at El Sistema tended to be established musicians. Some had studied their whole lives within El Sistema, while others had already been in the musical profession before El Sistema was even founded. Within that framework, Isandra's story was neither legible nor legitimate.

"Abreu was supporting me, while all the rest were stabbing me, telling me that I was no good," Isandra shared.

> I had to fight with an institution where there were only men. They looked at me all ugly, here as well as in Caracas. Many were fired because of the way they treated me. During one of my visits to Caracas I spoke to Andres. I had to bring him a few papers. He confronted me: "Do you really think you'll be able to do this?" I knew that he had played violin in the orchestra and was not that good. And I told him: "I'll tell you something. Maybe I don't know anything. But I have confidence in myself and I know that I can do it. And I also know that there are some musicians who are so bad that they end up working behind a desk,"

she concluded, with a direct affront to Andres, himself a musician behind a desk. "He was my enemy for life," Isandra remarked. Other male figures discouraged and resisted her. In her telling, she emphasized how Maestro Abreu punished them for mistreating her.

What stood out to me in these stories was how Isandra spoke back and fought for herself. If intuition described a momentary inspiration, an action that changed the course of a life, it also described a sense of knowing the right direction and putting sustained efforts towards it. In our conversations, Isandra frequently linked intuition to self-confidence and a belief in herself. In Isandra's case, her battles over the years with the patriarchal establishment were in the name of defending her hard-won núcleo, her living dream. Some interpretations would paint Isandra as ambitious and motivated, a masculine-inflected language. Her insistence on the term *intuition* did justice to the incredible amount of energy needed to overcome the social and institutional barriers that stood between her and her dream.

After she had the idea of starting a núcleo, Isandra went straight for the top of the hierarchical El Sistema pyramid – José Antonio Abreu. This was a strategic move that enabled her to leap above the many levels of institutional hierarchy that could prematurely slam the door shut on her project. Once she had support from the top, she was not as vulnerable to the resistance from people in positions of moderate power, such as Andres. Intuition combined instinct and strategy.

As the Las Panelas núcleo expanded over the years, attracting more and more students, the newspaper coverage shows how the musicians began rehearsing in front of Isandra's house, taking up the entire street with their chairs and music stands (Lopez 2013). Although the text in these clippings describes another music school in the process of being built, the project never materialized. After the deaths of Chávez (2013) and Abreu (2018), institutional and political instability hit Venezuela, and Isandra lost all institutional support.

In January 2022, Isandra was seeking support from the international community. I recently saw her plea for help on Facebook to rebuild the núcleo roof, and I offered a small amount. When we spoke, Isandra told me she thinks of me every time she sees the new roof of her núcleo. But, she said, it was hard asking people for building materials in such a climate of desperation. "When people don't have anything to eat, I can't ask them for money to buy a bag of cement. The businesses don't donate anything. Most of them have left. El Sistema is giving its last dead-man kicks. I am not ready to abandon what I put so much into," she said.

Outside of the institution, Isandra's family life was defined by strong relationships with other women, specifically her mother and daughters. "She supported me when I got pregnant at sixteen," Isandra said about her mother. "Of course, I'll take care of her in her old age." When Isandra's youngest son still lived in Las Panelas, he was the one to take care of his grandmother. Now it was Isandra who spent the nights with her. Beyond biological relationships of motherhood and care, Isandra also looked after other children in the community. Her acts of care in the community resemble what Alexis Pauline Gumbs (2016) calls practices of mothering, or acts of care in community that extend beyond biological mothering. When students came to Las Panelas, Isandra offered them meals. She told me about a couple of girls she had taken under her wing. They had been out on the street because their mothers had left for Colombia. They had started calling her mother.

"What guided you?" I asked her. "God. I only believe in him. I always ask him for everything. That's why I say it's a dream come true. Because it was just dreams. I dreamed of doing something big only I didn't know what it was. It was then up to me to fight with an institution where everyone is a man and they all look at me ugly." Isandra's belief in the power of God was intertwined with her belief in herself: "My belief in myself is part of intuition. I have never had my self-confidence on the floor."

Flashing Images

In my recent conversation with Isandra, I asked her directly whether she found intuition important in her life. "Yes. You know, my whole family calls me crazy. Me ha tocado ver cosas" (I've been destined to see things), she told me. One of her most vivid memories of seeing something was when she was a child, sick in bed. "Everyone was expecting me to die," she said to me. Then one day in the crack of a wall she saw the image of a woman holding a child. The following day she got out of bed and started walking, completely recovered. Later, when she was in church with her mother, she recognized her vision to be one of the saints: La Virgen de Coromoto.[2] At different points in Isandra's life, intuition appeared as a vision, a premonition of what was to come. For Isandra, *la virgen* was a vision that God sent her to help her recover.

Seeing that I was curious about her visions, Isandra told me another story. One time, she woke up in the middle of the night and saw someone sitting on her bed. She asked: "'But what happened? Do you have a problem? How nice you're not afraid to show yourself to me. Do you feel okay here?'" she had told the creature and continued the story: "I sat there and all of a sudden it disappeared." I responded with surprise and fascination. I realized then that my reactions were prompted mainly by Isandra's empathetic approach to the mysterious being on her bed. Instead of reacting with fear or distrust, she was concerned about the vision's well-being. Her empathy moved me, and I did not stop to think about whether the story sounded believable to me or not. Rather, I was focused on *how* Isandra was reacting and what that reaction said about her as a person. I thought about how intuition – and empathy – is cultivated, made, exercised, and practised (see E. Cook, this volume).

"You say 'wow,' but another person would say: 'she's crazy.'" Her words reminded me that I had forgotten to wonder about the veracity of the story, so captivated was I by the capacity for empathy that it illuminated. As a secular person, I would typically have found such an interpretation distant from my own habits of thought. But Isandra's story had, in the words of White (this volume), "deliver[ed] an affective charge that makes somatic sense in a way semiotic reasoning never could" (49). By the time I had a moment to make sense of her words, I was already enveloped in the charge – an experience I could not easily backtrack from without the help of my interlocutors, as in White and his colleague's examples of certain Buddhist priests who make sense of surprisingly moving experiences with evocative robots (see White and Katsuno 2021). There was something in the trust Isandra granted me as she was sharing her story that made it hard to dismiss or distance myself from her words. I realized then that she was telling me a story that made her vulnerable, that she could only share with a listener who made her feel safe. This trust entailed responsibility: I could not afford to turn back on her words, to distance myself from them later, for this would make my responses to her in the course of the conversation hypocritical. In writing now, I choose to remain close to my immediate reaction to her words at the time of our conversation instead of resorting to acquired academic habits of establishing analytical distance. One way of doing this would be to refrain from analysing her visions.

This religious vision was part of a constellation of events at key points in Isandra's life that had taken her in unexpected and improbable directions. I wished to remain open to the possibilities that such visions allowed her. To do so, I did not need to completely reorient my own belief system. I just needed to inhabit the question, what Mayanthi Fernando (2021), following Derrida, calls "the perhaps." The perhaps, in this case, was an openness to alternative potentialities unlocked through Isandra's visions. Isandra was revealing to me how such visions string a life together. Making space for hesitation in my work felt important when thinking about intuition, especially when my intuitive reactions in the moment of the conversation with Isandra distanced me from the habits of thought that shaped my own upbringing. It also helped me understand Isandra's reaching out towards religion as another instance of attempting to make do in the face of life's uncertainty. Fernando's invitation to linger in the question resonates with the provocation by White in the introduction to this collection: "What if the most constructive response to moments of ethnographic puzzlement and problematization was not the formulation of an answer but the cultivation of an affect?" (35).

"There is intuitive intelligence, which is not translatable by speech, and I am very intuitive, and I have a great deal of difficulty in logifying. ... Sometimes it happened that I said, when discussing with someone, 'I see,' but I cannot translate rationally what I was seeing." These are the words that Jacques Lacan's (1980, 27) patient shares in an interview with the famous scholar, describing the images that pass in his mind as a kind of cinema. Later in the interview, Lacan echoes back the patient's words, calling intuitions "images that pass through you" (31). Intuitive intelligence emerges from these frameworks as a type of thought process that does not rely on words or the *logos*. This way of seeing intuition seems to fit into the traditional definition of affect as somatic rather than semiotic, but Isandra's case also illustrates how feeling and meaning interact dynamically. Her stories were similarly about images that pass through you – we might call them intuitions. The specific moment of the vision was not always linguistically mediated but rather felt in the body, on the level of the skin. However, what struck me about Isandra's telling of the story is that if the instant of being affected by intuition was not linguistically mediated, her later interpretation that inserted the event into a portrait of herself and her life was indeed about meaning-making. In telling me about her visions, she was welcoming those visions as part of her life story and who she was as a person.

Future, Past

When I began writing this chapter, I told Julia, Isandra's daughter, and Alma about the topic, and they immediately got excited, confirming that intuition played an important role in their lives as well. They were visiting me in my childhood home in Sofia, Bulgaria. We were taking a walk in the park next to my mother's apartment, and I recorded the conversation while we were strolling around in the forest, our footsteps audible in the recording. Instead of attempting to gather unmediated ethnographic reflections, I asked the two musicians and old friends directly: "What is intuition for you?" It was an invitation to think through and theorize the concept together.

Julia answered first, with enthusiasm: "For me, it's what moves me to do great things," Julia said and laughed at her own bold statement. "You know how your mom was saying you need to find your own god? There are many gods. I believe in my intuition. It's too powerful. ...

Intuition always takes me in the right direction." Alma responded to my question second, mocking Julia:

> Well, after listening to the goddess of intuition, it is hard to say anything else. ... I would explain intuition as a feeling that makes us do things even though we are not convinced. ... Even when you feel like you are not doing things the way other people are doing them, intuition tells you it is possible. It's a tingling sensation that tells you to do things differently from how other people would do them, to not follow the crowd. ... Later, you think, this little voice guided me well. And it's not just a little voice – you feel it with your body. When something does not feel right, my stomach tightens. At first, I do not understand why my body behaves like that. Then I do my self-observation and think, that is why, because I'm not convinced.

In both Alma's and Julia's responses, intuition stood out as a feeling, frequently felt in the body, that propelled them forcefully in – or sometimes away from – a particular direction. This direction usually broke new ground, challenging the advice of others. It was a way of feeling a decision even when they, like the previously cited mother of the musician, did not have all the information needed to navigate a socially exclusive environment. What stood out in both responses was a conviction in the power of intuition to help them make the right decision. Rather than being accompanied by certainty, decisiveness, and speed, intuition in these testimonies was revealed as an unfurling of reasoning and bodily sensation that emerged slowly, sometimes painfully. On some level, Alma's and Julia's relationship to intuition sounded like a belief in a higher power that looked over them, protected them, and guided them. At the same time, this higher power was also deeply rooted in the self. "I believe in my intuition," Julia had said. If Isandra had comfortably situated intuition within God, for Julia and Alma, it was a process of finding "one's own god." For all of them, it was a story of women learning to trust their gut and fighting to break open paths that were closed, frequently guarded by others eager to preserve the status quo.

When I asked Julia and Alma to give me an example of how intuition had worked in their own lives, Alma and Julia both referred to intuition as the motor behind their decisions to move to Europe. Having grown up in barrios, they immigrated with few resources and, consequently, had taken enormous risks. Although they had a support network of friends from the orchestra who had already settled in Paris and were able to provide know-how, immigrating entailed many unknowns. The risk of this decision was especially high for Alma, who was partially blind. Alma and Julia became friends in the few months they shared an apartment together in Paris.

Julia's family and friends had picked up on these risks. "My mother and my brother both discouraged me from going to Paris because the 2015 attacks had just happened there and they were afraid. But I said, 'I am going. I already have a ticket and I'm leaving.' And they eventually supported me," Julia said with a smile.

"How did making that decision feel?" I asked her.

"I was still *en caliente* [on the spur of the moment]. When I first decided, I did not know if it would work out or not," she explained.

"Intuition was also part of my decision to immigrate," Alma reflected. "Ever since I began studying music, I knew I wanted to be a musician. When I was in the conservatory in Caracas, I felt stuck. I felt like I needed to seek something else; to get to know new places and rhythms." Intuition was a force that allowed Alma to break free from the feeling of being stuck, seeking opportunities beyond the educational environment she was in that did not allow her room to grow.

Unlike other stereotypical descriptions of intuition as a feeling of certainty, Alma and Julia spoke about vacillation. "There was a time when I was questioning my intuition a lot because I had many fears. I was seeing my future paths form, yet I was questioning my decision to leave Venezuela. I wanted to make sure I was doing it for my own self rather than for others." If at first Alma questioned her intuition, she had developed a new-found trust for it: "I believe that today I have begun to respect my intuition, to listen to it."

While Alma and Julia spoke of intuition very much as future-oriented, about how we see, imagine, and anticipate the future, they also crucially spoke of it as a way of making sense of the past. Reflecting on decisions that they saw as arising from intuition was a way of storying and building narratives about the past. Intuition, then, was as much about spontaneous decisions as about self-reflexive meaning-making. Retracing how intuition arose, through looking back at the past, is a way of making sense of events, creating meaning out of lived experience and interpersonal dynamics. Alma told me that only now, five years after settling in Paris, was she able to confirm that the decision to immigrate was the right one for her, that it was something she was doing for herself rather than for others. While still a musician at El Sistema, Alma had left home at a time of intense political and economic uncertainty in Venezuela. The leap of faith to immigrate served as a method of coping with the precariousness of daily life in Venezuela. Decisions based on intuition were validated only in retrospect, once

Alma and Julia could trace where those decisions had led them. Intuition, then, was not just a means for navigating challenging presents and unknown futures but also a way of reflecting on and story-ing the past and fluctuating modes of uncertainty.

As our conversation about intuition unfolded, Alma and Julia also spoke to me about the value of intuition when performing music. "At the moment of playing at a concert, I am not thinking," Julia, a violist, told me. Alma, a percussionist, explained that when performing she could focus on the melody of a piece without losing track of the beats. The ability to count beats in the back of her mind, without thinking of them consciously, was what she also called intuition, suggesting how intuition can be embodied through social practice. When I spoke about intuition to Angel, her cousin, he similarly found intuition meaningful in his own life, and especially when playing music: "When playing, everything is about making a decision *al instante* [instantly] and in these decisions intuition is important because you can never know the result (or how a piece will sound) before playing it." Intuition, then, was about being able to imagine and predict, to react on the spot to keep a piece of music together.

Coda

In this chapter, I see intuition as a case study in the social cultivation and reciprocal materialization of affect, a usually abstract theoretical concept. The notion of affect as method, or using "feeling as a means for generating insight" (White, this volume, 41), provides an opportunity to bridge a gap between the academic debates about affect, on one hand, and the affective energies that simmered in my fieldwork, on the other. Studying intuition offered me insight into how people summoned affect to think about their existence. These reflections have the unintended effect of engendering critiques of affect as we find it in the academy. For example, the way my interlocutors spoke about intuition challenged some of the binaries on which the definition of affect rested. In speaking about intuition, they painted more fluid boundaries between thinking and feeling. Intuition was an immediate, inexplicable feeling, at one point, and a mode of story-ing and analysing a life, at another. It was simultaneously about anticipation and the future and about making sense of the past. It was about making a decision, when lacking skills, while also recognizing that it was a decision enabled by the accumulation of experience. Intuition was an unstable, malleable concept that travelled between the socially constructed and the pre-conscious, the felt and the analysed, and the articulate and inexpressible. Most importantly, it inspired me to seek the social roots of intuition and the ways in which intuition functions in contexts that are gendered, racialized, and deeply permeated by structural violence and dispossession.

Building on the provocation in this volume's introduction, intuition offers a critique of institutional violence inflected through the experience of racialized, classed, and unequally gendered people. More than an analysis of these structures of violence, intuition as affect captures people's efforts and desires to overcome these very structures. In the experiences of my interlocutors, intuition as affect functioned in two opposite directions: on one hand, as a force pushing back against; on the other, as an aspiration towards, an orientation to the future, an overcoming, a transcendence. Intuition as affect carries the dual charge of critique: it identifies where power intersects with bodies, sometimes in ways that are limited to the somatic and are harder to translate into the semiotic, but it also points to how people reinvent themselves against the grain of violence to imagine alternative futures.

**

"People are dying without leaving anything behind," Isandra told me. Then, without saying anything more, she shared that recently she had been recording her own songs. The last one she recorded was *"Todo cambia"* (Everything Changes), a song originally recorded by Argentine singer Mercedes Sosa. At first, I did not recognize Isandra's voice; the recording was so professional and her voice so fluid. During our conversation, Isandra had shared the terrifying destruction and suffering in her community – people dying of COVID-19 and related diseases, of not having enough to eat. Her musical skills were humbling and filled me with admiration. She told me that the reason she chose to sing this song was because she herself had to change, adapting to changing circumstances. She was afraid of water – now she took swimming classes. She did not like plants – now she had a garden. Isandra's voice rose with a grounded quality, vibrating with a power that expanded with a crescendo, rising with every stanza.

NOTES

1 For example, see *You Already Know What to Do: Everyday Intuition for Relationships, Career and Spiritual Development,* by Sharon Franquemont (2007); *Radical Intuition: A Revolutionary Guide to Using Your Inner Power*, by Kim Chestney (2020); and *The Magic Path of Intuition,* by Florence Scovel Shinn (2013).

2 In this articulation, I am inspired by a graduate course on collaborative ethnography that I co-taught with Laura McTighe in the winter of 2021. The emphasis of the course is on methods as a site of theory and concept building in collaboration with interlocutors and colleagues, rather than purely as a means of gathering data.
3 La Virgen de Coromoto is popularly thought to be the patron saint of Venezuela.

REFERENCES

Adam, Charles, and Paul Tannery. 1964. *Oeuvres de Descartes (I–XI)* [Works of Descartes I–XI]. Paris: J. Vrin.
Baker, Geoffrey. 2014. *El Sistema: Orchestrating Venezuela's Youth*. Oxford: Oxford University Press.
Barnard, Chester I. 1968 [1938]. *The Functions of the Executive*, Vol. 11. Cambridge, MA: Harvard University Press.
Behar, Ruth. 2020. "Read More, Write Less." In *Writing Anthropology: Essays on Craft and Commitment*, edited by Carole McGranahan, 47–53. Durham, NC: Duke University Press.
Brennan, Teresa. 2004. *The Transmission of Affect*. Ithaca: Cornell University Press.
Calabretta, Giulia, Gerda Gemser, and Nachoem M. Wijnberg. 2017. "The Interplay Between Intuition and Rationality in Strategic Decision Making: A Paradox Perspective." *Organization Studies* 38 (3–4): 365–401. https://doi.org/10.1177/0170840616655483.
Caso, Antonio. 1982. *Antología filosófica* [Philosophical Anthology]. Mexico City: UNAM.
Chestney, Kim. 2020. *Radical Intuition: A Revolutionary Guide to Using Your Inner Power*. Novato, CA: New World Library.
Colina, Anne. 2011. Isandra Campos: "La coral es un sueño del que nunca quisiera despertar" [The Choir is a Dream I Never Want to Wake Up From]. *Nuevo Día* [New Day], 4 January 2011.
Cook, Emma E. "Serious Play and the Facilitation of Feeling in Food Allergy Advocacy in Japan." This volume.
Csordas, Thomas J. 2007. "Transmutation of Sensibilities: Empathy, Intuition, Revelation." In *The Shadow Side of Fieldwork: Exploring the Blurred Borders between Ethnography and Life*, edited by Athena McLean and Annette Leibing, 106–16. Malden, MA: Blackwell.
Dane, Erik, and Michael G. Pratt. 2007. "Exploring Intuition and Its Role in Managerial Decision Making." *Academy of Management Review* 32 (1): 33–54. https://doi.org/10.5465/AMR.2007.23463682.

Das, Veena. 1998. "Wittgenstein and Anthropology." *Annual Review of Anthropology* 27: 171–95.
Epstein, Seymour. 2010. "Demystifying Intuition: What It Is, What It Does, and How It Does It." *Psychological Inquiry* 21 (4): 295–312. https://doi.org/10.1080/1047840X.2010.523875.
Fernando, Mayanthi. 2021. "Modalities of the Perhaps: Secularity, Post-Humanism, Uncertainty." Virtual Lecture at McMaster University, 29 October 2021.
Franquemont, Sharon. 2007. *You Already Know What to Do: Everyday Intuition for Relationships, Career and Spiritual Development*. Louisville, CO: Sounds True.
Frondizi, Risieri. 1947. "El punto de partida del filosofar" [The Starting Point of Philosophizing], Editorial Losada, S.A. [Losada Publishers]. *Revista Cubana de Filosofía, La Habana [Cuban Journal of Philosophy, Habana]* 1 (2 (April, May, June 1947): 35–40. www.filosofia.org/hem/dep/rcf/n02p035.htm.
Gumbs, Alexis Pauline, ed. 2016. *Revolutionary Mothering: Love on the Front Lines*. Oakland, CA: PM Press.
Hardt, Michael. 2015. "The Power to be Affected." *International Journal of Politics, Culture, and Society* 28 (3): 215–22. https://doi.org/10.1007/s10767-014-9191-x.
Hoffman, Diane M. 2016. "Learning to See: Intuition and Perception in Fieldwork in Haiti." *Anthropology and Humanism* 41 (1): 28–38. https://doi.org/10.1111/anhu.12105.
Jager, Colin. 2006. "After the Secular: The Subject of Romanticism." *Public Culture* 18 (2): 301–21. https://doi.org/10.1215/08992363-2006-005.
Kahneman, Daniel. 2011. *Thinking, Fast and Slow*. New York: Farrar, Straus and Giroux.
Kemerling, Garth. 2011. "Plato: Education and the Value of Justice." *Philosophy Page*, 12 November 2011. www.philosophypages.com/hy/2h.htm.
Kondo, Dorinne. 2018. *Worldmaking*. Durham, NC: Duke University Press.
Lacan, Jacques. 1980. "A Lacanian Psychosis: Interview by Jacques Lacan." In *Returning to Freud: Clinical Psychoanalysis in the School of Lacan*, edited by Stuart Schneiderman, 19–42. New Haven, CT, and London: Yale University Press.
Lopez, Jarrinson. 2013. "Orquesta Sinfónica Las Panelas deleitó a su comunidad" [Las Panelas Symphony Orchestra Delighted Its Community]. *Nuevo Día [New Day]*, 23 July 2013.
Lufityanto, Galang, Chris Donkin, and Joel Pearson. 2016. "Measuring Intuition: Nonconscious Emotional Information Boosts Decision Accuracy and Confidence." *Psychological Science* 27 (5): 622–34. https://doi.org/10.1177/0956797616629403.
Lutz, Catherine. 1998. *Unnatural Emotions: Everyday Sentiments on a Micronesian Atoll and Their Challenge to Western Theory*. Chicago: University of Chicago Press.

Márquez, Gabriel García. 1981. "Gabriel García Márquez, the Art of Fiction No. 69." Interview by Peter Stone. *The Paris Review* 82 (Winter). www.theparisreview.org/interviews/3196/the-art-of-fiction-no-69-gabriel-garcia-marquez.

Massumi, Brian. 1995. "The Autonomy of Affect." *Cultural Critique* 31: 83–109. https://doi.org/10.2307/1354446.

McTighe, Laura. 2020. "Theory on the Ground: Ethnography, Religio-Racial Study, and the Spiritual Work of Building Otherwise." *Journal of the American Academy of Religion* 88 (2): 407–39. https://doi.org/10.1093/jaarel/lfaa014.

Online Etymology Dictionary. "Intuition." Accessed 2 August 2022. www.etymonline.com/search?q=intuition+.

Pilard, Nathalie. 2018. *Jung and Intuition: On the Centrality and Variety of Forms of Intuition in Jung and Post-Jungians*. London: Routledge.

Rodriguez, Nayma. 2011. "Escuela de música Las Panelas recibe apoyo del Sistema Nacional de Orquestas" [Las Panelas Music School receives support from the National System of Orchestras]. *NuevoDía [New Day]*, 14 March 2011.

Rodriguez, Nayma, and Joly Davalillo. 2010. "OSF y la coral Las Panelas cantarán por Venezuela" [OSF and Las Panelas choir sing for Venezuela]. *Nuevo Día [New Day]*, 22 October 2010.

Schleiermacher, Friedrich. [1799] 1996. *On Religion: Speeches to its Cultured Despisers*. Translated by Richard Crouter. Cambridge, UK: Cambridge University Press.

Shinn, Florence Scovel. 2013. *The Magic Path of Intuition*. Carlsbad, CA: Hay House.

Simon, Herbert A. 1987. "Making Management Decisions: The Role of Intuition and Emotion." *Academy of Management Perspectives* 1 (1): 57–64.

Stainova, Yana. 2019. "Enchantment as Method." *Anthropology and Humanism* 44 (2): 214–30. https://doi.org/10.1111/anhu.12251.

Stainova, Yana. 2021. *Sonorous Worlds: Musical Enchantment in Venezuela*. Ann Arbor: University of Michigan Press.

Stewart, Kathleen. 2011. "Atmospheric Attunements." *Environment and Planning D: Society and Space* 29 (3): 445–53. https://doi.org/10.1068/d9109.

Valera, Bernarda, and Pasante Unica. 2010. "Niños cantores de Las Panelas dieron serenata a Nuevo Día" [Singing children of Las Panelas serenade New Day]. *Nuevo Día [New Day]*, 5 August 2010.

Vargas, Rigel Olivares. 2005. "El concepto de intuición en Antonio Caso" [The Concept of Intuition in Antonio Caso]. *Iztapalapa* 58: 171–93.

White, Daniel, and Hirofumi Katsuno. 2021. "Toward an Affective Sense of Life: Artificial Intelligence, Animacy, and Amusement at a Robot Pet Memorial Service in Japan." *Cultural Anthropology* 36 (2): 222–51. https://doi.org/10.14506/ca36.2.03.

Chapter 2

Interiority Currency as Affective Method: Racialized Affect, Therapeutic Cultures, and Latin American Elites

ANA Y. RAMOS-ZAYAS

In the social sciences, *therapeutic culture* generally refers to the sociological and humanistic interest in psychology beyond cognitive and clinical interventions. It encompasses a varied spectrum of discourses, social practices, bodily sensations, and cultural artefacts that discursively and institutionally pervade everyday life and popular culture (see Nehring and Kerrigan 2019). Concepts like *self-knowledge, spiritual growth,* and *self-esteem* loosen from their scientific and religious moorings to become essential characteristics of neoliberal personhood and sociability (Ramos-Zayas 2012). Likewise, the study of *public feelings* in the humanities draws attention to how and why feelings and emotions – assumed to be a private, personal experience – influence politics and notions of social belonging and intimacy (Ahmed 2013; Berlant and Stewart 2019; Stewart 2007).

Early studies of therapeutic cultures and public feelings in anthropology centred on the impact of psychology on Western culture, assessing whether psychology's broadest consequences are emancipatory or repressive, and considering ways in which therapeutic culture serves late modern capitalism (Giddens 1991; Illouz 2007; Rose 1998). To different degrees, these debates draw on Foucault's idea that power is exercised not through overtly restrictive, coercive, or repressive means but rather indirectly; a language of therapeutic care rather than political control is what has come to define new governing logics and sociability (Foucault 1988, 16–49). The "technologies of self" through which individuals come to present themselves as ideal neoliberal subjects ground a politics of affect under emotional capitalism (Illouz 2007),[1] a condition of modernity characterized by the merger of therapeutic discourse and capitalist logic and, I would argue, racialization and racial projects in the Americas (Omi and Winant 1987).

From 2012 through 2017, I conducted ethnographic research to better understand the intersection of racialized affective worlds and neighbourhood-centred structures of feeling among wealthy white parents in Brazil and Puerto Rico. A focus on therapeutic cultures and public feelings in the everyday lives of these upper-class parents in the neighbourhoods of Ipanema (Brazil) and El Condado (Puerto Rico) serves as a point of departure to examine how affect can operate as ethnographic method and social critique. As examined elsewhere in relation to the Americas, perspectives, expressions, and representations of affect are always-already racialized or racializing (Berg and Ramos-Zayas 2015). Tracing *interiority currency* allows me to better understand how "racialized affect" operates methodologically and ethnographically and what it "does" to sociability.

In the first section of this chapter, I discuss what I am calling "interiority currency" in the context of my ethnographic encounters with Brazilian and Puerto Rican elites. A conduit through which vital emotions and structures of feelings get internalized and projected in ways that lubricate sociability and social hierarchies, interiority currency also accrues unequal power and value across class and race. In the second section, I introduce several ethnographic vignettes to illustrate how interiority currency – an affective capacity cultivated among my interlocutors – provides the optics to examine *inner worlds* in anthropology, an analytic that has remained a challenge to the discipline. In the conclusion, I consider how interiority currency as a precursor to racialized affect might offer new insight into the co-production of anthropological knowledge between ethnographer and interlocutors while also offering new methodologies in the field.

Interiority Currency: Bridging Vital Emotions and Structures of Feeling

My encounters with Ipanema and El Condado elites often reflected mutually produced, cultivated, and reinforced desires for a newly imagined intimacy and self-understanding. Socially explicit ways of feeling and expressing emotion figured throughout my interlocutors' testimonies, frequently trumping these individuals' sociological insights, contradictory experiences, and ambiguous observations. Encounters with Latin American elites in Ipanema and El Condado were simultaneously hyper-embodied and metaphysical. These upper-class parents always left me feeling that I had just engaged in conversations that were about the physical minutiae of body changes and conditions (the various incisions left from a cosmetic procedure, for instance), on one hand, and about the most esoteric understandings of the universal disembodied self, on the other. It was through these conversations that they measured and reflected on how our relationship, which some considered a friendship, matured over the time of my fieldwork.

These ethnographic encounters resonated with what Tomas Matza (2012) calls "psy-sociality," situations where "imagined intimate stranger relations in public are mimicked in therapeutically attuned settings" (28). Through this form of public intimacy, people feel free to share their inner struggles, personal problems, and even political traumas, which otherwise would remain hidden and unarticulated. In Ipanema and El Condado, forms of psy-sociality required that interlocutors and ethnographer alike divert their attention to inner linings of experience while producing alternative social orders, understandings of personhood, and expectations of what affect should be like, look like, and do.

When conducting fieldwork among Brazilian and Puerto Rican elites, I examined how such therapeutically infused sociality comes to exist and relate to affect, race, and privilege (Ramos-Zayas 2020). In my ethnographic analysis, *interiority currency* provided a means to access the inner-cultivation projects and social relations that modern capitalism encourages and that emerge when people shift their focus inward. During my fieldwork, I noticed how white elite parents in Brazil and Puerto Rico communicated psychological insights, meditated, went to ashrams or other spiritual travel, wrote journals and parenting blogs, participated in group therapy, or hired life coaches.[2]

Ipanema and El Condado were socially centred on a certain "feel" of a place akin to what Raymond Williams (1977) calls "structure of feelings," an affective atmosphere produced from an intuitive, pre-ideological sense of cohort and agreed upon social and cultural conventions of an era. A neighbourhood-based sociability among the white Latin American elites that I documented at length in *Parenting Empires* (2020) was forged on racialized forms of affect externalized and operationalized through interiority currency. As implied in the theoretical framework of "racialized affect" (Berg and Ramos-Zayas 2015), not all expressions of vital emotions function as the kind of currency that could be converted into cultural capital. We might better say that certain affects are more likely to be "empowering" and others more likely to be "liable." Interiority currency provides the methodological scheme and ethnographic analytics to examine the space through which systems of power – including race in the case of the Americas – and affect are co-produced, and how they are converted into forms of capital (or not).

As anthropologist Anand Pandian (2008) notes, spaces of interiority are made through moral dissension and ethical struggle with oneself, as individuals "come to populate themselves with the feelings of others" (468). Inspired by this understanding, I view *interiority* as a heightened attentiveness to one's inner lining and a process by which individuals became deliberate about self-cultivation. Crucially, however, individuals engage in this inward focus while simultaneously enacting broader social ideas about the arrangements of the state, the structure of cosmic time, and their participation in a metahistorical project. Notwithstanding its resonance with Bourdieu's notions of capital,[3] the word *currency* highlights the uneven, multidirectional flows of transactional social objects, including affect, and the vital emotions that hold together ordinary rituals and the feel of material and temporal spaces. Currency captures contemporary manifestations of social privilege by de-emphasizing refined tastes or explicit markers of wealth in favour of viewing privilege as the display of a strong sense of self and social ease (Gaztambide-Fernández 2009; Khan 2009). Currency, in this sense, centres not primarily on the accumulation of material goods, cultural objects, or beneficial social relations but on the adoption of lifestyles that foster the cultivation and appropriate projection of "self," such as participating in therapeutic or spiritual practices and pursuing happiness, emotional balance, personal growth, and professional fulfilment (Freeman 2014).[4]

Medical anthropologist and practising psychotherapist Rebecca Lester notes that the "self" is constituted in and through ongoing (and shifting) dialogues between two or more internally experienced aspects of the subject. This is what she calls "dialogic interiority" (Lester 2019, 231).[5] While such internal dialogue is reconceptualized as diversified and intra-relational among Lester's clients, which is also a characteristic of interiority currency, a crucial distinction is that interiority currency serves as a conduit for ongoing, multidirectional flows between vital emotions and structures of feeling, on one hand, and hierarchical forms of sociability, including racialized or classed affect, on the other. Interiority currency thus privileges how structures of feelings shape the continuous making and unmaking of interior spaces for particular social objectives, which operate in relation to personal discovery, sociability, and other forms of reflexive and embodied experiences.

Ipanema and El Condado have been historically associated with socially progressive sectors of the Brazilian and Puerto Rican elite, respectively. Most of the interlocutors in my project self-fashioned as politically or at least socially "progressive." They sustained those progressive identities through deliberate, interior-oriented practices of self cultivation, which served as strategies through which they could position themselves as ethical ("good people") in a geopolitical context in which wealth had been connected to corruption. This moral economy of privilege was not oblivious to social inequality, environmental pollution, and the competitive socialization of children or the affects behind philanthropic pursuits, for instance. While in the earlier years of development and neoliberalism in the Global South consumption was the prominent marker of well-being and middle-classness (O' Dougherty 2002), at the time of my fieldwork in 2012–17, elites in the specific neighbourhoods of Ipanema and El Condado were more concerned about mental health, seeking psychological counselling for themselves, working on their marriages, and raising happy children. There was an impetus towards depth and complexity, a salient language of popular psychology, and an overall confessional quality in local sociability that I initially attributed to similarities between the therapeutic and the ethnographic – or even to a spillover of the South American psychoanalytical tradition. Over time, I recognized how tone, themes, and the rhythm of conversations were infused with vital emotions and references to their attunement to the feel or ambiance of neighbourhoods.

Rather than viewing vitality as a metaphor for "energy" or a lack of cognition (Bens 2020), interiority currency focuses on how vital emotions manifest and infuse affective atmospheres and the feel of a place in a very material sense.[6] Interiority currency serves both as a space of confluence and as an analytical tool for interior and exterior sociality.[7] As analytical concept, it deliberately retains the view of affect in its constitutive association with class and racial hierarchies under emotional capitalism. Methodologically, interiority currency serves as a potential entry point into power relations. Vital emotions and structures of feelings in my fieldwork constituted one another and served as preconditions for interiority currency; moreover, such a process of internalization conditioned expressions of racialized affect (or the very racialization of affect).

Socially, interiority currency sheds light on the hierarchical ranking of interior worlds through which white Latin American elites set themselves apart both from the poor, whose affect was assumed to be flat and simplistic, and from other wealthy, consumption-driven individuals in their own countries, whose affect was considered superficial and shallow. As Jan Goldstein (2009) notes in the case of postrevolutionary France, by granting the self extraordinary cultural salience and providing a new criterion for ranking people, a new principle of structuring bourgeois society was established to replace the old social order.[8] By applying the concept of interiority currency as a practice drawn from interlocutors, my intention is to better demonstrate the multidirectional currents of subjective inner-world concerns – including embodiments of vital emotions and appraisals of structures of feelings – as they come to produce sociability and hierarchies in terms of a racialization of affect.[9]

The notion of personal freedom, through which therapeutic cultures increasingly help govern in traditional liberal democracies in the West (Rose 1998), is not widely invoked or shared in Latin America. Rather, it was the ease of managing complex, profoundly unequal social relationships and deploying a language of feelings and embodiments of racialized affect that situated therapeutic governance in the Global South in a broader context of negotiations between self-care and social obligations, views of privilege, and disadvantage. Interiority currency assumes that the so-called malleability of the self is in fact contingent on, and even dialectically related to, the place within a class and racial hierarchy in which the interlocutor is situated in the Americas.

Interiority Currency and Ethnographic Encounters

My interactions with Liliana González Padín, in Puerto Rico, and Beatriz Pissollo Itamar, in Brazil, illustrate how ethnographic encounters generated affects and feeling that did not resolve in traditional anthropological analytics but that, nonetheless, powerfully held cultural, ethical, and political worlds together. Both encounters allow me to explore how interiority currency operates empirically.

It was during my first visit with Liliana González Padín, an El Condado resident, that I was more clearly able to pinpoint what it was about the upper-class parents in Ipanema and El Condado that made interactions so affectively peculiar and the spaces they occupied so seemingly harmonious. I was dealing with mild anxiety over parking my rental car and not knowing if parking in the cul-de-sac near Liliana's weekend home in Dorado was legal. As I debated the parking situation with myself, Liliana opened her heavy, rustic entrance door. Wearing white loose linen pants, a flowy lavender tunic, and strappy leather sandals, she joyfully greeted me: "Welcome, welcome!" Considered a perfect example of *persona sencilla* (down to earth) by other interlocutors,[10] Liliana exuded a calmness and comfort in her own skin that I had come to expect from Latin American upper classes. "Maybe we can sit on the terrace. It's breezier there," she jovially suggested as we headed through the open-concept living room (underneath an impossibly high ceiling) to a beautifully landscaped terrace. "Is it okay if I leave the car parked there? I'm just noticing that the security guard has

Interiority Currency as Affective Method   89

come around twice, and I'm not sure if maybe I didn't park in a good spot ... or?" I felt frazzled as sweat drops formed on my neck, either from driving with a broken air conditioner or from fear that the security guard would think my silver Ford Fiesta rental was a stolen car, tow it, and leave me stranded in Dorado Beach. "That is not a problem at all," Liliana steadily assured me, putting me at ease, confident that my car would be there when I came out, and, even if it were not there, it would still not be a problem. Liliana gave mild-mannered directions to a woman I imagined was the *señora que limpia* (cleaning lady), as we sat on plush terrace furniture. The term *cuidarse* (to take care of oneself), which appeared in a range of Puerto Rican registries – from fitness to food quality, medical care, and general personal upkeep to a hegemonic integration with ambiance and a sense of well-being – applied to Liliana perfectly.

Liliana embodied the El Condado definition of down-to-earthness, conveying a sense of calm and Zen. Her warmth and poise could not be attributed to any one isolated trait or unique aspect of her temperament; in fact, describing her is helpful in conveying what I found to be a cultivated spiritual demeanour, confident diplomacy, and emotive disposition that constituted a certain form of white affect. Perhaps contributing to interiority currency in the case of *personas sencillas* like Liliana was the very material environment in which such affect was externalized. Personas sencillas generally expressed their down-to-earthness in contexts of understated comfort and in relationships with inanimate objects and curated spaces – spectacular-yet-tasteful wedding rings, home décor, solar panels, well-chosen paintings and photographs, and the ability to wear not only high couture but also, and more importantly, casual clothing, to name a few. They were perfect hosts, immediately calming and dictating the vital emotions and tone of the interaction without missing a cue or coming across as manipulative. Formations of a racialized (white) affect and images of personas sencillas, as the social manifestation of that affect, were instrumental to how class and racial privilege acquired legitimacy in a political economy characterized by profound inequality, residential segregation, and draconian austerity measures, as was the case of both Puerto Rico and Brazil during the time of my fieldwork. Liliana's attunement to ambiance and an embodied ease rendered it nearly impossible, even for a hyper-attuned social scientist, to catch any old-school snob. Was it Liliana's sense of aesthetics and temperament that created an ambiance, a rhythm or tone in our social encounter?

Analysing Liliana's affect acquires a more nuanced quality when I contrast her "ease" with my construction of a (parking) "crisis." Lauren

Berlant (2011) contrasts "slow death," the banal condition of being worn out by the activity of reproducing life, with crisis management, the dramas "that obscure the motives and temporalities of these aspects of [banal] living" (100). Was my propensity to drama a reaction to the slow death that I projected onto Liliana's domesticity?

In contrast to Liliana, Ipanema resident Beatriz Pissollo Itamar came across as "too negative" and "prone to worry" – at least, this is the reason why other Brazilian interlocutors found it difficult to establish *afinidade* (affinity) with her. While Beatriz was not necessarily an outcast, she knew that other Ipanema parents had difficulty reading her: "Have you heard that saying about the Corcovado having open, welcoming arms, but never closing them to embrace you? That's the carioca way. Here people tell you, 'Go to the beach, have an *agua de coco* and let the problems dissolve!' They can't deal with somebody else's dark spaces." When I mentioned the almost excessive willingness, even eagerness, of each person I knew in Ipanema to explicitly, in detail, lay out the machinations of their psychological self, including dark spaces, Beatriz clarified: "Oh yes, people here psychoanalyse themselves and each other ad nauseum. They really put themselves out there (*se expõe muito*). They describe their therapy sessions almost minute by minute. This gives you a false sense of closeness." I tried to push a bit to see how she reconciled her thinking about the simultaneously superficial forms of intimacy, on one hand, and the great psychological awareness that individuals seemed to have about each other's histories, on the other. Beatriz explained: "There is an Ipanema 'No,' which means that people see each other on the beach or run into one another, and are like 'Yes, yes, we need to meet! We'll have coffee!' But they know, and you should too, that that will never happen. It is a way of saying no without compromising carioca politeness, avoiding confrontation." This withdrawal from arguments was an aspect of the carioca structure of feeling that Beatriz interpreted as antisocial and disruptive to genuine sociality. The vital emotional energy Beatriz notices intersected with a structure of feeling which revolved around being together yet apart, a type of "collective solitude" (Pagis 2019).

Conversations with Beatriz brought forth images of what Berlant calls "the political depressive," an affect that seems to suggest detachment but that in reality consists of "navigating an ongoing circuit of optimism and disappointment" (Berlant 2011, 27). In her psychotherapy group, Beatriz targeted two seemingly contradictory objectives: to become less negative and to not care about others' opinions of her (as a negative person). While self-reflexivity involves evaluating oneself through the eyes of others, it was this social gaze that Beatriz had targeted as a problem to be overcome; her goal was to liberate herself from social expectations while remedying what that Ipanema social gaze, rooted in structures of feelings, evaluated was her problem (a negative outlook that contradicted Ipanema's optimistic, happy disposition). This therapeutic practice was oriented towards facing everyday social relations, to better deal with a social world that negated the disruptive nature of social responsiveness.

Whether it is forging an elite ambiance or identifying affective superficiality, Liliana González Padín and Beatriz Pissolo Itamar engaged in what Janelle Taylor (2005) calls "surfacing the body interior." Surfacing the body interior serves as a metaphor for how ethnographers and interlocutors give the interior a surface (as in surfacing a road) and bring the interior up to the surface. Taylor's framing points towards the range of practices and processes that materialize both bodily surfaces as significant sites within broader orders and surfaces that lie hidden beneath them. The materializing practices out of which bodies, publics, and economies are precipitated are influenced by Beatriz's social critique of intimate superficiality in Ipanema and by Liliana's image as a persona sencilla in El Condado. In both instances, their emotional and vital energies as solid members of a Latin American elite shaped the structure of feelings of the spaces they navigated while rendering social inequality and political economy somewhat invisible. Feeling more positive towards others, Liliana's skill and Beatriz's self-project, is arguably easier in a social world where one does not need to attend to others' social gaze, and one's sense of self is less dependent on others. This is a basic characteristic of how whiteness becomes affectively racialized (Berg and Ramos-Zayas 2015). Methodologically, we get to see the affective dimensions of racialization not only in momentary interpersonal dynamics but also in their afterlife, including, for instance, the post-fieldwork levels of sincerity and authenticity between interlocutors and ethnographer (Jackson 2010).

Importantly, interiority currency is decidedly historical and politically encumbered: unlike approaches that intend to bring an already-formed interiority to the surface, interiority capital highlights the grounding of that very interior according to social hierarchy and power. Engaging with but also questioning the unencumbered possibility of adopting affect as method, a consideration in this volume, the internalization of vital emotions and structures of feelings renders interiority currency available to sociological scrutiny and methodologically productive. The very ordinariness of interiority currency in my encounters sustained and provided the staging ground for a moral economy of privilege among Latin American elites that, when examined closely, came to constitute, over time, a structures-of-feelings archive. This process demands that ethnographers pay more attention to the "invisible contexts" in which racial, colonial, and imperial projects flourish in the Global South (see Comaroff and Comaroff 2006).

Inspired by Deleuze, Biehl and Moran-Thomas (2009) propose that we understand history not as a set of preconditions for being but as what interlocutors leave behind in order "to become" something new. They assume that because individuals in the Global South often abstain from situating their personal stories in broader colonial, imperial, and racial histories, they are leaving those histories behind. While few white upper-class Latin American interlocutors explicitly connected their lives to European racism or US hemispheric imperialism, they did filter ordinary life and self-cultivation through structures of feeling that came to serve as a social proxy for more explicit references to that more global history.

Structures of feeling in Ipanema and El Condado resonated with what Berlant and Stewart (2019) termed "ordinaries," those instances which offer records of affect and everyday meditations and manifestos. In fieldwork encounters with affect, we are required to direct our attention to the ordinary and how colonial histories, while sometimes hidden, are not absent. Anthropologist Ann Stoler (2004) encourages us to consider lapses in colonial hegemony and cruelty by observing instances in which ethics were important to colonial projects. Among the self-fashioned "progressive" Latin American elites I encountered in the field, there was a distinct moral economy and concern with being "good people." Drawing from Stoler (2004), we could view such concern as an example of how "imperial dispositions are marked by a negative space: that from which those with privilege and standing could excuse themselves" (256). This moral economy of privilege allows us to interpret an individual's propensity to view history from a psychological position rather than allude to the invisible contexts that would require them to contend with profound social inequality.

Interiority Currency and Racialized Affect as Methodology

The Ipanema and El Condado elites I encountered produced knowledge that carried a lot of weight, not only in their neighbourhoods but also in how I analysed, produced, and conveyed my own knowledge and insights about them. My relationships with Bruna Alves Teixeira and Maribel Seijo, two additional upper-class residents of Ipanema and El Condado, respectively, demonstrate how interiority currency offers a window into the racialized affective methods, and the powerful hidden feelings, of interlocutors.

Bruna Alves Teixeira's socialization into Ipanema's wealth involved transforming her explicit expressions of disgust towards dark, poor bodies into a more coded, neoliberal racial language akin to US multiculturalism. I trace this through an examination of "disgust" and "contempt" in Bruna's targeted self-growth trajectory.

Bruna's description of the day her doctor told her that she needed to have an emergency C-section at a public hospital was telling:

> We arrived at the Perinatal [municipal hospital], and there was a group of Blacks that had a super strong odor [um grupo de negros que tinha um cheiro super forte, super]. And pregnant women, we have that power of smell. I turned to my husband. "Mauricio, I don't want to have my son here." I began to cry right there, in the Maternity Ward. ... When the doctor arrived, she saw me crying, hysterically, my robe wet from all the tears. "What happened?" "I don't want to have my son here." "Where do you want to have your son?" "In the Casa de São Jose [a private hospital]" "Why?" "I don't know. I don't want to have my son here." She was very, very mad at me, and she told me afterward. She moved the whole birthing team to the São Jose, and it looked like a funeral, not a birth. At the moment I couldn't articulate a reason, the odor, the noise. ... In retrospect, I know that it was that I wanted a nice, beautiful, nice smelling world for my son to be born into.

Bruna's visceral narrative was exceptional in relation to those I heard from other Ipanema and El Condado upper-class parents, whose anti-Blackness was much more coded. Of the negative affects, contempt is an immensely powerful indicator of the interface between the personal and the social. Like the disgust it sometimes carries, contempt invokes collective sentiments, as individuals sharing similar social backgrounds may share their relationship to the object of contempt. Disgust hinges on proximity: when spatial or legal boundaries between racial or social groups are challenged, social hierarchy finds other ways of expression, including odour (Lawler 2005). Class and race were rarely as explicitly invoked in expressions of disgust as was in Bruna's case, a parenting instance in which it provided a morally sanctioned (and moralistic) endorsement of whiteness. It was Bruna's explicit allusion to blackness that most stood out. Whereas other upper-class residents of Ipanema and El Condado, when pressed, handled race with white gloves (pun intended) through narratives of diversity and inclusion, Bruna wanted to get into the messiness of racism in ways that were as unrefined and uncomfortable as they were genuine and unfiltered.

As a light-skinned Latin American woman myself, with life conditions Bruna might have considered on par with hers, I had a number of possibilities in terms of how I approached Bruna's confession. In this instance, adopting radical dishonesty as an affective methodological approach allowed me to moderate the repulsion of racism. Clearly, this is a strategy available to ethnographers who are more closely aligned with the class and racial backgrounds of their interlocutors. While such a strategy might seem purely performative, one must consider how the vital emotions the performance ignites (and how these intersect with structures of feeling) might also alter the methodological potential of affect; it would also alter interiority currency.[11]

Elites in El Condado and Ipanema, including Bruna's own Brazilian doctor, would be appalled by her explicit reference to Black bodies in terms of *cheiro* (stench), or at all. Nevertheless, Bruna was one of the few interlocutors who engaged with race affectively and viscerally felt racism as something she could not ignore. In the early years of fieldwork, Bruna seemed to appreciate our conversations as opportunities to work through something that was tremendously conflictive for her in how she parented her son.

One of the earlier times I recorded an interview with Bruna, I posed a general question about the aspirations she had for her son. If anything, this was a sort of "feel good" warm-up question for my interlocutors that yielded predictable answers like "finding their passion," "being happy," "getting a quality education," or some variation of these. Bruna's response was different:

> Listen, Ana, I am very racist. And I've suffered a lot as a consequence. I don't want my child to go through this. My father didn't like Blacks. ... It is very hard for me to get rid of that upbringing. ... It is fear. It is prejudice. It is acting like a crazy person [*uma coisa de louco*]. How can I get to like something I've been taught to dislike? [in tears]. I am telling you all this because you're not judging me, even though I've verbalized it already. Once I acknowledge that I am prejudiced, how do I change it? I don't want to change it. Because I don't want to admit it to anyone else. I simply want to keep that hidden inside. I don't want my son to be this way.

Given how racially fluent and superficial other liberal Ipanema residents were, Bruna felt alone in her anti-Black racism and the rawness of her feelings. This aloneness, guilt, and hidden racist feelings effectively led Bruna to locate racism within the "interiority" of the "self," away from collective institutions and structures. She wanted to understand the changes in her bodily sensations as early as possible and monitor the reactions they triggered by observing her inner experiences.

Perhaps it was partly because of her own lower-working-class origins, her ongoing processes of displacement and emplacement in Ipanema's high society, that Bruna engaged head-on with the messiness of race. For her, being anti-racist was not simply about becoming more cosmopolitan, crafting a liberal self-fashioning, or learning a socially acceptable vocabulary, at least initially. For Bruna, Ipanema was violent, and her own whiteness was unstable and deeply challenged in social interactions with "progressive" white elites with greater degrees of social and cultural capital.

My conversations with Bruna got much deeper in some ways, but between 2015 and 2016, her racial sincerity had been lost. She was now handling racial messiness with the same domesticated white gloves of other upper-class Brazilian and Puerto Rican interlocutors. A new, more modulated perspective on race had surfaced. Like other Brazilian parents in Ipanema, she became focused on teaching "racial fluency" to her child, which could and often did exist independently of actual anti-racist practices.[12] Interiority currency is specifically concerned with disciplinary modes of evidence-making, including an exploration of how people target areas of personal growth and conceptualize self-care. It also raises concerns about indiscriminately deploying affect as an ethnographic methodology or equitably assigning ethical value to our interlocutors' feelings and emotions. Bruna's inward turn, and her eventual renaming of racism as "anxiety," effectively transformed her genuine engagement with race into one that was more palatable and in alignment with modern capitalist multicultural expectations. Rather than assigning value to her various investments in whiteness, Bruna's biography requires that we emphatically examine the political economic and historical dynamics on which her feelings can become objects of ethnographic analysis.

At the urging of her boss at Petrobras, Bruna hired a life coach: "Because, I was so overwhelmed with my own prejudices, like I spoke to you about. ... [I learned that] all you can do is select where you put your energy, what you choose to focus on. I want to focus on growing as a human being, and better understanding my own internal schemas, what is preventing me from achieving happiness." Developing a language of individual psychology truncated any grammar of exploitation that could have emerged from Bruna's early embodied discomfort and emotional reactions to racism. Her experience of racism as a powerful inner lining of embodied sensation (disgust) was interrupted by a therapeutic strategy that pushed any possible social critique to the background, and individual happiness became the targeted personal goal.

Among elites in Ipanema and El Condado, the idea that happiness and the power to "manifest" alternative realities should be engineered from the inside out, rather than the outside in, took on the status of truism. "What does it mean for the theory and practice of social transformation," Berlant asked in a 1999 essay, "when feeling good becomes evidence of justice's triumph?" (cited in Hsu 2019, n.p.). Hence the irony that Bruna came to accept the way her life coach framed happiness as a journey of self-discovery rather than the natural by-product of engaging with the world, particularly the world of a Brazil in crisis.

***

"I don't think I could deal with the snobbishness and first-world problems of these people," a friend once remarked, echoing what other colleagues would also tell me upon learning of my research among white Latin American elites. Yet that is the irony of "studying up": most of my interlocutors had cultivated psychosocial selves that were engaging, profound, and even charming. I entered their spaces with the practised ease of someone who hangs out in places very similar to the ones the Ipanema and El Condado elites frequented. As an academic parent living in New York City (and Ipanema and El Condado during fieldwork periods), it was not uncommon for me to hang out at nice neighbourhood coffee shops with my laptop in the middle of a weekday or be (painfully) familiar with the world of playdates and the pressures of concerted child cultivation. If intimacy is a social good (Illouz 2008a), what does the relationship of "intimacy" between anthropologist and interlocutor tell us and whom or what does it serve?

Talking with Maribel was like talking with some of my closest academic friends – both fun and intellectually stimulating without pretension. Towards the official end of my fieldwork, in 2017, I was convinced that Maribel could tell that I was puzzled, if not explicitly judgmental, about her life choices. At the most basic level, I could not understand how she did not get bored staying at home, by herself, most of her weekdays. Sure, she attended Pilates classes, had lunch with friends she had known since elementary school, and participated in a long-standing book club. Still, if I had that much time, I often thought, I would become OCD about the position of the toilet paper on its tube or whether the kitchen sponge had been squeezed or not. Maribel did not come across as OCD. Was she an alcoholic? Bulimic? How do people who live in their head contend with the slow death of domesticity? Maribel was not one of those parents who considered planning the perfect Pokémon birthday party a space of creative self-expression. I found myself asking Maribel, on several occasions, if she had ever thought of going back to work or considered graduate school or even volunteering. She would answer that, even when she thought about it, there had never been enough (financial?) need to motivate her, nor had she identified a clear "path" or "passion" for herself.

Maribel's lack of a sense of competency and low-energy disposition baffled me. "I haven't put up that frame on the wall because [her husband] has been very busy"; "We haven't finished planting those pots because I will need help holding the plant while I put in the dirt"; "I will wait until the weekend so that [her daughter] can come with me to take the dog to the vet." I came to interpret these common attitudes towards the mundane as a low threshold for discomfort. Sure, nobody likes to have to juggle heavy grocery bags in one hand and a defiant toddler in the other, but oftentimes, for my interlocutors, these mundane discomforts were literally inconceivable. I found myself mourning the lives that some of these individuals, with all their resources, could have enjoyed had they better managed the tolerance for discomfort that public life requires – the discomfort of work politics, the discomfort of doing things because you have to and not because you want to, the discomfort of daring to take risks and enduring rejection, exhaustion, and pain. These instances highlighted for me the importance and inescapable ordinariness of affect (something central to an ethnographic praxis that is always funny and traumatic) about how anthropologists and their informants come to embody and interpret affect during ethnographic encounters.

At a rational level, the sadness I experienced towards Maribel, a wealthy, resourceful, and reasonably content woman, was paternalistic, condescending, and misplaced. It also resonated with what John Jackson (2010) calls a shift from "ethnographic authenticity to ethnographic sincerity," which requires us to ask what socio-cultural knowledge through participant observation might leave in its wake. Some could argue that Maribel's affect suggests certain elements of what we have medically come to understand as "depression." Yet I want to consider how approaching depression or anxiety as interiority currency, forging the racialized affect that contours structures of feelings and vital emotions, disrupts anthropological approaches to ethnographic materials and analytical disciplinary conventions. Such an analysis would require viewing depression and anxiety not as individual psychological (or even physical) illnesses but rather as relational "things" continually conjured within the contexts of shifting interpersonal, structural, and material relationships within which they do very particular kinds of work. At times, these "things" served as tools through which interlocutors executed interaction-management techniques of not letting another (including an ethnographer) exert an emotional influence.

Entertaining "depression" or "anxiety" as a type of emotional vitality brought back a question that had lingered from conversations with my colleague Ulla Berg when we were thinking through our "racialized affect" framework (Berg and Ramos-Zayas 2015): How much psychologizing can ethnographers do and how much extrapolation from the individual could we impose on the group without neglecting local history and political economy? This has been a difficult question for anthropologists interested in examining affect and interiority empirically, as the fear of generalizing and the limitations of translating intangibles into ethnographic writing always feel daunting.[13] How, exactly, do we cast an impression of the collective when an epiphany or insight into interiority emerges through individual interactions or self-reflection? How do we "scale up" or move across layers along the social scaffoldings we study?

We like to imagine that our informants' lives follow some kind of trajectory and that, by recognizing the social patterns behind a narrative arc, we might become better ethnographers. Interiority currency requires that we consider *what* it is that, to interlocutors, feels like progression. What would being "unstuck" feel like for Bruna, or resolving "doubt" in Maribel's case? If I felt that Maribel's commitments were noncommittal and her embodied capacities were unstable, what are the ethnographic tools one could use to write about disaffection, lack of reciprocity in relationships, or even "cruel optimism"? Viewing "anxiety," in Bruna's case, or Maribel's "depression" in relation to interiority currency allows ethnographers and interlocutors to use different logics to determine whether these negative affects are in fact negative: Are these affects intended to develop a new self? To recover an old self that feels to be slipping away? To unearth historical transcripts that were previously viewed as independent of the self or cover historical framings under inner-world cultivation? In Bruna's and Maribel's cases, I came to view anxiety and depression as subjective manifestations of social experiences rather than as overarching pathologies.[14] This challenged my expectation of their perpetual forward motion and offered alternative perspectives to how interlocutors create their futures and aspirations.

Tracing interiority currency, I was able to account for a regime of anticipation and the kinds of affordances that nudge individuals towards certain affective states more than others. Anticipation is a regime of being in time, of "becoming" (Biehl and Locke 2010), which encourages anthropologists and interlocutors to view the "now" in relationship to the "yet to come"; it stresses the recognition that what happens now will shape that future and aspirational self. But interiority currency does not view a separation between the "becoming" and a political economic history of imperial, colonial, and white supremacist projects associated with a temporal past or present; rather, it was precisely attentiveness to the hierarchical operations of racialized affect that encourages a fuller understanding of what "becoming" or the "yet to come" entailed. For my interlocutors, becoming was invariably anchored in specific political economies and entangled with social institutions, relations, and hierarchies. Interiority currency allowed my interlocutors and me to imagine ourselves beyond the present; I was able to uncover the historical markings of their (and my) aspirations and the fact that not everyone orients their process of becoming towards the future, which in fact tends to be the privilege of a few.

Racialized Affects as Ethnographic Methodology in the Americas

Ethnographic encounters with affect incite us to examine spaces for anthropological uncovering not only by attending to the researchers' feelings (Behar 1997; Stodulka, Dinkelaker, and Thajib 2019) but also by documenting how interlocutors' engagements with affect do critical work to produce, disrupt, or sustain social hierarchies. I also came to view interiority currency as necessarily co-produced between ethnographer and interlocutors. These optics allowed me to focus on an affective state and structure of feeling that were not just about analysing a reaction or describing a field site. Interlocutors' own practices of inquiry, temperamental dispositions, familiarity with therapeutic language and parenting trends, and search for symbolic authority challenged the analytics of fieldwork, forcing me to articulate more experience near and immediately relevant to conceptual work.

Uncovering the work of interiority currency allowed me to examine how Latin American white privilege was transformed into morally legitimate ways of being in the world, what I have elsewhere called a "moral economy of privilege" (Ramos-Zayas 2020). Scholars like Anthony Giddens (1991) argue that "life politics" (which includes such issues as self-realization, intimacy, and the good life in general) restructures older social divisions, including class and racial inequality. While a focus on interiority currency bestows fieldwork with uncertainty and angst, it also holds space for the collective labours and social histories against which individual subjectivities and hierarchical sociabilities are enacted in the Global South.

The challenge of empirically examining affect is not always, as has been assumed, a difficulty in "getting to interiority" or focusing on instances when interlocutors transfer their regular, everyday focus of attention from the social world to the inner linings of experience. As suggested by Danilyn Rutherford in a 2016 *Annual Review of Anthropology* article, "Affect theory seems to offer cultural anthropologists a way of getting to the bottom of things: to the forces that compel, attract, and provoke" (286). Interiority currency directs us to look beyond incidental markers of structural inequality; it reveals fundamental aspects of how people articulate a connection between a therapeutic or even cosmic and metaphysical self and their everyday classed and racialized social practices. The expression of racialized affects, grounded in a habitus of interiority currency, shows how a practised inward focus does not imply a silent, passive form of embodiment (e.g., Pagis 2019).

A turn inward requires, as therapeutic cultures show, an active doing that has to be validated by an audience to whom one projects a moral, enlightened self; that is, interiority currency always incorporates an element of sociality, and vice versa. Even when there is no common history or shared targeted area of personal growth, structures of feelings produce collective understandings of expectations about what is valued as interiority currency and turned into forms of capital.

Interiority currency allows us to trace affect and its hierarchical dimensions, particularly its always-already racialized aspect in the Americas. A question that emerges as we consider racialized affect as methodology is, How do we relate to interlocutors' inner worlds when their vital emotions reflect racism and classism? When studying embodied practices, ethnographers tend to focus on symbolic power – how mannerisms, appearance, and taste serve as cultural capital. Yet, in addition to projecting a competent subject to others, therapeutic cultural practices require participants to focus on the inner lining that, depending on an individual's position in race and class hierarchies, permits breaks in one's attention to the social gaze (for the privileged) or not (for the marginalized). A focus on interiority currency enables ethnographers to consider how, in the case of white elites in the Americas, practices of self-cultivation afford the power to transcend contextual constraints and step away, if temporarily, from the social gaze in a way not available to marginalized populations.

Ethnographic encounters where anthropologist and interlocutor negotiate the meaning of truth and orient themselves towards each other in physical space also become instances in which colonial, imperial, and racial power matrices get unearthed and, perhaps, even grappled with. These instances raise critical questions: What is the place of affect in the sphere of social justice, assuming affect has its own criteria of value, definitions of the good life, and concerns with personal satisfaction? Could we determine if affect is "justly" distributed? Attention to interiority currency directs us to how racialized affect manifests in contexts of elite status and white privilege; in such instances, racialized affect seems to assume its own criteria of value.

Recognizing the theoretical and empirical value of interiority currency not only allows us to examine the social centrality of inner worlds and therapeutic cultures, but also to view ethnographic fieldwork around both topics of affect and inequality more robustly. The very preconditions and expressions accumulated or depleted from interiority currency demonstrate that not all inner-world cultivations result in fulfilment and growth. Indeed, ethnographers must perpetually adjust their direction of travel, aspirations, and anticipation in ethnographic encounters with racialized affect. The narratives and affects we share in the field are not merely a reflection of a momentary interaction, but a form of practice that does something important for and *to* us – scaffolding and guiding the potentiality for new neoliberal selves.

NOTES

1 Additionally, Zhang (2020) shows how increasing concern with self-work in China is ultimately about creating a self that is better able to handle family and social relationships, rather than a turn towards individualism.
2 By the 1980s, wellness and well-being in Brazil and Puerto Rico referred not to physical health but to the search for happiness (positive psychology) and quality of life. This intensified in the 1990s with a boom in the study of positive emotions (Galinha and Ribeiro 2005).
3 Following the logic of capital described by Bourdieu, a certain emotional habitus is increasingly a prerequisite to enter and play in additional fields. Surpassing traditional forms of cultural capital, such as wine tasting or familiarity with high culture, emotional capital mobilizes the least reflexive aspects of habitus and the most embodied part of cultural capital (Bourdieu 2018a, 2018b, 1990).
4 These practices and their affective dimensions are part of a neoliberal cultural economy of flexibility and a changing social order; as Carla Freeman (2014) rightfully notices in the case of Trinidad, "they reflect a new ethos of living, working, partnering, parenting, and self-definition that for many also bear unmistakable spiritual elements" (201).
5 Lester shows that mental health patients participate in practices of creating and maintaining their own experiences of affect within different atmospheres

and institutions, whose purpose is to reshape the emotional, behavioural, sensory, and interpersonal lives of participants (Lester 2019, 110).
6 For approaches that view "energy" in relation to emotion or vitality, see, for instance, Collins (1993) and Vora (2015). For an excellent critique of the use of energy and vitality as a metaphor for affect, see Bens (2020).
7 Polsky (1993) argues that the modern welfare state normalizes marginalized social groups by subjecting them to the help of experts, such as clinicians, psychologists, and social workers. The assumption is that, without these "social technicians," people cannot govern themselves, become self-sufficient, or develop healthy relationships and positive self-esteem.
8 In her reading of Freud, Eva Illouz (2008b) notes, "Freud argues that if class determines emotions, emotions may play an invisible but powerful role in social mobility. ... Freud implicitly relies on a model in which psychic development *may disturb and invert* the traditional hierarchical supremacy of money and social prestige" (198).
9 The symbolic interactionist tradition has focused on self-understandings, self-meanings, and self-concepts as the social products of greatest interest to social scientists (e.g., Goffman 1978). Yet it tends to undermine the public self, the self that is visible and known to others or what social scientists have traditionally accepted as contained within the cultural category of personhood.
10 *Persona sencilla* refers to someone who, despite having the wealth and material resources to justify pretentiousness, was unassuming, modest, and colloquial (e.g., a lack of affectation, using popular language and phrases that were below the linguistic level they had access to). Being a persona sencilla needed to result from a clear choice rather than from a lack of options due to material constraints. Persona sencilla was also different from *persona humilde*, which pointed to someone's humble, unfavourable economic origins.
11 Stern (2013) explores clinical psychoanalysis as a social space. Through the "thinking-with others" that occurs in this space, ideas meet and are transformed together. Despite potential applicability to the ethnographic encounter, where ethnographer and interlocutor might engage in multi-directional forms of knowledge production, however, the assumption should not be that "thinking-with others" – or "feeling with" (De Antoni, this volume; De Antoni and Dumouchel 2017), for that matter – is power-neutral.
12 In her study of Afro-Brazilians in Bahia, Hordge-Freeman (2015) considers racial fluency to be "as much about the diverse strategies people use to identify and manage racial situations as it is a reflection of the different ways that people define themselves and others" (138).

13 The notion of "social suffering" (Kleinman, Das, and Lock 1997) has been useful in elucidating the close linkage of personal problems with societal problems, and thus showing how social suffering resists the categorization of anxiety and depression as principally psychological, individual, or medical.
14 Chua (2014) shows how the 1990s' liberalization of the Indian economy has linked notions of the "good life" to consumption and other displays of wealth in the communist state of Kerala. This has increased anxiety and suicide rates, while also authorizing new subjectivities and interventions. Thus, rather than terminating life, suicide generates new ways of living.

REFERENCES

Ahmed, Sara. 2013. *The Cultural Politics of Emotion*. Edinburgh: Edinburgh University Press.
Behar, Ruth. 1997. *The Vulnerable Observer: Anthropology That Breaks Your Heart*. Boston: Beacon Press.
Bens, Jonas. 2020. "Vitalism and Its Discontents: Use and Misuse of the Energy Metaphor in Affect and Emotion Research: A Reply to Hicks." *Global Discourse: An Interdisciplinary Journal of Current Affairs* 10 (1): 37–40. https://doi.org/10.1332/204378919X15762350233091.
Berg, Ulla D., and Ana Y. Ramos-Zayas. 2015. "Racializing Affect: A Theoretical Proposition." *Current Anthropology* 56 (5): 654–77. https://doi.org/10.1086/683053.
Berlant, Lauren. 2011. *Cruel Optimism*. Durham, NC: Duke University Press.
Berlant, Lauren, and Kathleen Stewart. 2019. *The Hundreds*. Durham, NC: Duke University Press.
Biehl, João, and Peter Locke. 2010. "Deleuze and the Anthropology of Becoming." *Current Anthropology* 51 (3): 317–51. https://doi.org/10.1086/651466.
Biehl, João, and Amy Moran-Thomas. 2009. "Symptom: Subjectivities, Social Ills, Technologies." *Annual Review of Anthropology* 38: 267–88. https://doi.org/10.1146/annurev-anthro-091908-164420.
Bourdieu, Pierre. 1990. *The Logic of Practice*. Stanford: Stanford University Press.
– 2018a. "Cultural Reproduction and Social Reproduction." In *Knowledge, Education, and Cultural Change: Papers in the Sociology of Education*, edited by Richard Brown, 71–112. London and New York: Routledge.
Bourdieu, Pierre. 2018b. "The Forms of Capital." In *The Sociology of Economic Life*, edited by Mark Granovetter and Richard Swedberg, 78–92. New York and London: Routledge.
Chua, Jocelyn Lim. 2014. *In Pursuit of the Good Life: Aspiration and Suicide in Globalizing South India*. Berkeley: University of California Press.

Collins, Randall. 1993. "Emotional Energy as the Common Denominator of Rational Action." *Rationality and Society* 5 (2): 203–30. https://doi.org/10.1177/1043463193005002005.

Comaroff, Jean, and John L. Comaroff. 2006. "Figuring Crime: Quantifacts and the Production of the Un/Real." *Public Culture* 18 (1): 209–46. https://doi.org/10.1215/08992363-18-1-209.

De Antoni, Andrea, and Paul Dumouchel. 2017. "The Practices of Feeling With the World: Towards an Anthropology of Affect, the Senses and Materiality – Introduction." *Japanese Review of Cultural Anthropology* 18 (1): 91–8. https://doi.org/10.14890/JRCA.18.1_99.

Foucault, Michel. 1988. "Technologies of the Self." In *Technologies of the Self: A Seminar With Michel Foucault*, edited by Luther H. Martin, Huck Gutman, and Patrick H. Hutton, 16–49. Amherst: University of Massachusetts Press.

Freeman, Carla. 2014. *Entrepreneurial Selves*. Durham, NC: Duke University Press.

Galinha, Iolanda, and J.L. Pais Ribeiro. 2005. "História e evolução do conceito de bem-estar subjectivo" [History and Evolution of the Concept of Subjective Well-Being]. *Psicologia, saúde e doenças* 6 (2): 203–14.

Gaztambide-Fernández, Ruben A. 2009. *The Best of the Best: Becoming Elite at an American Boarding School*. Cambridge, MA: Harvard University Press.

Giddens, Anthony. 1991. *Modernity and Self-Identity: Self and Society in the Late Modern Age*. Stanford, CA: Stanford University Press.

Goffman, Erving. 1978. *The Presentation of Self in Everyday Life*, Vol. 21. London: Harmondsworth.

Goldstein, Jan. 2009. *The Post-Revolutionary Self: Politics and Psyche in France, 1750–1850*. Cambridge, MA: Harvard University Press.

Hordge-Freeman, Elizabeth. 2015. *The Color of Love: Racial Features, Stigma, and Socialization in Black Brazilian Families*. Austin: University of Texas Press.

Hsu, Hua. 2019. "Affect Theory and the New Age of Anxiety." *The New Yorker*, 25 March 2019. www.newyorker.com/magazine/2019/03/25/affect-theory-and-the-new-age-of-anxiety.

Illouz, Eva. 2007. *Cold Intimacies: The Making of Emotional Capitalism*. Cambridge, UK: Polity.

Illouz, Eva. 2008a. *Saving the Modern Soul: Therapy, Emotions, and the Culture of Self-Help*. Berkeley: University of California Press

Illouz, Eva. 2008b. "Emotional Capital, Therapeutic Language, and the Habitus of 'The New Man'." In *Sexualized Brains: Scientific Modeling of Emotional Intelligence from a Cultural Perspective*, edited by Nicole C. Karafyllis and Gotlind Ulshöfer, 151–78. Cambridge, MA: MIT Press.

Jackson, John L., Jr. 2010. "On Ethnographic Sincerity." *Current Anthropology* 51 (S2: S279–87). https://doi.org/10.1086/653129.

Khan, Shamus. 2009. *Privilege: The Making of an Adolescent Elite at St. Paul's School*. Princeton: Princeton University Press.

Kleinman, Arthur, Veena Das, and Margaret Lock, eds. 1997. *Social Suffering*. Berkeley: University of California Press.

Lawler, Stephanie. 2005. "Disgusted Subjects: The Making of Middle-Class Identities." *The Sociological Review* 53 (3): 429–46. https://doi.org/10.1111/j.1467-954X.2005.00560.x.

Lester, Rebecca J. 2019. *Famished: Eating Disorders and Failed Care in America*. Berkeley: University of California Press.

Matza, Tomas. 2012. "'Good Individualism'? Psychology, Ethics, and Neoliberalism in Postsocialist Russia." *American Ethnologist* 39 (4): 804–18. https://doi.org/10.1111/j.1548-1425.2012.01396.x.

Munem, Bahia. 2014. "Expulsions and Receptions: Palestinian Iraq War Refugees in the Brazilian Nation-State." PhD diss., Rutgers University.

Nehring, Daniel, and Dylan Kerrigan. 2019. *Therapeutic Worlds: Popular Psychology and the Sociocultural Organisation of Intimate Life*. London; New York: Routledge.

O'Dougherty, Maureen. 2002. *Consumption Intensified: The Politics of Middle-Class Daily Life in Brazil*. Durham, NC: Duke University Press.

Omi, Michael, and Howard Winant. 1987. *Racial Formation in the United States*. New York; London: Routledge.

Pagis, Michal. 2019. *Inward: Vipassana Meditation and the Embodiment of the Self*. Chicago: Chicago University Press.

Pandian, Anand. 2008. "Tradition in Fragments: Inherited Forms and Fractures in the Ethics of South India." *American Ethnologist* 35 (3): 466–80. doi: 10.1111/j.1548-1425.2008.00048.x.

Polsky, Andrew J. 1993. *The Rise of the Therapeutic State*. Princeton, NJ: Princeton University Press.

Ramos-Zayas, Ana Y. 2012. *Street Therapists: Race, Affect, and Neoliberal Personhood in Latino Newark*. Chicago: University of Chicago Press.

Ramos-Zayas, Ana Y. 2020. *Parenting Empires: Class, Whiteness, and the Moral Economy of Privilege in Latin America*. Durham, NC: Duke University Press.

Raymond, Williams. 1977. *Marxism and Literature*. Oxford; New York: Oxford University Press.

Rose, Nikolas. 1998. *Inventing Our Selves: Psychology, Power, and Personhood*. Cambridge, UK: Cambridge University Press.

Rutherford, Danilyn. 2016. "Affect Theory and the Empirical." *Annual Review of Anthropology* 45: 285–300. https://doi.org/10.1146/annurev-anthro-102215-095843.

Stern, Donnel B. 2013. "Relational Freedom and Therapeutic Action." *Journal of the American Psychoanalytic Association* 61 (2): 227–56. https://doi.org/10.1177/0003065113484060.

Stewart, Kathleen. 2007. *Ordinary Affects*. Durham, NC: Duke University Press.

Stodulka, Thomas, Samia Dinkelaker, and Ferdiansyah Thajib, eds. 2019. *Affective Dimensions of Fieldwork and Ethnography.* Cham, Switzerland: Springer Nature.

Stoler, Ann Laura. 2004. "Affective States." In *A Companion to the Anthropology of Politics*, edited by David Nugent and Joan Vincent, 4–20. Malden, MA: Blackwell Publishing.

Taylor, Janelle S. 2005. "Surfacing the Body Interior." *Annual Review of Anthropology* 34: 741–56. https://doi.org/10.1146/annurev.anthro.33.070203.144004.

Vora, Kalindi. 2015. *Life Support: Biocapital and the New History of Outsourced Labor.* Minneapolis: University of Minnesota Press.

Zhang, Li. 2020. *Anxious China: Inner Revolution and Politics of Psychotherapy.* Oakland: University of California Press.

Chapter 3

The Devil Is in the Details: Affect and Creativity in Discerning Illness and Demonic Possession in Contemporary Italy

ANDREA DE ANTONI

On that day in July 2019, the perfect blue blessing of the sunny Sicilian sky in the early afternoon brought a torrid curse with it.[1] We found shelter from the scorching sun sitting at a small bar table under a parasol, directly on the street. The neighbouring cathedral was also protecting us with its shade. Dr Vitale, an extremely well-mannered man in his early sixties was sipping his espresso. I opted for an iced coffee. Shaken.

Dr Vitale, a generalist doctor, was the first medical specialist who started assisting the local exorcist, Brother Gentile, in his practice more than ten years before.[2] Although he had always been a practising Catholic "up to that time," he explained, "I did not even know that certain things existed." Brother Gentile contacted him because he was a member of the parish and asked him to check the conditions of a young woman who, apparently, was possessed by the devil. That was the first time Dr Vitale took part in a Catholic exorcism. He recalled the suffering and screaming of the woman, as well as his "shock" in witnessing "deep wounds similar to scratches" suddenly appearing on the woman's body when the devil manifested during the exorcism, just to disappear once the séance was over. Witnessing such a suffering and symptomatology, which he "was not able to explain despite" his "medical knowledge and experience," opened him to the possibility that "maybe there is something that cannot be explained by biomedicine." That encounter stimulated his "scientific curiosity," but above all, he "felt the need to help that woman and other people like her, because," he added, "I am a doctor."

Dr Vitale was the first member of what, over the following years, became the "medical team" (*equipe medica*) that assists Brother Gentile in the Psycho-Spiritual Diagnostic Centre (Centro Diagnostico

Psico-Spirituale) created by the exorcist in the mid-2000s. I could meet Brother Gentile only some months after I met Dr Vitale, for he travels the world to deliver his experience-based knowledge on, and to deliver people from, the "Evil One." He was a short, bald friar, whose disarmingly kind smile was adorned by a bright white beard that reached his chest. His humble brown-grey robe and sandals were not enough to disguise sparks of a somehow amused and inquisitive curiosity in his firm eyes, resting behind his big glasses. He emanated a balanced, deep, warm, and kind aura that made me think of holiness, topped with a pinch of self-effacing irony.

There are many reasons why Brother Gentile is a celebrity among Catholic exorcists. Born in 1941, friar since 1957, nominated as an exorcist by the bishop in 2000, and in charge of organizing and coordinating training programs for other exorcists across the whole of Sicily, he is considered one of the most experienced and knowledgeable decans in the world. In addition to his long experience as an exorcist – he told me that he performs 1,500 exorcisms per year and that he witnessed the final liberation of fifty-five people in the previous three years (2016–9) – he holds a university degree in philosophy and one in religious studies. Thus, he is generally considered one of the most educated "intellectual" exorcists whose competency is deeply rooted both in theology and in academic rational thinking. He has been actively involved in the National and International Association of Exorcists, where his status increased even further after the founder, the extremely influential Father Gabriele Amorth (1925–2016), passed away.[3]

Yet, likely the main reason why Brother Gentile is so highly regarded is that he is the founder of the aforementioned Regional Centre that, besides being responsible for the education and training of new exorcists, is one of the examples of an institution that carries out what exorcists call "differential diagnosis" (*diagnosi differenziale*), or "discernment" (*discernimento*): the practice of distinguishing between demonic possession and (mental) illness. Exorcists are very conscious of the difficulties of their ministry, including the challenges of differentiating what they call "spiritual issues" from illness, perceived as grounded in nature. Although the centre is not unique in Italy, it is probably the one that features the highest degree of systematized collaboration between exorcists, laypeople, and biomedical practitioners.

Collaboration between exorcists and biomedical practitioners has been strongly recommended by the Vatican throughout history (Young 2016). Presently, the General Directives (*Praenotanda*) in the new version of the Ritual of Exorcism, called *Of Exorcisms and Certain Supplications* (*De exorcismis et supplicationibus quibusdam* 2004, *DESQ* hereafter),[4] which presently regulates the practice of Catholic exorcism, clearly state that

> [r]egarding the necessity of using the Rite of Exorcism, the Exorcist will make a prudent judgment after diligent inquiry, ... having consulted, to the extent possible, experts in spiritual matters and, if necessary, in the science of medicine and psychiatry, who have a sense of spiritual realities. (17)[5]

Such collaborations are not always possible, because medical practitioners willing to volunteer for collaboration are not always available. In addition, as the last words in the preceding quotation suggest, exorcists are supposed to work with specialists who are preferably Catholic or who, at the very least, do not exclude a priori the theoretical possibility of demonic possession. Yet such people are not always easy to find.

Brother Gentile had become increasingly frustrated in his work as an exorcist because demonic possession is not, as he explained, "talked about at universities and barely even during seminaries," even though Catholic exorcists continuously witness people healing through exorcisms. He wished that specialists in biomedicine and scholars in general were more open, even just towards investigations of such phenomena. As he told me, speaking as if he were imaginatively addressing medical practitioners:

> I do not demand that you [physicians, psychiatrists, and psychologists] *believe* in the existence of the devil or diabolic possessions. But, at least in your intellectual honesty you should be able to say that "certain – at least for us [physicians, etc.] – "pathologies" ... we do not know how or why, but they [the sufferers] ... heal through what Catholics call exorcisms. How that happens, we do not know.

This "unknown" indicated by Brother Gentile and the "unexplainable" pointed out by Dr Vitale are the focus of this chapter. I argue that focusing on the work of affects can constitute a starting point to investigate such unknowns, for affects and affective methods are exactly what enabled my interlocutors' uncovering of the devil and possession, as well as their critical views on biomedicine. I focus on differential diagnosis, as it constitutes the moment in which the realities of both possession and (mental) illness explicitly emerge through and are shaped by diagnostic practices (see Csordas 1994; Good 1994; Mol 2002). By focusing on how diagnostic processes happen in practice, I shed light on the institutionalized procedures employed by both medical and religious specialists to – borrowing Annemarie Mol's (2002) words – "enact" illness and possession, respectively. I also consider how the interplay between affects, bodily perceptions, and decision-making (re)constituted the boundaries between two ontologies – "biomedicine" and "religion" – which are generally perceived as oppositional. Finally, I argue that focusing on affective methods such as those exercised by exorcists and their collaborators can provide a new direction to explore the *unknowns* to which my interlocutors pointed, as well as uncover new findings for the anthropology of spirit possession and religious healing.

Uncovering Diagnostic Work and Affective Methods

Diagnosis and its consequences have long been under examination by medical anthropology and social studies in general. Research has discussed the role of diagnostic "labelling" in the transformation of both social practices and individual identities, focusing mainly on the political and social spheres that underlie the formation of labels and diseases (Brown 1990; Brown, Lyson, and Jenkins 2011; Jutel 2015) and the production and redistribution of biomedical authority related to diagnostic categories (Armstrong 2011; Kirmayer 1994).

A consequence of such approaches has been the deconstruction of the belief that medical science mirrors nature, and that diseases are something "out there" waiting to be uncovered through objective scientific observation (Good 1994; Mol 2002). Yet such a focus on classification and labelling has tended to overlook the practicalities of diagnostic processes, including their embodied and experienced dimensions.

However, phenomenological approaches (Crapanzano 1973; Csordas 2002; Good 1994; Stoller 1995) have shown that the reality of illness – be it biomedically defined disease or spirit possession – emerges in bodily experiences intersubjectively shaped through interactions between the specialist and the sufferer. Such approaches have relativized both diagnostic categorizations and illness experiences, embedding them in socio-culturally meaningful worlds (Kleinman 1980). This has led to a phenomenological model of mental illness and spirit possession that relies on universal concepts, such as "idioms of distress" (Nichter 1981), "culture-bound syndromes," or "cultural concepts of distress" (Kaiser and Weaver 2019), and that is generally accepted in anthropology and transcultural psychiatry. According to this model, experiences of suffering are signified and narrativized through intersubjective encounters that entangle experiences with cultural models accepted by the actors, in which the biomedical model is one of various possibilities (Csordas 1994; Good 1994; Kirmayer 2004; Seligman 2014). Furthermore, the reality of cultural models – operating within what Foucault (1984) calls "regimes of truth" – is grounded in embodied experiences and relies heavily on the efficacy of healing. This process also allows for the renegotiation of personal and cultural histories through embodied memories (Csordas 1994, 2002; Good 1994; Stoller 1995). Thus, such approaches understand all cultural models as equally valid, but relying on notions of metaphor or interpretation of experienced symptoms, they tend to reproduce epistemologies of illness and suffering rather than demonstrating how the realities of illness ontologies "hang together" (Mol 2002).

Medical anthropologist Annemarie Mol's (2002, 2008) work has been influential in developing a praxeological approach to illness ontologies. In developing her methodology, she suggests focusing on how humans and non-humans "do" illness and disease and, among various possibilities, she claims:

> There may (but need not be) a script available for doing a disease. ... At different times and places scripts are staged in various ways. If there is no script, actors improvise. (Mol 2002, 32)

Mol's radical empiricism leads her to ditch the Goffmanian play/stage metaphor (Goffman 1959), for it "may be taken to suggest that there is a backstage, where the real reality is hiding." To her, "In the act, and only then and there, something *is* – being enacted" (33, emphasis in original).

While the focus on enactment is fundamental to understanding how disease ontologies are shaped and hang together through situated practices, glossing over specialists' repertoires of knowledge can be misleading. The specific actions that specialists perform at a particular moment are generally informed by and derived from a certain kind of knowledge and a range of possible skills that specialists have acquired and draw from. When medical specialists diagnose, they do not perform a spell or divination. That knowledge becomes one of the agents that enables situated enactments. In this sense, if the metaphor of knowledge as a "script" can lead to misunderstandings, perhaps relying on ideas of *procedures* can be helpful.

The idea of "diagnostic work" (Büscher, Goodwin, and Mesman 2016) can be useful here, for it allows seeing diagnos*ing* as the entanglement of knowledge, procedures, and situated enactments, while accepting that the relation is "not merely the enactment of a linear logic following from preset classifications or solutions" (Risør and Nissen 2018, 23).

Here, I am primarily interested in the embodied and affective dimension of diagnostic work. In fact, "Long before machines are put to use clinicians diagnose with their senses" (Mol 2008, 39). Yet, besides a few ethnographic accounts of the sensory and embodied dimensions of diagnosing (Gardner and Williams 2015; Goodwin 2010; Moreira 2006), such dimensions – not to mention the affective one – have barely been taken into consideration.

An exception to this trend is the work of anthropologist Berhnard Hadolt (2018), who, in his analysis of pre-symptomatic genetic testing and counselling in Austria, has argued that "a focus on affect as a generative force for sociality can foster our understanding of diagnostic practices" (143). His research shows that affective coordination between counsellor and counselee constitutes the basis that affords the enactment of diagnostic procedures, where the counsellor "guides the counselling while the counselee follows" (Hadolt 2018, 143). He also warns against a strong dichotomization between rationality and emotionality, for "when looked at from the perspective of affective flows both rationality and emotionality emerge as culturally specific solutions to coordination problems" (144).

In this chapter, I build on the aforementioned approaches to offer reflections on how illness and possession realities and ontologies emerge through "diagnostic work" in the correspondences between exorcists, medical practitioners, and sufferers. I show that affective attunements not only become the ground for diagnostic procedures, rationality, and emotionality but that they also ground the very existence of illness and the devil. In other words, I argue that the border between the two apparently oppositional ontologies of religion and biomedical science, as well as the one between "faith and reason" (Csordas 2017, 303), emerge as *results* of affective attunements among actors. I show that the role of affective attunements or, as I prefer, practices of "feeling with" (De Antoni and Dumouchel 2017) the sufferer, becomes all the more important once the enactments of the sufferer's body "break" diagnostic procedures. In fact, when procedures break, medical practitioners are forced to improvise and resort to "forms of consciousness or knowledge that exceed the cognitive – forms that are sensory, bodily, affective" (Livingston 2012, 27).

From a methodological perspective, thus, my aim is to contribute to the anthropology of diagnosing, of spirit possession, and, more broadly, to theories of affect by integrating the phenomenology of the body and bodily perceptions with approaches focusing on enactments as the ground for "doing" ontologies. In doing so, I advocate for a more emergent, affect-based praxeological approach that sheds light on *how* ontologies are formed and hang together. In fact, the practice of attending to the workings of affects or, more specifically, the "affective methods" of interlocutors – one of the central notions in this volume – becomes paramount not solely because affective methods are what allow for new discoveries and critiques by my interlocutors but also because they enable new anthropological discoveries and critiques more broadly through processes of ethnographic uncovering. Following *how* affects work and what they *do* (rather than discussing what they are) can be useful for a critique of an anthropology that analyses diagnosing, healing practices, and spirit possession in terms of idioms of distress and cultural models.

Roman Catholic exorcism can provide a unique insight in this sense, for one of its characteristics is the "church's complete acceptance of psychiatry," because, as Csordas (2017) writes, "in practice mental illness must be professionally ruled out or deemed to be copresent before a problem is recognized as due to demonic affliction" (295). In other words, the case of Catholic exorcism is unique because medical practices and practitioners are part of the institutionalized processes of discernment between possession and mental illness. Therefore, "the standard formulation of ethnopsychiatry that recognizes psychotherapy and religious healing as equivalent or alternative ways of addressing affliction cannot be applied" (Csordas 2017, 295). In the next sections, I shed light on how such ontologies emerge and are negotiated, starting from how diagnostic procedures work.

Discerning Procedures

Scholarly and especially ethnographic research on Roman Catholic exorcism is scarce. While the main focus has been on historical change (Young 2016), recent research has examined its contemporary revival, with a particular focus on how discourses about exorcism have been reshaped in relation to modernity, secularization, and the media (De Antoni 2015; Giordan and Possamai 2018; Hauke 2006). As for strictly anthropological research, beyond a few articles (Csordas 2017; De Antoni 2017, 2022), the only extensive ethnographic research is Talamonti's (2005) work. While providing interesting accounts of some of the sufferers' stories and of how a famous exorcist operated in practice, Talamonti's work mainly focuses on interpretations of ritual practices from a symbolic aspect. In addition, sociological research has shown that collaboration between an exorcist and a psychiatrist in Italy "rests on particular mechanisms of exchange of legitimacy between the religious and the medical fields, with mutual recognition and autonomy" (Giordan 2020, 109).

According to the Catechism of the Catholic Church (2012), *exorcism* refers to events "when the Church asks publicly and authoritatively in the name of Jesus Christ that a person or object be protected against the power of the Evil One and withdrawn from his dominion" (§1673). The solemn exorcism, called a "major exorcism," "can be performed only by a priest and with the permission of the bishop" and is a ritual "directed at the expulsion of demons or to the liberation from demonic possession" (§1673).

The *DESQ* limits the use of exorcisms exclusively to cases of possession, which it recognizes according to four main signs: (1) aversion to the sacred, (2) speaking languages that were before unknown to the victim, (3) revealing information that the victim is not supposed to know, and (4) manifesting exceptional strength. Such signs, however, "may constitute simple indicators and therefore should not necessarily be considered as coming from the devil" (*DESQ*, 28).

In addition to such textually institutionalized signs of possession, Father Amorth described symptoms that vary within a wide though limited range. He pointed out that "the two areas most commonly affected by evil influences are the head and the stomach," adding that the hypothesis of being in front of demonic possession needs to be considered "[i]f the pain travels, now to the entire stomach, then to the kidneys, later to the ovaries, etc., defying the understanding and remedies of medicine … , while blessings prove very efficacious (Amorth 1999, 32).

Three points can be surmised from this explanation. First, more than the body parts in which pain is experienced, the unusual features of pain can be possible signs of possession. Second, biomedical diagnoses and treatments are already taken into consideration in the exorcist's diagnostic work. In fact, those who arrive "at an exorcist's door have already tried every possible medical test and remedy"; thus, "it is easy for the exorcist to discover the medical diagnosis, what therapy was attempted, and with what results" (Amorth 1999, 32). Third, the final diagnosis depends on the efficacy of the treatment. While the presence of medically unexplained symptoms or the initial failure of medical treatment opens possibilities for the hypothesis of possession, it is the efficacy of prayer, blessings, or exorcism that (de)stabilizes its reality.

In addition, there are psychological and behavioural signs, although they are considered less easy to identify. Works by both exorcists (Amorth 1999; Babolin 2014) and psychiatrists who collaborate with their International Association (de Ezcurra 2019), clearly warn about the difficulties in discerning possession from conditions such as psychotic disorders, including schizophrenia, dissociation and hysteria, neurotic disorders, as well as personality or mood disorders, especially major depression.

This perceived grey area is the reason why the *DESQ* warns that exorcists "should not too easily believe that someone is possessed by a demon, when the person may be labouring under some illness, especially of a psychological nature" (14). It is also the reason why exorcists tend to choose their collaborators among professional psychiatrists or psychologists: they are the ones who have the duty and responsibility of tracing the boundaries of mental illness. Whatever falls beyond those boundaries – for example, any medically unexplained symptom – could possibly be perceived as a sign of a "spiritual disorder."

Generally speaking, exorcists collaborate with one or two trusted medical practitioners. When people visit an exorcist there are several possibilities (see Figure 3.1). In most cases, the exorcist does not find any mental or spiritual disorders, and he suggests that the supplicant undergo a Catholic life, regularly confess, attend Mass as much as possible, and live "in God's light." In some cases, the exorcist might suspect disorders of a mental or spiritual nature or both. In cases he thinks disorders have an exclusively psychiatric or medical/natural cause, he suggests that the supplicant visit a medical specialist. He might refer the person to a specialist he trusts, but he will not interfere with the supplicant's choice: once the colloquium is over, that person is beyond the exorcist's interest. If the exorcist exclusively suspects some disorder of a demonic nature, he will start with what exorcists call "exorcistic therapy" – typically weekly, biweekly, or monthly meetings in which an exorcism is conducted and which can continue for years.

Yet, if the exorcist suspects the possibility of a mental disorder in addition to a disorder of demonic nature or if he is not sure about his judgment, he refers the supplicant to one of his trusted medical practitioners. The doctor's judgment is what determines the supplicant's condition, thus bringing it back to the aforementioned binary, although all the exorcists and medical practitioners I talked with reported that there is a minority of cases in which disorders of a medical nature coexist with spiritual disturbances. In these cases, supplicants undergo medical treatment and exorcisms, namely, what Brother Gentile called "integrated therapy." All exorcists claim that cases of demonic possession are extremely rare. Although there are no official statistics, both exorcists and medical practitioners report that

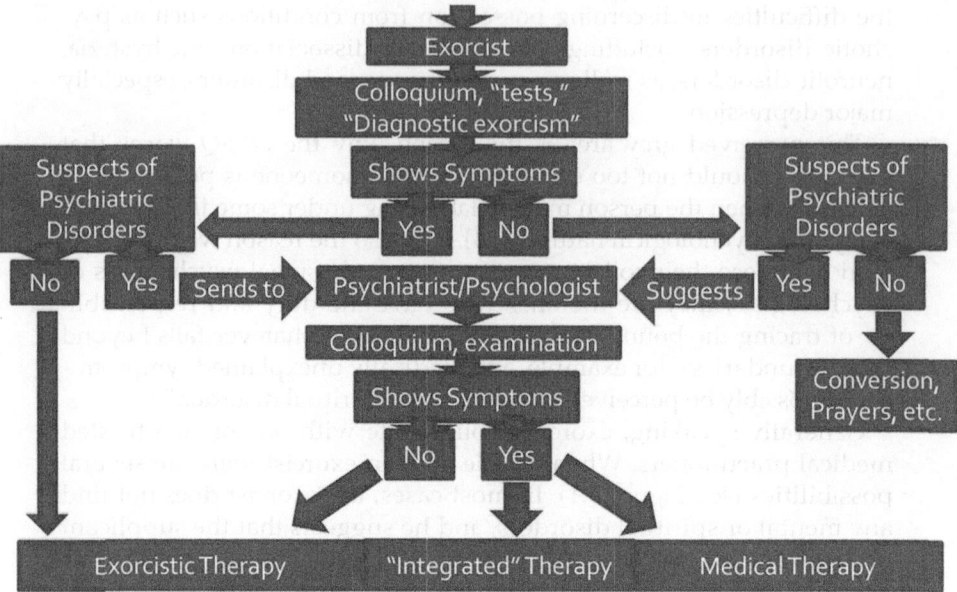

Figure 3.1. Differential diagnostic process (general) flowchart.

those cases fall within the range between 2 and 5 per cent of the totality of supplicants with whom they had colloquia (see also Giordan and Possamai 2018).

In terms of diagnostic procedures, the ones employed by exorcists parallel the ones employed by medical practitioners. Both work based on "colloquia," which consist primarily of interviews with the sufferer. Exorcists might employ "tests" to "uncover the devil" in case they suspect demonic disturbances. Such tests vary enormously, but they generally include praying with the supplicant to see their reactions, as people who suffer from demonic disturbances tend to experience issues with praying, such as an inability to concentrate, dozing off, or more or less violently refusing to pray at all. Other tests might include sprinkling holy water on the supplicant, giving mental (i.e., silent) commands to the devil, mentally praying for the supplicant, or performing a so-called diagnostic exorcism, namely, a short exorcism, which could also be performed mentally, to establish final proof of any demonic presence.[6] If the supplicant negatively or violently reacts to such tests, the exorcist may choose to investigate further.

Brother Gentile reported people reacting to holy water as though it was burning them, or people immediately showing negative reactions when the exorcist imposed a crucifix on their back without them supposedly knowing and without touching them:

> Or, for example, you put the Bible close to them and you hear the words "take that bunch of paper away!" Not even love for the Bible. ... It leaves you at least suspicious that there is something that, evidently, goes beyond pathology.

Such situated reactions are not sufficient to determine a case of exorcism, though. Exorcists also draw on interviews to unearth any clue of possible demonic disturbance from the phenomenological field of the patient's everyday life and personal history, especially in suspicious cases. Typically, any previous experiences with the "occult" or "occultism" would trigger suspicion.[7] In addition, behavioural symptoms connected to aversion to the sacred are seen as possible signs of possession. Brother Gentile mentioned a woman who wanted to have communion, but she could not, for her legs would stiffen and she would not be able to stand up or walk or, if she did get the Eucharist, she would feel the urge to spit it out. As Brother Gentile explained:

> If people pray, they have issues. If they do not, they feel well. This is already an element that makes you think, isn't it? [Laughs]. ... Then, with experience ... their gaze. Sometimes it is a hateful gaze that ... you don't find it in a sick person ... toward the exorcist! And it makes you suspect that there is something slightly different. It is all small, small elements put together [dots the air with his fingers]. Naturally, the more there are of those elements, the more perfect the diagnosis becomes. And, of course we do the whole anamnesis of a person. ... We have to collect all those elements, starting from early childhood ... reconstructing everything and seeing what can be a psychological problem – conditionings, etc. – and understand what emerges from the whole picture, which can make one at least *suppose* a diabolic action.

Rather than considering a specific symptomatology of possession as though it was one condition, the diagnostic procedure on the exorcist's side aims at identifying a whole constellation of clues of possession, which mainly consist of situated negative affects entangled with interactions with sacred objects, or people and with specific events in the sufferers' personal histories. It is the situated emergence of negative affects in the sufferer feeling with specific (sacred) objects or people that grounds the possible reality of demonic action (see also De Antoni 2017, 2022). Exorcists' diagnostic work, then, relies on enacting possession through "affirming" it, by means of eliciting specific negative affective reactions. Possession and the devil emerge as the result of such reactions.

Conversely, biomedical specialists tend to identify signs that exclude mental illness. Psychiatrists who collaborate with the International Association of Exorcists have painstakingly refined diagnostic criteria for discernment. For instance, an article written by one of these psychiatrists and recently circulated within the association (de Ezcurra 2019), proposed some criteria to discern when certain conditions are mental illnesses or not. Obviously, in their own diagnostic practice, medical practitioners follow the procedures indicated by the *Diagnostic and Statistical Manual of Mental Disorders*. Yet, there are some cases in which this is not possible.

The article explains in great detail how to discern between each of the aforementioned mental disorders and possible demonic action. Yet, the most general criteria or conditions that "break" the standard procedures for diagnosing and, thus, enacting illness can be summarized as follows: (1) Sufferers/patients have a "normal" life outside of the "crises." Namely, possible signs of possession, such as the external personality or physical symptoms, appear only during exorcism séances and do not influence everyday life. (2) The "crises" themselves are limited to exorcism séances or to getting in contact with the sacred. (3) Sufferers do not heal or improve through medical treatment, or their condition worsens, or drugs have a contrary effect to what it is supposed to be. (4) Sufferers improve through prayers and exorcisms. (5) There is an absence of delusional or histrionic self-centred speech structures. (6) Sufferers do not have a history of mental illness. (7) The beginning of symptoms can be related to a moment in which sufferers had contacts with "occultism."

Similar to the procedures employed by exorcists, such criteria (perhaps with the exception of number 5) do not point to specific symptoms. They are focused on anamnesis – the practice of documenting the sufferer's illness history – and suggest unveiling certain elements in the phenomenological field of the sufferer's everyday life and behaviours ("crises") that need to be entangled with a specific ritual/therapeutic assemblage.

As Mol (2002, 27) pointed out, "[w]hen doctor and patient act together in the consultation room, they jointly give a shape to the reality of the patients'" symptoms. Procedures to enact mental illness, here, *break* because patients and their bodies do not "collaborate" with biomedical procedures and treatments, thus disallowing the enactment of mental illness. This is what opens the way to considerations of possession as, at this point, biomedical specialists seek to improvise within their diagnostic work. This is where following how situated affects work becomes crucial to developing an anthropology of diagnosis.

The Devil's Doctor

The centre created by Brother Gentile organizes collaborations with medical specialists and laypeople assigned to different stages, the last of which is Brother Gentile. It was created out of necessity, for when Brother Gentile started his ministry, he quickly found himself overwhelmed with requests. He organized a filtering system so that he could deal exclusively with serious cases.

As explained in Figure 3.2, the first stage is called the Listening Centre, managed by lay volunteers from the parish. Supplicants phone a call centre and explain their situations. The volunteer listens, provides advice, and, in many cases, organizes a colloquium. In most cases, the sufferer is satisfied with the advice and with simply having been listened to. Yet, if volunteers suspect any possible demonic influence, they schedule an appointment with Brother Gentile's medical team. Roughly 10 per cent of the supplicants access the second stage.

The medical team is composed of two generalist doctors (the aforementioned Dr Vitale and his wife), one male forensic psychopathologist and criminologist in his mid-sixties, and one female psychotherapist in her early seventies. Brother Davide, a friar in his late forties, is also part of the team. He is trained as a clinical psychologist, has a background in the psychology of education, and is actively involved in projects supporting deprived adolescents and young couples. His role is unique, for he acts as both a medical and a religious specialist, although he is not the official exorcist. Brother Gentile also joins the meetings.

The team meets monthly, each time assessing two to three "complicated cases." The group collectively listens to the supplicant and goes through diagnostic procedures. Brother Gentile performs an exorcism in cases he deems it appropriate. The rest of the team assists and intervenes in case there are violent reactions. This stage provides the team with the final assessment of the supplicant's condition. If the supplicant reacts to the exorcism and any demonic entities manifest themselves through the supplicant's body, the supplicant accesses the final stage, the therapeutic one. The therapy is carried out by the two friars, and it consists of exorcisms, by Brother Gentile, and spiritual/psychological

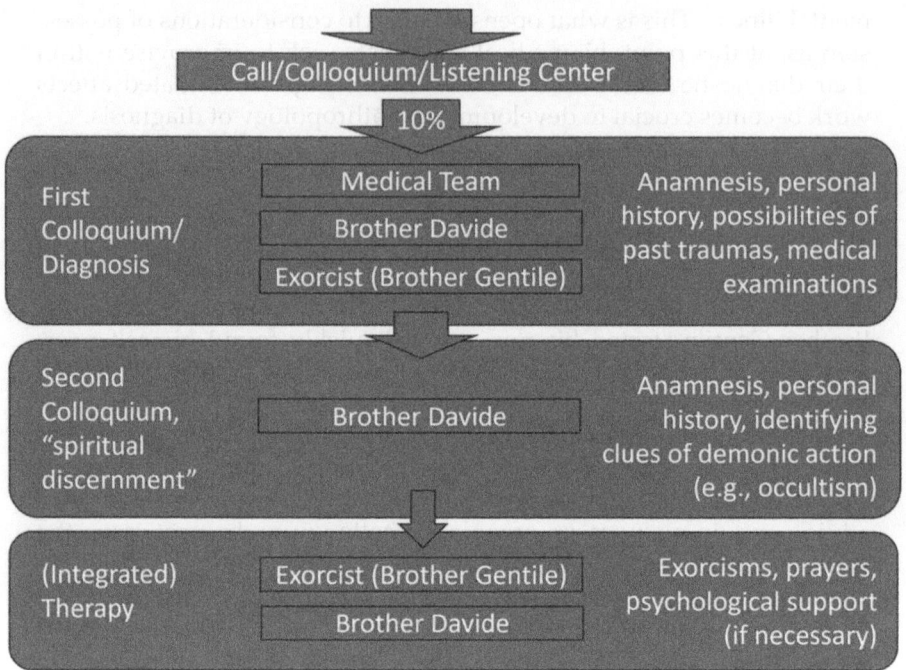

Figure 3.2. Centre stages flowchart.

support, carried out by Brother Davide, depending on the sufferer's needs.

Brother Davide's unique position, including his experiences in educational projects that constantly put him in touch with youth from difficult socio-economic backgrounds and who had very traumatic experiences, enabled him to participate effectively within both biomedical and religious ontologies. Perhaps unsurprisingly, he did not feel that they contradicted each other. He patiently explained to me how the reality of biomedical and spiritual disorders can coexist. Once I realized that I could freely ask questions, I asked about his opinion about the vast amount of psychological literature that tends to reduce possession states to trauma. He promptly replied:

> There are some traumas, especially the ones during childhood, which become a locus for an "opening" to possession. … In that case, the traumatic event is actually what causes that kind of symptomatology. But, from my perspective, the symptomatology is tied to divine action. Whereas for

the skeptical diagnostician, that condition relates to an issue of fixation, neurosis, [etc.]. …. Clearly, any therapeutic intervention in that case will be totally ineffective.

Brother Davide inhabited a world in which psychological or biomedical disorders could not only coexist as separate conditions but also complement each other, sometimes shaping codependent conditions of causation. Traumatic events and memories could become an "opening" for the devil to sneak in. The difference was defined by therapeutic efficacy. Needless to say, the integrated therapy offered by the Centre would work on both fronts:

> A trauma is a trauma. … You obviously work on the aspects of healing from a trauma perspective. Yet, if there is no concurrent intervention based on exorcisms, you will never be able to do that work, because evil will confuse all the dimensions more and more. It will put the traumatic experience more and more under the spotlight, repeatedly pushing it in front of the person. … So, the person will always be *exposed* to the traumatic event because the Evil One keeps on operating.

In Brother Davide's view, therefore, although trauma and possession are ontologically distinct, they might exist in a co-causal relation. This would not be possible without some common ground underlying both conditions. Understanding this common ground constitutes the first step into the unknown at which Brother Gentile pointed, for it is fundamental to unveil how the two ontologies are shaped. Interestingly, accounts by medical practitioners can offer a clearer perspective on this.

Dr Vitale explained that, during the anamnesis, he looks at sufferers' "family history – whether parents are alive, dead, or divorced – because these are all traumas that, obviously, we need to take into account." The team also relies on medical examination results taken elsewhere that supplicants submit:

> So if, from a medical perspective, we think that, after all, those traumas are not particularly significant, (s)he is a capable person, etc., physically healthy, or (s)he underwent a lot of examinations, this often happens. … And there is nothing that comes out from those examinations … MRI of the brain, all good. CT scan, all good, etc. Then we start thinking.

If the first diagnostic step does not reveal any possible pathology, the team delves into the "reasons why the sufferer believes that they are spiritually disturbed from a spiritual perspective." In case the sufferer mentions negative affective reactions in relation to the sacred in everyday life, they start suspecting possible issues of a spiritual nature. Yet "these are signs. ... They are not pathognomonic; they do not indicate to us that that person is surely [possessed]. ... However, they are signs to take into account." Up to this point, therefore, there is a degree of certainty about the supplicant's condition as not caused by natural reasons, but possession is still only a theoretical possibility. Procedures to enact illness ultimately break as a consequence of reactions to the exorcism, and this is what gives way to another kind of diagnostic work.

The "unexplainable" hinted at by Dr Vitale is what paved the way for his uncovering of the devil. Besides the aforementioned "scratches," he reported swellings appearing and moving under the supplicant's skin and disappearing under the exorcist's command, and a woman with rheumatoid arthritis who could barely walk who started jumping, running, and screaming.

These are cases in which the sufferers' bodies not collaborating *broke* procedures and did not allow him to enact biomedical illness *as he was used to doing*. This is fundamental: his shock and surprise were not only the consequence of a procedure that did not work but also of his own body, habituated and enskilled in biomedical practice and a certain kind of diagnostic work. This allowed the sufferer's body, which did not conform to Dr Vitale's experience, to appropriate authority and power by carrying out its own actions and "become the devil":

> You understand straight away when a person is really [possessed]. Because their face is ugly, really ugly. ... "Ugly" because he [the devil] changes you a bit. ... Facial features stay the same, because the face itself cannot change. But you see a person who becomes evil. ... The eyes redden, their face become tense, they are full of hatred. You really get that feeling. And it upsets you. ... Now I laugh because, you know ... but the first few times, I was afraid. ... Look, for me saying these things ... it is not easy, because I have a rational mentality. I did many years of university studies, you know?

The performance of certain affects by the sufferer's body, then, became the ground for the reality of the devil and possession. Dr Vitale, unable to enact illness through his habitual diagnostic work and forced to improvise, had to rely on other more embodied ways of knowing. His habitual mode of diagnostic work already implied a certain degree of affective attunement with the sufferer. Yet the impossibility of enacting a certain procedure made him susceptible to affective becomings in the supplicants, to a modality of "feeling with" the supplicant: "You really get that feeling," and "it upsets you." In other words, the doctor's modality of attending to and feeling with the sufferer, enskilled through practice and enacted through situated diagnostic work, is what enabled the supplicant's affects to, in Ahmed's (2004) framing, spread.

Indeed, such a modality of "feeling with" the patient is usually employed – although often implicitly – by medical specialists. For instance, Dr Gioia, a female psychiatrist, clinical psychologist, and psychotherapist in her fifties, and collaborator with an exorcist in Central Italy, explained to me that

> even psychiatrists, when they are with patients, they feel various things. Empathy, even nervousness is possible. ... The psychiatrist wonders why (s)he feels like that, and (s)he uses it [for diagnosis or therapy].

During her career, Dr Gioia worked in clinics for drug addicts and in public mental health clinics, and she "saw quite a few things, you know, collaborating with the police, or the firefighters." Nevertheless, talking about her first experience in dealing with a person – a woman in her thirties – who then turned out to be possessed, she told me that for the first time in thirty years she got really afraid, simply by being with her and listening to her stories. The woman presented no signs of psychopathology but she had physical symptoms that were too incongruous with one another to identify them as a biomedical condition. Dr Gioia explained that, in the case of illness,

> there is a continuum and it is explainable. In other cases, laboratory examinations ... are syntonic with that determined disease. ... The patient responds to pharmacological therapy and so on. There is order even in illness. ... Instead, in those cases there is madness, one could barely talk about illness.

Also in this case, the patient's body broke the diagnostic procedures, thus making it impossible for Doctor Gioia to enact her usual diagnostic work and, consequently, excluding the reality of biomedical conditions. Furthermore, the woman's life was characterized by repeated encounters with cult-like ceremonies and poltergeist-like phenomena in her house. She used to find herself paralysed in bed alone, repeatedly feeling orgasms beyond her will, and she was obsessed by thoughts that, sometimes, tended to be blaspheme but, more importantly, "she felt that they were ego-dystonic," namely, perceived as external and against her will. Furthermore, "there was rage toward herself or her children, which appeared suddenly without reason." Dr Gioia was so struck by the woman that she spent three whole days listening to her. Eventually, she was shaken by how she ultimately felt: "Saying it was like my bones froze would not be enough, but I cannot find other ways to say it. ... I felt the chill in my spine for the very first time."

In this case, the doctor's modality of feeling with the patient, of attuning to her, possibly enhanced by the failure in enacting disease and the prolonged time of diagnostic work, led to an affective state from which the reality of the devil and possession emerged. They emerged through specific, negative feelings that Dr Gioia perceived as exclusively hers, but they were also the result of feeling with the patient through enskilled diagnostic work. Most importantly, it was precisely these affects that enabled Dr Gioia to start her upsetting *uncovering* of the devil and of the limits of biomedical rationalities. Similar to Dr Vitale – and, incidentally, to all the medical practitioners who collaborate with exorcists whom I met – it was this process of uncovering through affective methods, rather than through faith or belief, that opened her to the possibility of possession. It was diagnostic work as an affective practice that allowed her to become entangled with while, at the same time, actively shaping the *unknown*.

Feeling Diagnostic Work and the Shape of the Unknown

Are biomedical and religious ontologies mutually exclusive? My main argument in this chapter is that they are not. This echoes the findings of phenomenological approaches, which have shown that embodied and intersubjective experiences are central to identifying both spirit possession and illness (Crapanzano 1973; Csordas 2002; Good 1994; Stoller 1995). However, my point here is that the collaboration between medical practitioners and exorcists enabled the phenomenological and ontological realities of mental illness and demonic possession to emerge through "diagnostic work" (Büscher, Goodwin, and Mesman 2016) – namely, through *practice*. As Stoller (1995) argued, embodied experiences can become crucial sites for negotiating memories and power relations. In contemporary Italy, bodily enactments have become the ground for defining the distinction between possession and illness. In this process, affective attunements and feeling with specific (sacred) humans and objects became the ground for the emergence of these realities. Affects grounded and shaped processes of ontological emergence, and their ungraspable nature – their manner of eluding the realm of discourse – not only enabled the smooth performance of diagnostic procedures (Hadolt 2018) but also facilitated the very emergence of both illness and the devil. These processes, however, were made possible and shaped by broader assemblages with which affective attunements between specialists and sufferers were deeply entangled.

Diagnostic procedures formed a key element of such assemblages. While the diagnostic criteria employed by exorcists aimed at "affirming" possession by finding signs of possible demonic activity, the ones employed by medical practitioners focused on excluding the possibility of mental illness. In other words, exorcists followed a relatively institutionalized procedure to enact possession, whereas medical specialists focused more on cases in which procedures to enact illness break. This assumes an apparent division of roles and distribution of responsibilities in which each specialist follows diagnostic procedures within their respective fields.

These two sets of procedures suggest the conflictual existence of different interpretive frameworks that have been referred to in traditional anthropological analytics in several ways: as "systems of knowledge" (Crapanzano 1973), "cultural models," "medical systems" (Csordas 1994), or as "regimes of truth" (Foucault 1984). From these perspectives, the two diagnostic systems appear as embedded in two ontologies that hang together separately (Mol 2002). However, my interaction with interlocutors from seemingly two "distinct" worlds suggests that they worked through and worked with similar ambiguities, while sharing affects and consternation. Therefore, such procedures also enabled the creation of a common ground between the two worlds by enabling and directing specific situated enactments through diagnostic work. Although exorcists and medical practitioners enacted different conditions, they were also trying to reduce ontological uncertainty and indeterminacy by performing very similar diagnostic work: following symptomatic criteria and investigating the phenomenological field of everyday life and personal history through anamnesis. As a result of these procedures, exorcists and medical practitioners' *actions*, as well as their modalities of attending to and feeling with sufferers, paralleled each other.

This was possible because the collaborative practice of the Centre was implicitly permeated by the primacy of modern medicine. In fact, on one hand, the devil and possession were possibilities that came into play once the "reality" of mental illness was excluded, and the whole institutionalized assemblage of practices created for this purpose sheds light on a certain degree of anxiety, of urgency to exclude the presence of mental illness. On the other hand, even the jargon employed by exorcists was permeated by biomedical terms. This, in turn, was the result of the progressive modernization of such collaborative practice that has been carried out since the implementation of the *DESQ* (De Antoni 2015; Giordan 2020).

That said, it may be helpful to again return to Mol (2002) and her reminder that it is enactments during diagnostic practice that shape the reality of illness. Exorcism deals with bodies that do not collaborate with dominant biomedical diagnostic procedures, "breaking" those procedures and forcing medical practitioners to improvise through other, more embodied ways of knowing. Before becoming "possession," the sufferers' conditions were unexplained symptoms. The reality of the devil started emerging through a specific kind of diagnostic work grounded in affective methods, exactly because medical practitioners were entrained and enskilled in feeling with the sufferer during the diagnostic process. The beginning of "doing possession" depended on specific negative affects (fear, feeling uncomfortable, chills, etc.) that emerged in this process. Attending to the practitioners' affective work and methods can serve as a way to push ethnographic uncovering towards a critique of analytics focused solely on biomedical rationalities. In fact, it was exactly the process of attending to affects that allowed my interlocutors to uncover the realities of possession.

Exorcists – and especially Brother Davide – mixed biomedical and religious procedures comfortably with no particular anxiety towards unexplained symptoms. This allowed them to consistently follow *some* procedure, excluding their own affective dimension, to "objectively" evaluate each case and act accordingly. Nevertheless, they enacted possession through specific diagnostic work (e.g., tests) which elicited specific negative reactions and feelings in the sufferer. In turn, the sufferer's affective reactions and bodily changes affected both the exorcist and the medical practitioners, thus becoming central to the emergence of the shared reality of possession and the devil. Therefore, situated affects "spreading" (Ahmed 2004) from the sufferer to the specialists were fundamental in shaping differential diagnoses and possession states because they became the ground of improvisation and the "existential ground" (Csordas 1994) of the devil. Biomedical and spiritual ontologies, along with the realities of illness and possession, thus, were constantly shaped and hung together because they emerged *as a result* of situated processes of "feeling with" other actors (including non-humans) and diagnostic work.

Could such an emergent perspective on situated affective correspondences and diagnostic work lead to a new phenomenological understanding of the "unknown" that Brother Gentile pointed at? If it can, then it can shape an anthropology of healing processes and well-being and of how spirit ontologies affect people's everyday life. One way it might do so is by illustrating how both the production of ethnographic knowledge and the understanding of affect become possible through somatic attunements, rather than exclusively through cognition and its corollary applications of "theory" in anthropology and "diagnosis" in healing. In this sense, ethnography and diagnostic work reveal shared practices of attunement to the experiences of others as a process of discernment and uncovering. To the degree that such affective practices were more deliberately acknowledged as distinct methods of connecting somatically with the states of others, anthropologists, healers, and institutionalized medical practitioners might find increased capacity for collaboration and mutually productive critique.

NOTES

1 This article is based on ethnographic data collected through fieldwork (2014–19) with Catholic exorcists and their collaborators throughout Italy. I repeatedly met and interviewed ten different Catholic exorcists and six of their collaborators. In addition, I attended and gave a lecture at the 10th Course on Exorcism and Deliverance Prayers in Rome (Regina Apostolorum University, 2015), where I spoke with even more practitioners, and I regularly took part in exorcisms as a helper at an undisclosed location in Central Italy. I am grateful to all the exorcists, medical practitioners, laypeople involved as helpers, supplicants, and possessed people who shared their stories with me, as well as to the Japanese Society for the Promotion of Science that made this research possible (Grant numbers 15K16905 and 21H00650).
2 Although Brother Gentile is a very famous and essentially a public figure, I decided to use a synonym in this article, as I did for all the other people mentioned in this chapter. I use the appellative "Brother" rather than "Father," because Brother Gentile is a friar, and friars see themselves as a Brotherhood. Brother Gentile belongs to a subgroup of the Franciscan order, which observes extreme poverty as well as a series of behavioural restrictions in everyday life.
3 Father Amorth was the official exorcist of the Diocese of Rome from 1986 to 2000 and contributed enormously to the popularization of exorcism. He published several books on his experiences as an exorcist and encounters with the devil, two of which were (reportedly) translated into eighteen languages. He appeared in countless national media features and international documentaries, and he founded the National Association of Exorcists in 1990, which became International in 1993, and has grown exponentially since then.

4 Originally, exorcists used the so-called *Roman Ritual* (*Rituale Romanum*), written in Latin, which dates back to 1614, although it was revised several times, with the last edition dating back to 1952. Yet, as a consequence of the modernization process, the Vatican issued a revised rite of exorcism on 26 January 1998, making it the last of the church's liturgical books to be updated after the Second Vatican Council. This new version, which regulates present-day exorcism and should be used by all exorcists, is the *DESQ*. On the history of the *DESQ*, see De Antoni (2015) and Hauke (2006).

5 Official texts issued by the Catholic Church are divided into numbered paragraphs and have no specific authors. It is customary practice to refer to them through their titles and, in case of direct quotes, reporting the paragraph rather than the page number. I adopt this practice throughout the chapter.

6 The possibility or legitimacy of carrying out diagnostic exorcisms on first timers has long been discussed within the association, for the *DESQ* seems to discourage it, as it could have a potentially negative impact, especially on people who suffer from psychiatric disorders (De Antoni 2015; Hauke 2006). Nevertheless, many exorcists employ it. Brother Gentile did not employ it in the early stages of the diagnostic process.

7 Among exorcists, *occultism* refers to any (religious) practice perceived to go against the Catholic doctrine. While some practices such as worshipping Satan and the practice of reiki have been institutionally declared as causing demonic possession, others such as New Age practices, (transcendental) meditation, spiritism (including the Ouija board), certain kinds of rock or metal music, yoga, traditional magic, etc. can all be included into the umbrella-term *occult*, depending on the judgment of the exorcists. Exorcists do not consider such practices as deterministic causes of possession. Rather, they see them as something that "opens the door to the Evil One."

REFERENCES

Ahmed, Sara. 2004. *The Cultural Politics of Emotion*. London; New York: Routledge.

Amorth, Gabriele. 1999. *An Exorcist Tells His Story*. Translated by Nicoletta V. Mackenzie. San Francisco: Ignatius Press.

Armstrong, David. 2011. "Diagnosis and Nosology in Primary Care." *Social Science & Medicine, Sociology of Diagnosis* 73 (6): 801–7. https://doi.org/10.1016/j.socscimed.2011.05.017.

Babolin, Sante. 2014. *L'esorcismo. Ministero Della Consolazione* [Exorcism: Ministry of Comfortation]. Padua, Italy: Edizioni Messaggero Padova.

Brown, Phil. 1990. "The Name Game: Toward a Sociology of Diagnosis." *The Journal of Mind and Behavior* 11 (3/4): 385–406.

Brown, Phil, Mercedes Lyson, and Tania Jenkins. 2011. "From Diagnosis to Social Diagnosis." *Social Science & Medicine* 73 (6): 939–43. https://doi.org/10.1016/j.socscimed.2011.05.031.

Büscher, Monika, Dawn Goodwin, and Jessica Mesman. 2016. "Ethnographies of Diagnostic Work: Introduction." In *Ethnographies of Diagnostic Work: Dimensions of Transformative Practice*, edited by Monika Büscher, Dawn Goodwin, and Jessica Mesman, 1–14. Basingstoke, UK, and New York: Palgrave Macmillan.

Crapanzano, Vincent. 1973. *The Ḥamadsha: A Study in Moroccan Ethnopsychiatry*. Berkeley, CA: University of California Press.

Csordas, Thomas J., ed. 1994. *Embodiment and Experience: The Existential Ground of Culture and Self*. Cambridge, UK: Cambridge University Press.

Csordas, Thomas J. 2002. *Body, Meaning, Healing*. Basingstoke, UK, and; New York: Palgrave Macmillan.

Csordas, Thomas J. 2017. "Possession and Psychopathology, Faith and Reason." In *The Anthropology of Catholicism: A Reader*, edited by Kristin Norget, Valentina Napolitano, and Maya Mayblin, 293–304. Oakland: University of California Press.

De Antoni, Andrea. 2015. "The Politics of Spirits and the Legacy of the Exorcist: The Historical Construction of Discourses of Spirit Possession in Contemporary Japan and Italy." *Ritsumeikan Social Sciences* 106: 27–69.

De Antoni, Andrea. 2017. "Sympathy from the Devil: Experiences, Movement and Affective Correspondences During a Roman Catholic Exorcism in Contemporary Italy." *Japanese Review of Cultural Anthropology* 18 (1): 143–57. https://doi.org/10.14890/jrca.18.1_143.

De Antoni, Andrea. 2022. "She Talks to Angels: Spirit Becomings, Embodied Memories and Affective Imagination Skills in Catholic Exorcism in Contemporary Italy." In *Re-Creating Anthropology: Sociality, Matter, and the Imagination*, edited by David N. Gellner and Dolores P. Martinez, 108–25. Abingdon, UK: Routledge.

De Antoni, Andrea, and Paul Dumouchel. 2017. "The Practices of Feeling with the World: Towards an Anthropology of Affect, the Senses and Materiality – Introduction." *Japanese Review of Cultural Anthropology* 18 (1): 91–8. https://doi.org/10.14890/jrca.18.1_91.

de Ezcurra, Héctor. 2019. *La diagnosi differenziale tra i disturbi psicopatologici e l'azione straordinaria del demonio (seconda parte) [Differential Diagnosis Between Psychopathological Disorders and Extraordinary Demonic Activity (Part Two)]*. A.I.E. Associazione Internazionale Esorcisti Press Office.

Ecclesia Catholica. 2004. *De exorcismis et supplicationibus quibusdam* [Of Exorcisms and Certain Supplications]. Rome: Libreria Editrice Vaticana.

Foucault, Michel. 1984. "Truth and Power." In *The Foucault Reader*, edited by Paul Rabinow, 51–76. New York: Vintage.

Gardner, John, and Clare Williams. 2015. "Corporal Diagnostic Work and Diagnostic Spaces: Clinicians' Use of Space and Bodies During Diagnosis." *Sociology of Health & Illness* 37 (5): 765–81. https://doi.org/10.1111/1467-9566.12233.

Giordan, Giuseppe. 2020. "Diagnosing the Devil. A Case Study on a Protocol Between an Exorcist and a Psychiatrist in Italy." In *The Social Scientific Study of Exorcism in Christianity*, edited by Giuseppe Giordan and Adam Possamai, 95–110. Cham, Switzerland: Springer.

Giordan, Giuseppe, and Adam Possamai. 2018. *Sociology of Exorcism in Late Modernity*. Cham, Switzerland: Palgrave Macmillan.

Goffman, Erving. 1959. *The Presentation of Self in Everyday Life*. New York: Doubleday Anchor.

Good, Byron J. 1994. *Medicine, Rationality and Experience: An Anthropological Perspective*. Cambridge, UK: Cambridge University Press.

Goodwin, Dawn. 2010. "Sensing the Way: Embodied Dimensions of Diagnostic Work." In *Ethnographies of Diagnostic Work: Dimensions of Transformative Practice*, edited by Monika Büscher, Dawn Goodwin, and Jessica Mesman, 73–92. Basingstoke, UK, and; New York: Palgrave Macmillan.

Hadolt, Bernhard. 2018. "A Desire for Knowing: Ontological Uncertainty, Diagnostic Evidence and Generative Affectivity in Pre-Symptomatic Genetic Counselling." In *Diagnostic Fluidity: Working with Uncertainty and Mutability*, edited by Nina Nissen and Mette Bech Risør, 129–47. Tarragona, Spain: Publicacions URV.

Hauke, Manfred. 2006. "The Theological Battle over the Rite of Exorcism, 'Cinderella' of the New Rituale Romanum." *Antiphon* 10: 32–69.

Jutel, Annemarie. 2015. "Beyond the Sociology of Diagnosis." *Sociology Compass* 9 (9): 841–52. https://doi.org/10.1111/soc4.12296.

Kaiser, Bonnie N., and Lesley Jo Weaver. 2019. "Culture-Bound Syndromes, Idioms of Distress, and Cultural Concepts of Distress: New Directions for an Old Concept in Psychological Anthropology." *Transcultural Psychiatry* 56 (4): 589–98. https://doi.org/10.1177/1363461519862708.

Kirmayer, Laurence J. 1994. "Improvisation and Authority in Illness Meaning." *Culture, Medicine, and Psychiatry: An International Journal of Cross-Cultural Health Research* 18 (2): 183–214. https://doi.org/10.1007/BF01379449.

Kirmayer, Laurence J. 2004. "The Cultural Diversity of Healing: Meaning, Metaphor and Mechanism." *British Medical Bulletin* 69 (1): 33–48. https://doi.org/10.1093/bmb/ldh006.

Kleinman, Arthur. 1980. *Patients and Healers in the Context of Culture: An Exploration of the Borderland Between Anthropology, Medicine, and Psychiatry*. Berkeley: University of California Press.

Livingston, Julie. 2012. *Improvising Medicine: An African Oncology Ward in an Emerging Cancer Epidemic*. Durham, NC, and London: Duke University Press.
Mol, Annemarie. 2002. *The Body Multiple: Ontology in Medical Practice*. Durham, NC: Duke University Press.
Mol, Annemarie. 2008. *The Logic of Care: Health and the Problem of Patient Choice*. London; New York: Routledge.
Moreira, Tiago. 2006. "Heterogeneity and Coordination of Blood Pressure in Neurosurgery:" *Social Studies of Science* 36 (1): 69–97. https://doi.org/10.1177/0306312705053051.
Nichter, Mark. 1981. "Idioms of Distress: Alternatives in the Expression of Psychosocial Distress: A Case Study From South India." *Culture, Medicine and Psychiatry* 5 (4): 379–408. https://doi.org/10.1007/BF00054782.
Risør, Mette Bech, and Nina Nissen. 2018. "Configurations of Diagnostic Processes and Practices: An Introduction." In *Diagnostic Fluidity: Working with Uncertainty and Mutability*, edited by Nina Nissen and Mette Bech Risør, 11–32. Tarragona, Spain: Publicacions URV.
Seligman, Rebecca. 2014. *Possessing Spirits and Healing Selves: Embodiment and Transformation in an Afro-Brazilian Religion*. New York: Palgrave Macmillan.
Stoller, Paul. 1995. *Embodying Colonial Memories: Spirit Possession, Power, and the Hauka in West Africa*. New York; London: Routledge.
Talamonti, Adelina. 2005. *La carne convulsiva. Etnografia dell'esorcismo* [The Convulsive Flesh: An Ethnography of Exorcism]. Naples, Italy: Liguori.
US Catholic Church. 2012. *Catechism of the Catholic Church*. 2nd ed. Vatican City: Libreria Editrice Vaticana.
Young, Francis. 2016. *A History of Exorcism in Catholic Christianity*. London: Palgrave Macmillan.

Chapter 4

Serious Play and the Facilitation of Feeling in Food Allergy Advocacy in Japan

EMMA E. COOK

"Sharing a meal, you can communicate," a man in his early twenties said during an online workshop in 2021 that I co-facilitated with Atopicco Network for Children of the Earth (hereafter Atopicco). Atopicco is an authorized non-profit organization (NPO) in Japan which supports people with allergic disease. The man participating in the workshop was struggling with a feeling of obligation to socialize with co-workers and visit business contacts over food and asked attendees for advice on how to deal with his food allergies at work. He had a sense that his allergies produced discomfort and unease in others. He felt that they inhibited communication and the development of congenial relationships, and he worried that not eating the same food as others would mark him as a different and potentially difficult colleague, which would adversely affect his job and career. Many people with food allergies who attend Atopicco workshops and events have similar concerns: How will others view them? How will their inability to eat everything put in front of them affect how they are perceived? How can they make others understand that they are not being fussy or difficult but instead need to take care to avoid an allergic reaction? Given the possibility of suffering a severe allergic reaction requiring medical treatment, taking precautions when eating out is not a choice but a necessity. Finding ways to communicate this understanding to others and then managing the affects that result are thus primary concerns.

In Japan, as in many other places where charities and NPOs focus on allergic diseases, facilitating an understanding of what food allergies are and what they entail is a significant part of advocacy work. Atopicco has been specifically focused on food allergies and other allergic diseases, including eczema and asthma, since 1993.[1] In addition to running a telephone support line, they have cultivated working relationships with food manufacturers, convenience store brands, and supermarket groups. The managing director of the NPO, Tomomi Akagi, has written a column on allergy for House Foods Group, a popular food company specializing in Japanese curry, since 2017 (Akagi n.d.). She has also written articles for the Nihon Keizai newspaper (Japan's leading financial newspaper) since 2018 (Akagi 2018, 2020a, 2020b, 2020c) and published a range of books on allergic disease for the public (Akagi 2005, 2014, 2019). Prior to the pandemic Tomomi was also travelling regularly around the country giving lectures and running workshops on allergic disease to diverse audiences.[2] The NPO aims, as outlined on a web page titled "Towards Acceptance, Empathy and Tolerance" (Juyō to kyōkan, soshite kanyō e), to provide support for patients and their families; to help people and nature coexist, with diverse values accepted; and to create a society where everyone can live together (Atopicco n.d.-a).

In line with this volume's aspirations outlined in the introduction, my aim in this chapter is to explore how interlocutors engage with terms that anthropologists have themselves extensively theorized, to move towards collaborative forms of critique, grounded foremost in affective responses and practices. There exists a significant body of research on the importance of empathy – as a specific emotional orientation towards another's experience – in health care and patient advocacy, as well as in theoretical literature in anthropology, which I discuss later in the chapter. I focus specifically on how NPO staff highlight and engage with empathy in their engagement with patients and why they choose not to focus on it specifically as a goal of their advocacy work, favouring instead the cultivation of a broad range of affects and feelings that might more constructively move people towards positive action. This accords with their ethos that while encouraging feeling in others is good for expanding understanding, telling others what those feelings *should be* is not. In other words, the NPO's use of empathy is applied as a heuristic strategy to position the NPO in a supportive role towards the person with allergies (or their guardian) and create a space where allergic sufferers feel understood. Of course, the NPO's activities to educate the public *can* lead to the development of empathy *for* allergic sufferers, but what staff primarily seek is to move people to help make life more equitable for food allergy sufferers and thus encourage a broader acceptance of a diversity of experiences, identities, and values in Japanese society. One of the ways they have begun to do this is through the medium of play.

Affective Advocacy and Play

In the lectures and workshops that I have seen Atopicco's director Tomomi host, affect is intimately integrated into her work. She usually introduces herself by first speaking about her own experiences of food allergies and of raising a son with food allergies thirty years ago, before there was any mandatory allergen labelling or public knowledge about them in Japan. There is an immediacy in this information. It is not dry data or facts but a recounting of lived experience that invites listeners to imagine what it might be like to live with food allergies. In the workshops and events I have participated in since 2015, Tomomi consistently seeks to engage intimately with her audience and to facilitate – and allow for – a range of affects and feelings in participants. This is often done in terms of using personal stories as well as through the practice of encouraging the sharing of impressions in the latter half of workshops. For example, she often distributes pens and sticky notes and asks participants to write down their thoughts and feelings, individually or in partnership with others in small groups, before sharing with the rest of the room.

Since 2017 Tomomi has also been facilitating workshops in which participants (usually food manufacturers, food cooperatives, university students studying childcare, or nutritionists) play a card game called Ranran Lunch, which helps participants imagine eating out with allergies. It is through this game that this chapter explores how serious practices of play[3] facilitate understanding in ways that are deeply intimate but not, surprisingly, always necessarily "empathetic" as anthropology has traditionally understood it.

The game itself was created by a paediatric allergist in 2011 as part of a research project focused on improving quality of life (QOL) among food allergic patients, and a free download is available on Japan's Ministry of Health, Labour and Welfare website (MHLW, n.d.). It was thereafter printed by Atopicco in collaboration with the Nippon Foundation for their Food Allergy Patient Support Project. The card game is described on Atopicco's website in two ways: first, "Ranran Lunch: Thinking about food allergies: a tool that promotes understanding of food allergies among the general public" (Atopicco n.d.-b) and, second, "A campaign where adults play and think seriously" (Atopicco n.d.-c). The organizers advise groups to play the game and subsequently do a workshop or study session about food allergies, suggesting that participants discuss what they both learned *and* felt while they played. Aimed squarely at adults while being simple enough for children to play, the cards have a dual purpose: to get adults to have fun and relax through play and prompt learning about allergens in common dishes through a simulated experience of eating out with allergies. This playful simulation helps cultivate an understanding – cognitively, affectively, and (potentially) emotionally – of the experiences and feelings of those with food allergies.[4] It encourages non-allergic people in wider society to be aware, knowledgeable, and engaged. The game thus relies on facilitating an awareness of what those with food allergies experience when eating out. However, the practice of playing also engenders a variety of affects that may then be leveraged towards empathic ends.

Where empathy has been taken up in anthropology and broader academic discourse, it is often understood as something to "have" or "cultivate," especially in advocacy and in health care contexts (e.g., Halpern 2001; Miller 2015). Defying a neat definition, empathy has most commonly been understood as a capacity in which we are able to "gain a first-person perspective on another's thoughts and feelings, as if we were experiencing and understanding the world through his or her vantage point" (Hollan and Throop 2011, 3). A cursory look at Ranran Lunch might lead a person to assume that the point of the game is to engender empathy in players. However, as noted above, Atopicco does not necessarily seek to develop empathy in others and dictate its content but, rather, to cultivate feelings that can be leveraged towards educational – and only *potentially* empathic – ends. In a conversation about their philosophy, Tomomi stressed that moving people to take positive *action* for those with food allergies is the ultimate aim. Empathy is something that they, as staff of the NPO, foster for the experiences of the people on whose behalf they work, and although empathy can move one to action, it is action itself that they feel is most important. Therefore, rather than focusing on the content of a particular emotion (e.g., empathy) they instead focus on process: how feelings can be facilitated through specific "affective arrangements" (Slaby, Mühlhoff, and Wüschner 2017), in this case through playing a card game, to stimulate learning and understanding, and ultimately move people to take action with positive effects. In this way the NPO thereby works towards reducing the social difficulty that those with allergic disease experience in daily life.

I propose that if in scholarship on empathy we focus only on *having* empathy or cultivating empathy in – and for – others, we risk thinking of empathy as a stable emotion from which people act. However, affects, feelings, and emotions are not stable categories from which we act but are instead far more fluid. Moreover, affects are not only rooted in bodies but instead emerge from particular contexts and "arrangements" (Slaby, Mühlhoff, and Wüschner 2017; Slaby and Röttger-Rössler 2018). Therefore, while advocacy can and often does emerge from, and include, feelings of empathy for others, contrary to literature that seeks to understand what empathy "is" or that suggests that empathy is a quality that individuals possess or need to cultivate more of to understand (and advocate for) others, I argue that it is instead more productive to trace *how* affects and feelings are mobilized in efforts to increase knowledge, understanding, cooperation, and action.

To illustrate this, I first describe a workshop that I attended in 2017 during Atopicco's yearly summer camp for people with allergic diseases.[5] In doing so, I trace out how the card game Ranran Lunch facilitates a range of feelings and imaginings through the process of play that have educational effects that potentially go beyond *serious* (i.e., non-play) workshops that impart knowledge but do not affect people in the same way. Rather than featuring extensive anthropological theories of empathy first in the chapter, followed by ethnographic data that might otherwise "demonstrate" or "deconstruct" it, I have chosen to sandwich academic discussions on empathy in the middle of the chapter. This structure serves to highlight how such theoretical work on empathy, while instructive in and of itself, is of limited use as theory to my interlocutors in their advocacy efforts. The final section bookends this discussion by presenting impressions and feelings from a range of other workshops that food allergy study groups have put on, which have been uploaded to Atopicco's website, to illustrate how non-allergic people have engaged with the game. Although these comments are discursively mediated and not directly captured by me in the ethnographic moment, the affect-rich impressions are valuable because they demonstrate the ways that convivial affect generated through playful experiences is converted into understandings of allergy. This chapter thus explores how the serious play that is engendered by Ranran Lunch is taken up as an affective practice for facilitating ethical learning experiences, such as about food allergy realities, that do not always fit anthropology's traditional engagements with empathy.

Serious Play and the Facilitation of Feeling

It was 3:30 p.m. on the second day of a three-day summer camp in August 2017, held at an arts centre that has a camping ground. It was another hot and sticky day, and I was feeling tired. As I moved into the air-conditioned room, I suppressed a yawn and paused briefly near the door. Adults were slowly trickling in and taking seats at rectangular tables. They had enjoyed the previous session as a "free session," where they could create art or get together to share coffee and cake at an attached restaurant. Some people were quietly chatting; others were sitting in silence. The feeling of the room was quietly expectant but with lower energy compared to the morning when people filed into a workshop with employees from McDonald's Research Centre and were chattering animatedly. I joined a table with two women and two men who were sitting quietly. The two men nodded to me and said hi, and one of the women turned to me and asked about the teen workshop I had just facilitated.[6] Tomomi picked up the microphone and started to introduce the session, telling us that we were going to play a card game. There was a quiet murmur of what seemed to be mostly curiosity in response, and she began her introduction of the card game as follows:

> When I was raising my child [who had allergies] we didn't have these cards. So I stood at the whiteboard and wrote about food allergies to explain it [to teachers, parents, and others], but that's embarrassing, isn't it? But with these cards, although you can't teach a lot about allergies with them, it introduces what it really feels like (*jissai ni donna kanji de aru ka tte iu no o shōkai shiteiru*). And the game can be used to start a discussion or do a workshop. It's not for people to think about, but to experience/feel (*taikan shite morau*).

As she started explaining the rules, there was a rumble of confusion in the room and at my table as we all tried to figure out how it worked. It is a simple game once people get the hang of the rules. There are fourteen cards with the top seven allergens (in Japan) listed on them[7] and six "allergy-free" cards. Fifty other cards depict meals in five different cuisine categories demarcated by five different colours: Japanese, Western (including US and Italian dishes), Chinese, Ethnic (in which Vietnamese and Indonesian dishes predominate), and Snacks (see Figure 4.1). The allergen cards are distributed among the players, and the menu cards are put in the centre of the table. Players play rock, paper, scissors to decide who will start, and then the game moves clockwise around the table.[8] Players pick up a menu card and consider whether the allergens that they have (on the cards they were given at the beginning) are in that dish or not. If it is safe to eat, they keep the card; otherwise, they put it at the bottom of the pile and pick another. The aim is to get one card of each colour, and the first player to get five cards of different colours wins the game.[9]

As players began to understand the rules of the game, an acknowledging symphony of "ahhhs" rippled around the room. But there was still confusion for some, as a counterpoint of "eeeeh?" also punctuated the soundscape. Reading the room, Tomomi suggested we do a practice run. One of the women at my table raised her eyebrows and commented in a quiet weary voice to us, "We're adults, but it's a card game…?" She seemed to express a feeling that she was too adult to play and that a card game was a bit too frivolous to be spending time on,

Figure 4.1. Ranran Lunch card game. The picture shows the front page of the printed instruction booklet, the five types of menu cards (blue through red), and three of the allergen cards (egg, peanuts, and wheat).
Photo by author.

especially with so serious a topic as allergies. Implicit was a criticism that the time could be better spent.

As we began playing rock, paper, scissors to start the game, laughter started to ring out across the room, and the air became full of chattering voices. At our table the energy picked up. The rock, paper, scissors rounds were quick, as people in Japan have practised this decision-making tool regularly since they were young. I struggled to keep up. I am fine one-on-one, I feel compelled to note, but when it is a rapid-fire round with multiple participants, it takes me time to figure out if I have won the round or lost. This elicited surprise and chuckles, and Sasaki, a woman in her early thirties, kindly explained the result with a grin at my ineptitude. As people began turning over menu cards, exclamations of surprise rang out around the room, along with "Really?!" One of the men in my group, Morioka, who was playing with an egg allergy (i.e., he had the egg allergen card) was, for example, shocked that egg is in hamburgers. Soon after, Sasaki leaned in towards a card and then suddenly veered back in her chair as she realized that a meal she thought was safe actually contains milk (her child is not allergic to milk), and Yamamura, a woman in her early forties whose child has a milk allergy, keenly leaned into the table in response and exclaimed to us, "Oh, there's loads of milk in it, loads!" Although allergy parents are knowledgeable about allergens, they develop expertise related to their children's allergies and are not necessarily aware of what other allergens are in the foods they choose, which led to several exclamations of surprise during the game.

After going through the practice round we started playing "for real." As we set up the cards for a new round the atmosphere had distinctively shifted from the start: the talk at the table had become animated and jovial. Yamamura, who had lamented at the beginning that she was not so keen to play a game, now had a big smile on her face and energetically injected, "It's fun/interesting (*omoshiroi*) after all!" Contrary to the beginning of the session, people were relaxed, and Kawai, a man in his mid-thirties teased Morioka, a man in his mid-forties, for choosing a set of cards that contained lots of vegetables.[10] Everyone at the table chuckled in response. Animated discussions developed about what certain dishes were, where they were from, and what was in them. As we shared our food knowledge Sasaki expressed wonder at menu items like the Indonesian dish nasi goreng and reflected, "We always eat 'safe foods' so we don't choose foods we don't know. I don't know what some of these are!"

When the game came to an end Tomomi guided the room to begin sharing our impressions (*kansō*).[11] She encouraged us to share both the things we had felt (*kanjita koto*) and learned as we played, and as they were shared, she wrote them on a whiteboard. People commented on the lack of choice they had concerning what they wanted to eat and that it was hard to know what is in a dish just by looking at it. A number of people raised the issue of not knowing what is in seasonings, and some suggested that there is also an issue of common-sense knowledge (*jōshiki*): for some it is common sense that egg is in hamburgers; for others it was a revelation. One woman, a veteran of the summer camps, complained that a lot of the Western dishes on the cards would likely actually contain butter, but the card did not say that there was milk in it. Tomomi responded by saying that while that's true, it is also true that you cannot assume that you know what is in a dish by looking at it, and therefore you always have to check ingredients at the restaurant. She reiterated to the room that the point of the cards is to help non-allergic people feel and imagine the difficulties of choosing dishes when eating out. By doing so she suggested that they can then understand that while there might be lots of options available on the menu, it does not mean that someone with food allergies can choose any of them. By eliciting impressions from playing the game, the workshop organizers who are using the game can then, she said, add information to aid comprehension of food allergies.

Play, and the various affects engendered through the process of playing, facilitated the development of conceptual knowledge. This is done not just by the content presented on the cards themselves or by sharing information about ingredients. Through encouraging an atmosphere of fun and enjoyment, there was an openness to uncovering other people's experience. The post-play practice of encouraging people to share their impressions to the group – whether that was surprise at their limited knowledge of ingredients or frustration that the cards were not accurate enough – then turned participants' attention to learning and knowledge acquisition. The result was a specific "affective arrangement": "a material-discursive formation as part of which affect is patterned, channeled, and modulated" and in which numerous actors are brought "into a dynamic orchestrated conjunction so that these actors' mutual affecting and being affected is the central dimension of the arrangement from the start" (Slaby, Mühlhoff, and Wüschner 2017, 3). Although the card game was carried out over a short period and with people who were already more knowledgeable about allergies than the general public, many participants were nevertheless deeply affected by their realizations about allergens that they or their children had not needed to be careful of. By engaging in play these adults were given space to exclaim, veer forwards and back in their seats as they were overcome with surprise or shock, and laugh and tease each other while, at the same time, discovering information about allergens on the cards. The affective energies of the experience were then channelled through the practice of sharing impressions and discussing the knowledge they gained in more detail with the group towards potentially empathic ends. The possibility of producing affective resonances, including those leading towards empathy, was thus integral to the transformational power of the card game and the workshops. But how has anthropology understood empathy? I shift gears now, moving away from affective practices of advocacy, to briefly explore how empathy has been theorized anthropologically. I then return to the role of play in cultivating a range of affects for advocacy and the ways my interlocutors in Japan themselves felt about the role of empathy in health advocacy.

Beyond (Having) Empathy?

There have been multiple analytical framings and definitions of empathy, emerging from social psychology, social neuroscience, health care and advocacy, international relations, philosophy, and cultural anthropology, among others.[12] Definitions vary, with some scholars focusing on cognitive aspects and others on the affective-somatic (Preusche and Lamm 2016). How these definitions are applied also varies considerably. Social psychologist Dan Batson (2009), for example, identifies eight different ways in which empathy is often used. For the cultural psychiatrist and anthropologist Kirmayer (2008, 458), "[t]o empathize is to understand another's experience through feeling or thinking something similar oneself. Empathy reflects the willingness to meet, engage, and be moved by the other – whether that other is an esthetic object or a person." In this understanding empathy is rooted in a "feeling with" (Kirmayer 2008, 471).[13] It also requires effort (Hollan and Throop 2008; Hoppe 2018). Some suggest that empathy is only possible if one has had similar experiences to the person in question, and Fainzang (2007, 7) suggests that "empathy is a way of knowing; sympathy is a way of relating." Others argue it can be a mediating relation (Pedwell 2014). Halpern (2001), a professor of bioethics, argues that empathy is both cognitive *and* affective: it is about resonating or attuning emotionally *and* imagining how the other person (or in her work, patients) feels about or views a situation. As she states, "[i]n empathy, emotional resonance can set the tone, but imagination work must be done to unify the details and nuances of the patient's life into an integrated affective experience" (88; see also, Hoppe 2018; Preusche and Lamm 2016).

Empathy in anthropology specifically has often been understood as a methodology related to the production of particular types of knowledge (Davies and Stodulka 2019; Fainzang 2007; Hoppe 2018; Kirmayer 2008; Walter 2019). Kirmayer (2008, 457) has argued that understandings of empathy in anthropology have been shaped by the endeavour to "produce narratives or texts that convey another's world in a seamless and evocative way." This, he suggests, "introduces systematic distortions into our understanding of empathy as situated practice." Hollan and Throop (2011), meanwhile, have argued that empathy has been understudied in anthropology, and they note the difficulties of differentiating empathy from other behaviours such as compassion, pity, or sympathy (see also Nussbaum 2001). They also remind the reader that empathy is not necessarily always understood or experienced positively in all cultures (see also Bubandt and Willerslev 2015). More recently, Throop and Zahavi (2020), drawing on phenomenology, suggest basic empathy is a face-to-face "immediate experiential encounter with another living being's bodily and embedded experience in the world" (292). They advise readers that imaginative perspective taking (or projection) is different from basic empathy, and that although we can think of empathy on a continuum, we should be careful not to collapse different types of social cognition related to understanding others into empathy.[14]

Disagreements as to what empathy consists of and how we should define it notwithstanding, empathy often emerges in academic discourse – especially in research that focuses on illness – as something to be cultivated or as a necessary solution to particular social problems (e.g., see Batson 2018; Guidi and Traversa 2021; Halpern 2001; Head 2012; Hoffman 1989; Miller 2015; Roberts 2021; Segal and Wagaman 2017, Thornber 2020). Yet there are also acknowledged limits to empathy (Head 2016; Hollan and Throop 2011; Kirmayer 2008; Kitanaka 2021; Throop 2010a, 2010b). Hoppe (2018) argues that empathy is highly complex due to the problematic of shared experience, the multiplicity of experience, and the fact that feelings are dynamic processes, not fixed states. Medical anthropologist Junko Kitanaka (2021) argues that people living with dementia in Japan are now beginning to think beyond empathy to focus instead on "rights," corresponding to debates that have emerged in other countries about the limits and ethics of actions based on emotion. Moreover, social scientists Son et al. (2019) have argued in the context of medical education in Japan that the diversity of patient perspectives complicates the endeavour of cultivating and using empathy, as does the power dynamics inherent in doctor–patient relations. They also suggest that it is unclear which definition – and understanding – of empathy should be used in medical education and that there needs to be a more reciprocal model of empathy put in place in medical education to mitigate against empathy being used as a strategy to convince patients to remain within a medical framework (Son et al. 2017, 2019).

What stands out among the diverse theoretical perspectives outlined above is a gap in understanding that persists between these analytical formulations of empathy and the affective intensities by which empathy is managed and modulated towards various ethical ends. Focusing on the work being done by Tomomi and her team, I have found that the anthropological theorizing of empathy – of what it consists of, can be defined as, and the conditions for *having* it – are conceptually compelling but not particularly helpful in understanding the affective dimensions of Tomomi's engagement with empathy in her advocacy work. This gap might be posed as a critical reminder of the need for anthropologists to consider the work that highly conceptual academic theorizing accomplishes and for whom.

Serious Play and the Facilitation of Feeling   143

As noted above, Atopicco explicitly lists empathy (along with acceptance and tolerance) in its working philosophy. However, Tomomi tells me that they prefer not to focus on the "having" of particular emotions such as empathy (*kyōkan o motsu*) but instead focus on what can be done to create conditions of acceptance to allow people with diverse experiences and values to live well together. Empathy can be (and often is) a part of this: it can, as anthropologists have often conceived of it, be a methodology that generates particular types of knowledge. However, Tomomi emphasized to me in conversation that while they, as staff of the NPO, have empathy for people on whose behalf they work, cultivating empathy in their advocacy work is not the goal because *having* empathy is not necessarily a prerequisite for action on behalf of allergic people. Food manufacturers may, for example, get a feeling for, and come to see, an untapped potential for increased profit if they lead the way with better labelling, or clearer information provision, or food ranges that are allergen-free. But to do this, they need to first get a feel for and understanding of the issues and needs of food allergic customers. Developing an empathic understanding can be part of this, but as Bubandt and Willerslev (2015) show, empathy does not necessarily lead to positive action. For Tomomi, allowing for, and facilitating, a range of feelings through a simulated (playful) experience such as the card game can, she thinks, help people come to understand what the issues are, which can then lead to action to improve allergic peoples' daily lives. In the following discussion, I turn to comments made by non-allergic people who have played the game in educational workshops to illustrate how different individuals have engaged with and taken away different messages from the game: while some focus on the fun of the game, others describe how they came to a better understanding of food allergy realities and felt motivated to take action on behalf of those with allergies.

Ranran Lunch: Feeling and Understanding through Play

On the Atopicco website there is a dedicated section titled Topics (Atopicco n.d.-d.), where one can glean a sense of the various responses to the Ranran Lunch game in non-allergic people. These responses offer both supporting and countervailing perspectives on the game compared to the interlocutors I played with during the in-person workshop. Atopicco asks workshop organizers to keep a record of – and send in – the impressions (*kansō*) section of the event, which they then post on their website. These are curated by the workshop organizers, but they can still provide a sense of how people engaged with the game and what they consequently felt and understood. For example, some people focused on the feelings of enjoyment:

> At first, I wondered what kind of card game it was, but when I started playing it, it was fun. (Atopicco Topics, 5 July 2017 entry)
>
> In a short period of time I could easily enjoy and understand about allergies. (Atopicco Topics, 5 July 2017 entry)
>
> It was great to be able to study without being formal/stiff. (Atopicco Topics, 19 September 2017 entry)

Here the focus was on the participants' own enjoyment of playing a card game, and on how a relaxed and playful environment enabled them to study and more deeply understand allergies.

Other participants commented on things they noticed about themselves or about other people who do not have food allergies:

> Through the game it was good that I noticed some points about myself. I was able to think as if I had a food allergy myself. (Atopicco Topics, 19 September 2017 entry)
>
> A person without allergies may be saying cruel/thoughtless (*kokoronai*) words. I want to share [the card game] with people without allergies so that they can understand their [people with allergies] feelings. (Atopicco Topics, 16 January 2018 entry)

The first quote illustrates how the game enabled players to imagine themselves in the situation of having a food allergy, which could potentially lead to (empathic) understanding of another. The second illustrates that playing the game enabled a player to imagine the feelings of people with food allergy, inspiring them to share the game for educational purposes and stop people from saying cruel things. This player imagined what it might be like to have food allergies and wanted to take action to share that knowledge with others to make life easier for sufferers.

Other participants focused their comments on the difficulties they felt allergic people experienced:

> I didn't understand the difficulty/hardship (*kurō*) because there are no people with allergies around me [in my daily life], but I thought [from playing the game] that it is so difficult. (Atopicco Topics, 24 August 2017 entry)

Serious Play and the Facilitation of Feeling   145

> Sharing the feelings of people with allergies I realized that it is very difficult to think about the menu. (Atopicco Topics, 20 July 2017 entry)

> I learned that people with allergies are always struggling with danger. Eating is my only pleasure, but people with allergies can't just enjoy it ... (Atopicco Topics, 1 December 2017 entry)

> During the game, when I chose the card I felt [what it was like to have an] allergy, and I wondered if allergic children always feel like this? (Atopicco n.d.-d.)

In these comments we can see a specific focus on feelings: on fear, hardship, danger, and enjoyment (or the lack thereof) and how, through playing the game, people came to new understandings about what they thought eating out with food allergies might be like: difficult, hard, fearful, unenjoyable.

Finally, some participants focused specifically on how what they had felt had moved them to think about specific changes they might undertake, such as this comment from a person who works in a children's centre:

> Since there was a place to exchange opinions after having fun playing [the card game] together, I was able to have a sense of intimacy. It was also good to be able to consider what would make it easier [for people] to participate in the food experience program at the children's center etc. and to hear questions and hints/tips about activities from the organizer [of the workshop]. (Atopicco Topics, 20 January 2018 entry)

These quotes demonstrate engagement with different experiential aspects of the game. Some focus only on themselves and what they felt (that it was fun, relaxed, stimulating). Others began to extrapolate from the game what allergic people might be feeling and experiencing (fear, difficulty, hardship). Others still began to think about what changes they might enact. The card game, and the impressions section of the website, created space for these responses without specifically stipulating what participants *should* learn or feel. Rather, through the specific material-discursive "affective arrangement" of the card game and the workshop, affects and feelings emerged and were engaged with in different ways.

Empathy, as noted above, is usually understood to be about putting yourself in the shoes of another, to understand another person's experience. One could understand these varied responses to the game simply as a form of empathic resonance, but it would be more accurate to understand the game as a way of facilitating a range of affects that can then be harnessed towards a more public understanding of allergies. As Halpern (2001, 91) has argued, "Experiencing emotion guides what one imagines about another's experience, and thus provides a direction and context for learning." The materiality of the game – sitting with allergen cards and menu items and making decisions based on what ingredients one thinks are in the meal – makes it different to just asking someone to imagine that they are in a restaurant with a menu in hand. The game invites a visceral experience that listening to a lecture lacks. In the workshop I attended participants responded to and *with* each other. Through play they moved, laughed, were surprised, and became excited in their explanations and exclamations. They teased each other, and then during the impressions section, they sobered as they listened to and shared various feelings, impressions, thoughts, and opinions. The comments on the website show that for some, an empathic understanding emerged; for others, a focus on the fun they felt as they gained new knowledge was predominant.

Conclusion

Through the practice of play, Ranran Lunch affectively moved participants and prompted energetic discussions about allergens in common menu items, even for those with lived experience of food allergies. In this regard, the card game did more than simply provide information; it also leveraged affective intensities that were generated towards an awareness of the difficulty and frustrations that people with allergies might themselves feel when eating out and living with their allergies. Play encourages people to "feel with" others and thus temporarily inhabit another reality (De Antoni 2017; Noddings 2013). Simultaneously, the materiality of the game facilitates the "feeling with" that emerges. Thus, rather than creating workshops where an expert provides all the information and education and participants passively listen, the practice of playing the game, and the affects and feelings that emerge through play and imagination, facilitate the development of allergy knowledge by encouraging simulated forms of reflection, adding energy and significance to those reflections, and (potentially) motivating one to take action.

In the discussion following play, the workshop is oriented towards converting participants' feelings into a more intimate knowledge of food allergies. For Tomomi, then, this form of education is about mitigating a problem that is often discussed: how to help non-allergic people understand what it is like to live with food allergies. Although only a partial reply to this problem, the cultivation of affects to facilitate knowledge acquisition, and ideally action, is one that Atopicco understands to be both an effective and ethical response.

While Tomomi and the NPO Atopicco are trying to facilitate an imagination of "what it might be like" for those with allergies by eliciting a range of feelings via play, they do so to increase general awareness – leading hopefully to positive action – rather than as a call for empathy per se. In this, empathy is employed less as a practice of cultivating feelings and more as an exercise of making feelings public (Latour and Weibel 2005). By having an expansive understanding of shared feeling beyond a focus on cultivating empathy and not telling people what they should do or feel, Atopicco potentially mitigates some of the polarizing tendencies observable in other places around the world. For example, as nut bans in UK schools have shown, although some people respond empathetically and adhere to the restrictions, they can also lead to the production of negative affects. Proposed bans have been met with anger and frustration in some parents with non-allergic children, with some claiming that with a ban, "There isn't much we can give them to eat" (Burrows 2018). Rather than helping such parents to empathize positively with those who struggle to find safe foods for their children, they are instead angry at limitations being put on them by others. Although these bans may help those with nut allergies (and their parents) feel safer, they can consequently foster unhelpful feelings because they can alienate non-allergic people, setting up an us-versus-them dynamic and making the wider goal of education, awareness, and understanding harder to achieve.[15]

In Japan, where people with food allergies are sometimes seen as potentially difficult or fussy when enquiring about allergens or stating food needs, enabling non-allergic people to imagine how it feels for just a short time, in a low-stakes playful atmosphere with no demands attached, encourages the development of knowledge that works through affect, feeling, and imagination as an ethical response towards increasing awareness and understanding. Facilitating and allowing for a range of feelings through the practice of serious play may thus be productive not just for uncovering what others with food allergies might be experiencing but also for creatively helping bring about positive social change.

NOTES

1 The director of Atopicco, Tomomi Akagi, began her activities while working for the Japanese Recycling Movement Citizen's Council, which was organized by citizens to address environmental issues. As a parent of a child with allergies, who was herself struggling, she researched and learned about ecology, the environment, and health. She initially set up Atopicco Network for Children of the Earth within the Recycling Movement and began a telephone consultation service and a magazine (Ushiyama 2020). In 2002 Tomomi and the staff working on Atopicco were made redundant, and they consequently created an independent organization. In 2003 they were incorporated as an NPO (Ushiyama 2020). As Ushiyama states, one of the defining aspects about Atopicco is that, contrary to many citizens' or activist groups, Tomomi (and Jun Yoshizawa, her co-director) work for the organization full-time. That being said, finances are always extremely tight; they often run at a loss (Ushiyama 2020), and Tomomi spends considerable time each year writing research grant applications and looking for ways to continue financing their work.

2 Information can be found in its yearly business reports on its website, www.atopicco.org/about.html, and through the page that lists her public lecture engagements, www.atopicco.org/activity/lecturer/

3 Izumi-Taylor et al. (2010) have argued that in childhood education in Japan play is understood as something that enables children to develop knowledge. However, contrary to the idea seen in, for example, the United States, that play is itself a form of children's work (based on the philosophy of Maria Montessori), in the early education context of Japan it is primarily about developing social skills, an orientation to group cooperation, and a state of heart/mind. It is thus about emotional and social development rather than learning per se. By contrast, Izumi-Taylor and colleagues found that adult play was understood as being for enjoyment, with American respondents talking about play in terms of "fun feelings" and Japanese respondents linking it to "the state of one's heart (spirit, mind, lightheartedness)" (3). For both adults and children in Japan, play is "a source of possibility" (5). The idea of play being simultaneously fun and serious is not something unique to Atopicco's framing of the game but can be seen in other contexts in Japan. For example, William H. Kelly (2002) has talked of the seriousness with which individuals apply themselves to training in karaoke. Rupert Cox (2002), meanwhile, has suggested that there is often a "logical structure to play" (170) and an attitude of serious application, in contrast to ideas in the West that play is spontaneous and unstructured. For Cox this can be traced back to the *Kojiki* (Record of Ancient Matters, 712 BCE), wherein *asobi* (play)

Serious Play and the Facilitation of Feeling   149

can be seen to have two contrasting aspects: one as festive, amusing, and light-hearted and the other as disciplined and serious. The attitude of seriousness that Atopicco invokes in playing games is thus part of a cultural repertoire of play that asserts that play need not be unstructured and spontaneous but can be fun *and also* serious and implemented for learning. Although seriousness in play is often related to rules, or learning the correct way (e.g., to do karaoke, if we take Kelly's example), in the context of the Ranran Lunch card game, the seriousness is applied more towards learning about the *serious* nature of living with allergies via a simulated experience. The format of the workshop (described in the main text) facilitates this kind of *serious play*.

4   I follow practices in scholarship on the anthropology of affect, discussed in the Introduction, which treats affects as somatic sensations that can crystallize into emotions when they are experienced through socially fixed conceptual categories, such as "empathy."

5   Since 1995 Atopicco has organized a yearly summer camp for children with allergic disease and their parents. Parents who attend have their own schedule of events, including workshops with, for example, food and skincare manufacturers, and convenience store brands, as well as workshops on disaster relief efforts, among others. I have attended this summer camp since 2015, although the camp was held online in 2020 and 2021 due to the COVID-19 pandemic.

6   Since 2017 I have been co-running support workshops with Atopicco oriented towards teenagers and young adults with food allergies.

7   In March 2023, walnut was added to the required allergen list, so there are now eight allergens that must be labelled.

8   Playing *janken* (rock, paper, scissors), is very common in Japan and is practised in a multitude of contexts to decide something in an egalitarian way: who will go first in a game, who will get to be the first to choose the sweet they want from those available, who will do the cleaning or take the garbage out, who will pick up the bill, who will drink in a drinking game, and so on. This form of play is thus used to determine priority to choose (to do something or not to do something), and it is often used not just in typical play settings (i.e., playing a game) but also as a way to playfully decide serious things.

9   If there is no one with five different colored menu cards, then whoever has the highest number of different colored cards wins. If everyone has the same number of different colored cards, then the person with the most points wins.

10 The teasing centred on Morioka choosing a set of cards that looked healthy. In his forties, Morioka was an average size, neither over- nor underweight. Yet the bodies of middle-aged men (and women) have become increasingly

scrutinized for the risks of lifestyle related to metabolic illnesses, often dubbed *metabo* in Japan (e.g., see Borovoy 2017; Manzenreiter 2012). By teasing him about choosing vegetables over other options (such as meat dishes), Kawai may also have been drawing, tongue-in-cheek, on recent discourses of so-called herbivorous men (*sōshokukei danshi*) who are supposed to prefer vegetables over meat, which euphemistically also suggests sexual appetites, or lack thereof. Such herbivorous men are thought to embody a more "feminized masculinity" in Japan (Castro-Vázquez 2019, 267).

11 At Atopicco, and in Japan generally, sharing impressions (*kansō*) is a common practice at the end of lectures and workshops. Often this includes each member sharing short impressions in the last few minutes of the event, but at Atopicco sharing impressions sometimes features as part of the workshop itself.

12 See, for example, Batson (2009, 2018), Blum (2018) Bubandt and Willerslev (2015), Decety and Ickes (2009), Deigh (2018), Fainzang (2007), Gieser (2008), Gruen (2013), Halpern (2001), Head (2012), Hollan (2012), Hollan and Throop (2008, 2011), Kirmayer (2008), Kitanaka (2020, 2021), Marshall and Hooker (2016), Ozoliņš (2015), Pedwell (2014), Preckel, Kanske and Singer (2018), Preusche and Lamm (2016), Roberts (2021), Roughley and Schramme (2018), Schramme (2018), Segal and Wagaman (2017), Throop (2010a), and Throop and Zahavi (2020).

13 However, in the context of care, Noddings (2013, 30) argues that "feeling with" is more than empathy in that it incorporates reception whereas empathy, she suggests, is often a projection of oneself into the "object of one's contemplation" to reach understanding. Bubandt and Willerslev (2015), drawing on Wispé's work, have suggested that "feeling with" more accurately describes sympathy, whereas "feeling into" is a more accurate description of empathy. De Antoni and Cook (2019), meanwhile, have argued that "'feeling with' implies a stronger focus on the practice-based 'affective correspondences.' … It focuses less on 'what is what' and more on 'how' that 'what' emerges and comes into shape within the social" (144).

14 Groark (2020, 294) and Maibom (2020, 295–6), in their separate comments to the article, caution however, that relying on a definition of empathy that limits it to face-to-face experiential encounters considerably narrows the scope of our understandings of empathy, and they both suggest that it is not representative of how empathy is commonly understood in society. In response, Throop and Zahavi (2020) suggest that "empathy" is a technical word with a relatively short history and that the way we understand and use terms need not be the same as that which a layperson would understand. Furthermore, for them, the key takeaway was to insist on not collapsing different aspects of social cognition into "empathy" and to suggest that

phenomenology gives us useful insights on social cognition that should be taken into account in work on empathy (Throop and Zahavi 2020, 301–2).
15 It should be noted that charities such as Allergy UK and Anaphylaxis Campaign in the United Kingdom also oppose nut bans – or blanket bans of any allergen in any context – because bans are not reflective of the wider world and can provide a false feeling of safety and security. Moreover, there are many allergens other than nuts, and it is impossible to restrict all allergens. They instead advocate for allergy education and awareness (e.g., see www.allergyuk.org/living-with-an-allergy/at-school/faqs-for-parents/). Food allergy specialists from around the world also do not recommend blanket allergen bans (e.g., see Waserman et al. 2021).

REFERENCES

Akagi, Tomomi. 2005. *Arerugī to tanoshiku ikiru* [Living Happily With Allergies]. Tokyo: Gendai Shokan.
Akagi, Tomomi. 2014. *Gakkō kyūshoku arerugī shikobōshi manyuaru: Sensei oya kodomo to hajimeru kiki kanri* [School Lunch Allergy Accident Prevention Manual: Crisis Management Beginning With Teachers, Parents, and Children]. Tokyo: Gōdō Shuppan.
Akagi, Tomomi. 2018. "Ensoku ni oyatsu 'dame' shōgakkō, arerugī taisaku de" [Elementary Schools That Prohibit Snacks for Excursions: For Allergy Measures]. *Nihon Keizai Shimbun*, 23 January 2018. Accessed 18 July 2022. www.nikkei.com/article/DGXMZO29423400W8A410C1CC0000/.
Akagi, Tomomi. 2019. "Arerugī hyōji ni kanren shita: Shokuhin kaishū to kanja no go shoku jittai" [Related to Allergy Labeling: Food Recalls and Patients' Accidental Ingestion]. *Shokuhin to kagaku [Food and Science]* 61 (2): 63–8.
Akagi, Tomomi. 2020a. "Arerugī meguru shakai to no atsureki: Kodomo no kokoro ni kizu" [Conflict With Society Around Allergies: Wounds to Children's Hearts]. *Nihon Keizai Shimbun*, 9 June 2020. Accessed 18 July 2022. www.nikkei.com/article/DGXMZO60088750Y0A600C2TCC000/.
Akagi, Tomomi. 2020b. "Arerugī-ko muke kyanpu kaisai: Saigai shien ni mo chūryoku" [Holding a Camp for Allergic Children: Focusing Also on Disaster Support]. *Nihon Keizai Shimbun*, 21 June 2020. Accessed 18 July 2022. www.nikkei.com/article/DGXMZO60088830Y0A600C2TCC000/.
Akagi, Tomomi. 2020c. "Shokuhin hyōji, jittai ni awasete arerugī kanja-ra uttae" [Food Labeling and Actual Conditions: Allergic Patients' Complaints]. *Nihon Keizai Shimbun*, 23 January 2020. Accessed 18 July 2022. www.nikkei.com/article/DGXMZO54758630T20C20A1CR8000/.
Akagi, Tomomi. n.d. "Akagi Tomomi san no koramu" [Akagi Tomomi's Column]. Accessed 18 July 2022. https://housefoods-group.com/sustainability/health_nutrtion/allergy/column/akagi.html.

Atopicco. n.d.-a. "Juyō to kyōkan, soshite kanyō e" [Towards Acceptance, Empathy and Tolerance]. Accessed 18 July 2022. www.atopicco.org/philosophy.html.

Atopicco. n.d.-b. "Shokumotsu arerugī o kangaeru: Ranran Ranchi" [Thinking About Food Allergies: Ranran Lunch]. Accessed 18 July 2022. www.atopicco.org/topic/lunch/index.html.

Atopicco. n.d.-c. "Shokumotsu arerugī kanja shien purojekuto" [Food Allergy Patient Support Project]. Accessed 18 July 2022. www.atopicco.org/joint/lunch.html.

Atopicco. n.d.-d. "Topics." Accessed 18 July 2022. www.atopicco.org/topic/.

Batson, C. Daniel. 2009. "These Things Called Empathy: Eight Related but Distinct Phenomena." In *The Social Neuroscience of Empathy*, edited by Jean Decety and William Ickes, 3–16. Cambridge, MA: The MIT Press.

Batson, Dan. 2018. "Empathy, Altruism, and Helping: Conceptual Distinctions, Empirical Relations." In *Forms of Fellow Feeling: Empathy, Sympathy, Concern and Moral Agency*, edited by Neil Roughley and Thomas Schramme, 59–77. Cambridge: Cambridge University Press.

Blum, Lawrence. 2018. "A Moral Account of Empathy and Fellow Feeling." In *Forms of Fellow Feeling: Empathy, Sympathy, Concern and Moral Agency*, edited by Neil Roughley and Thomas Schramme, 142–62. Cambridge: Cambridge University Press.

Borovoy, Amy. 2017. "Japan's Public Health Paradigm: Governmentality and the Containment of Harmful Behavior." *Medical Anthropology* 36 (1): 32–46. https://doi.org/10.1080/01459740.2016.1148033.

Bubandt, Nils, and Rane Willerslev. 2015. "The Dark Side of Empathy: Mimesis, Deception, and the Magic of Alterity." *Comparative Studies in Society and History* 57 (1): 5–34. https://doi.org/10.1017/S0010417514000589.

Burrows, Thomas. 2018. "'The Only Nut Ban Should be the Head': Parents Blast Primary Headteacher's 'Ridiculous' Proposal to Completely Bar NUTS From School Grounds." *The Mail Online*. Accessed 28 January 2022. www.dailymail.co.uk/news/article-5234339/Primary-school-Exeter-bans-nuts-school-grounds.html.

Castro-Vázquez, Genaro. 2019. "Japanese Men's Embodied Culinary and Eating Practices: Health, Bodyweight Control, and the Male Self." *The Journal of Men's Studies* 27 (3): 265–86. https://doi.org/10.1177/1060826518815148.

Cox, Rupert. 2002. "Is There a Japanese Way of Playing?" In *Japan at Play: The Ludic and the Logic of Power*, edited by Joy Hendry and Massimo Raveri, 169–85. London and New York: Routledge.

Davies, James, and Thomas Stodulka. 2019. "Foreword: Pathways of Affective Scholarship." In *Affective Dimensions of Fieldwork and Ethnography*, edited by Thomas Stodulka, Samia Dinkelaker, and Ferdiansyah Thajib, 1–6. Cham, Switzerland: Springer Nature.

De Antoni, Andrea. 2017. "Sympathy from the Devil: Experiences, Movement and Affective Correspondences During a Roman Catholic Exorcism in Contemporary Italy." *Japanese Review of Cultural Anthropology (JRCA)* 18 (1): 143–57. https://doi.org/10.14890/jrca.18.1_143.

De Antoni, Andrea, and Emma E Cook. 2019. "Introduction: Feeling (in) Japan: Affective, Sensory and Material Entanglements in the Field." *Asian Anthropology* 18 (3): 139–53. https://doi.org/10.1080/1683478X.2019.1633061.

Decety, Jean, and William Ickes, eds. 2009. *The Social Neuroscience of Empathy*. Cambridge, MA: The MIT Press.

Deigh, John. 2018. "Is Empathy Required for Making Moral Judgments?" In *Forms of Fellow Feeling: Empathy, Sympathy, Concern and Moral Agency*, edited by Neil Roughley and Thomas Schramme, 245–64. Cambridge, UK: Cambridge University Press.

Fainzang, Sylvie. 2007. "Anthropology and Medicine: Empathy, Experience and Knowledge." In *Facing Distress: Distance and Proximity in Times of Illness*, edited by Els van Dongen and Ruth Kutalek, 1–20. Berlin: LIT Verlag.

Gieser, Thorsten. 2008. "Embodiment, Emotion and Empathy: A Phenomenological Approach to Apprenticeship Learning." *Anthropological Theory* 8 (3): 299–318. https://doi.org/10.1177/1463499608093816.

Groark, Kevin P. 2020. "Comment on Throop and Zahavi, Dark and Bright Empathy: Phenomenological and Anthropological Reflections. *Current Anthropology* 61 (3): 294–5.

Gruen, Lori. 2013. "Entangled Empathy: An Alternative Approach to Animal Ethics." In *The Politics of Species: Reshaping Our Relationships With Other Animals*, edited by Annette Lanjouw and Raymond Corbey, 223–31. Cambridge: Cambridge University Press.

Guidi, Clarissa, and Chiara Traversa. 2021. "Empathy in Patient Care: From 'Clinical Empathy' to 'Empathic Concern'." *Medicine, Health Care and Philosophy* 24 (4): 573–85. https://doi.org/10.1007/s11019-021-10033-4.

Halpern, Jodi. 2001. *From Detached Concern to Empathy: Humanizing Medical Practice*. Oxford: Oxford University Press.

Head, Naomi. 2012. "Transforming Conflict: Trust, Empathy, and Dialogue." *International Journal of Peace Studies* 17 (2): 33–55. www.jstor.org/stable/41853034.

Head, Naomi. 2016. "A Politics of Empathy: Encounters with Empathy in Israel and Palestine." *Review of International Studies* 42 (1): 95–113. www.jstor.org/stable/26618548.

Hoffman, Martin L. 1989. "Empathy and Prosocial Activism." In *Social and Moral Values: Individual and Societal Perspectives*, edited by Nancy Eisenberg, Janusz Reykowski, and Ervin Staub, 65–85. London: Routledge.

Hollan, Douglas. 2012. "Emerging Issues in the Cross-Cultural Study of Empathy." *Emotion Review* 4 (1): 70–8. https://doi.org/10.1177/1754073911421376.

Hollan, Douglas, and C. Jason Throop. 2008. "Whatever Happened to Empathy?: Introduction." *Ethos* 36 (4): 385–401. https://doi.org/10.1111/j.1548-1352.2008.00023.x.

Hollan, Douglas, and C. Jason Throop. 2011. "The Anthropology of Empathy: Introduction." In *The Anthropology of Empathy: Experiencing the Lives of Others in Pacific Societies*, edited by Douglas Hollan and C. Jason Throop, 1–24. New York; Oxford: Berghahn Books.

Hoppe, S. 2018. "A Sorrow Shared is a Sorrow Halved: The Search for Empathetic Understanding of Family Members of a Person With Early-Onset Dementia." *Culture, Medicine and Psychiatry* 42: 180–201. https://doi.org/10.1007/s11013-017-9549-4.

Izumi-Taylor, Satomi, Ingrid Pramling Samuelsson, and Cosby Steele Rogers. 2010. "Perspectives of Play in Three Nations: A Comparative Study in Japan, the United States, and Sweden." *Early Childhood Research and Practice* 12 (1): 1–12. https://ecrp.illinois.edu/v12n1/izumi.html.

Kelly, William H. 2002. "Training for Leisure: Karaoke and the Seriousness of Play in Japan." In *Japan at Play: The Ludic and the Logic of Power*, edited by Joy Hendry and Massimo Raveri, 152–68. London and New York: Routledge.

Kirmayer, Laurence J. 2008. "Empathy and Alterity in Cultural Psychiatry." *Ethos* 36 (4): 457–74. https://doi.org/10.1111/j.1548-1352.2008.00027.x.

Kitanaka, Junko. 2020. "In the Mind of Dementia: Neurobiological Empathy, Incommensurability, and the Dementia Tojisha Movement in Japan." *Medical Anthropology Quarterly* 34 (1): 119–35. https://doi.org/10.1111/maq.12544.

Kitanaka, Junko. 2021. "Limits of Empathy: The Dementia Tōjisha Movement in Japan." *Journal of the History of the Behavioral Sciences* 57 (3): 266–72. https://doi.org/10.1002/jhbs.22098.

Latour, Bruno, and Peter Weibel, eds. 2005. *Making Things Public: Atmospheres of Democracy*. Cambridge, MA: The MIT Press.

Maibom, Heidi. 2020. "Comment on Throop and Zahavi, Dark and Bright Empathy: Phenomenological and Anthropological Reflections." *Current Anthropology* 61 (3): 295–6.

Manzenreiter, Wolfram. 2012. "Monitoring Health and the Body: Anthropometry, Lifestyle Risks, and the Japanese Obesity Crisis." *The Journal of Japanese Studies* 38 (1): 55–84. www.jstor.org/stable/41337598.

Marshall, George, Robert Ellison, and Claire Hooker. 2016. "Empathy and Affect: What Can Empathied Bodies Do?" *Medical Humanities* 42 (2): 128–34. https://doi.org/10.1136/medhum-2015-010818.

MHLW. n.d. "Kādogēmu ranran ranchi [Card game Ranran Lunch]." Accessed 18 July 2022. www.mhlw.go.jp/topics/bukyoku/iyaku/syoku-anzen/kodomo/lunlun.html.

Miller, Sonya R. 2015. "Fostering Informed Empathy Through Patient-Centred Education About Persons With Disabilities." *Perspectives on Medical Education* 4 (4): 196–9. https://pubmed.ncbi.nlm.nih.gov/26183247/.

Noddings, Nel. 2013. *Caring: A Relational Approach to Ethics and Moral Education*. Berkeley; Los Angeles: University of California Press.

Nussbaum, Martha C. 2001. *Upheavals of Thought: The Intelligence of Emotions*. Cambridge, UK: Cambridge University Press.

Ozoliņš, Jānis T. 2015. "Empathy and Care." In *Foundations of Healthcare Ethics: Theory to Practice*, edited by Joanne Grainger and Jānis T. Ozoliņš, 70–84. Cambridge, UK: Cambridge University Press.

Pedwell, Carolyn. 2014. *Affective Relations: The Transnational Politics of Empathy*. Basingstoke, UK: Palgrave Macmillan.

Preckel, Katrin, Philipp Kanske, and Tania Singer. 2018. "On the Interaction of Social Affect and Cognition: Empathy, Compassion and Theory of Mind." *Current Opinion in Behavioral Sciences* 19: 1–6. https://doi.org/10.1016/j.cobeha.2017.07.010.

Preusche, I., and C. Lamm. 2016. "Reflections on Empathy in Medical Education: What Can We Learn From Social Neurosciences?" *Advances in Health Sciences Education* 21 (1): 235–49. https://doi.org/10.1007/s10459-015-9581-5.

Roberts, Jessica. 2021. "Empathy Cultivation Through (Pro)Social Media: A Counter to Compassion Fatigue." *Journalism and Media* 2 (4): 819–29. www.mdpi.com/2673-5172/2/4/47.

Roughley, Neil, and Thomas Schramme. 2018. "Empathy, Sympathy, Concern and Moral Agency." In *Forms of Fellow Feeling: Empathy, Sympathy, Concern and Moral Agency*, edited by Neil Roughley and Thomas Schramme, 3–56. Cambridge, UK: Cambridge University Press.

Schramme, Thomas. 2018. "The Role of Empathy in an Agential Account of Morality: Lessons from Autism and Psychopathy." In *Forms of Fellow Feeling: Empathy, Sympathy, Concern and Moral Agency*, edited by Neil Roughley and Thomas Schramme, 307–26. Cambridge, UK: Cambridge University Press.

Segal, Elizabeth A., and M. Alex Wagaman. 2017. "Social Empathy as a Framework for Teaching Social Justice." *Journal of Social Work Education* 53 (2): 201–11. https://doi.org/10.1080/10437797.2016.1266980.

Slaby, Jan, Rainer Mühlhoff, and Philipp Wüschner. 2017. "Affective Arrangements." *Emotion Review* 11 (1): 3–12. https://doi.org/10.1177/1754073917722214.

Slaby, Jan, and Birgitt Röttger-Rössler. 2018. "Introduction: Affect in Relation." In *Affect in Relation: Families, Places, Technologies*, edited by Birgitt Röttger-Rössler and Jan Slaby, 1–28. London; New York: Routledge.

Son, Daisuke, Takuya Matsushige, Miho Ushiyama, Yosuke Hatakeyama, Jimpei Misawa, Mayumi Asahina, Junko Iida, Chikako Inoue, Giichiro Oiso, Yoshio Kashida, Satoshi Kodama, Hiroshi Nishigori, Hideki Nomura, Yoji Hirayama, Shin Hoshino, Hiroshi Yoneda, Shun-ichiro Izumi, and Yasushi Miyata. 2017. "Wākushoppu: 'Kyōkan to 'kanja shiten': Igaku kyōiku e no shisa' kaisai hōkoku" [Workshop Report: Empathy and 'Patients' Perspectives": Suggestion for Medical Education]. *Igaku kyōiuku (Medical Education)* 48 (5): 311–14. https://doi.org/10.11307/mededjapan.48.5_311.

Son, Daisuke, Jimpei Misawa, Miho Ushiyama, Yosuke Hatakeyama, and Takuya Matsushige. 2019. "Iryō-sha kyōiku ni okeru 'kanja shiten' ni fuzui suru sho kadai to jukugi apurōchi no kanōsei" [Challenges for Understanding "Patient Perspectives" and the Application of the Deliberative Approach in the Education of Health Professionals]. *Hoken iryō shakaigaku ronshū (Medical Sociology Collection)* 29 (2): 74–84. https://doi.org/10.18918/jshms.29.2_74.

Thornber, Karen Laura. 2020. *Global Healing: Literature, Advocacy, Care*. Leiden, The Netherlands: Koninklijke Brill NV.

Throop, C. Jason. 2010a. "Latitudes of Loss: On the Vicissitudes of Empathy." *American Ethnologist* 37 (4): 771–82. https://doi.org/10.1111/j.1548-1425.2010.01284.x.

Throop, C. Jason. 2010b. *Suffering and Sentiment: Exploring the Vicissitudes of Experience and Pain in Yap*. Berkeley: University of California Press.

Throop, C. Jason, and Dan Zahavi. 2020. "Dark and Bright Empathy: Phenomenological and Anthropological Reflections." *Current Anthropology* 61 (3): 283–303. https://doi.org/10.1086/708844.

Ushiyama, Miho. 2020. *Incorporating Patient Knowledge in Japan and the UK: A Study of Eczema and the Steroid Controversy*. London; New York: Routledge.

Walter, Anne-Marie. 2019. "Embodying Ineffable Concepts: Empathic Intimacy as Tool for Insight." In *Affective Dimensions of Fieldwork and Ethnography*, edited by Thomas Stodulka, Samia Dinkelaker, and Ferdiansyah Thajib, 143–56. Cham, Switzerland: Springer Nature.

Waserman, Susan, Heather Cruickshank, Kyla J. Hildebrand, Douglas Mack, Laura Bantock, Theresa Bingemann, Derek K. Chu, Carlos Cuello-Garcia, Motohiro Ebisawa, David Fahmy, David M. Fleischer, Lisa Galloway, Greg Gartrell, Matthew Greenhawt, Nicola Hamilton, Jonathan Hourihane, Michael Langlois, Richard Loh, Antonella Muraro, Lana Rosenfield, Sally Schoessler, Mimi L.K. Tang, Brenda Weitzner, Julie Wang, and Jan L. Brozek. 2021. "Prevention and Management of Allergic Reactions to Food in Child Care Centers and Schools: Practice Guidelines." *Journal of Allergy and Clinical Immunology* 147 (5): 1561–78. https://doi.org/10.1016/j.jaci.2021.01.034.

Chapter 5

On Moral Thresholds: Shi'i Zakirs and the Surface Tension of Public Affect in Pakistan

TIMOTHY P.A. COOPER

How do we know when we have gone too far? Any answer is likely to be radically subjective, yet the notion of passing a point of no return is a shared one, related to the drawing of boundaries through which selves and others are identified. To pass a point of no return can permanently alter a relationship, sever an attachment important or beneficial to the transgressor, or result in a moment of reorientation towards practices previously abhorred. An awareness of the constitution of the "middle ground" is not always a product of moderation. Contemporary political and religious life in an era of mass mediation is characterized by its interfaces, such as outrage, heightened sentiment, or controversy. In this context, remaining on the middle ground while the poles of order and disorder realign involves heightened attention not only to how things are but also to the changing boundaries of how they might be. To operate at the threshold of public affect entails a sense of intuition to moral dangers that lie just outside of immediate perception.

This chapter examines the social place of *moral thresholds*. These recall William Mazzarella's (2017, 200) description of the feeling of being moved to respond within the bounds of a sense of responsibility that characterizes the unruly interactions between affect and ethics, as well as its impasses (204). As a social anthropologist, I am part of a discipline that continues to debate how and where to locate the formation of moral orientation, whether as the result of being face-to-face with difference, the aggregation of virtues and values, or a means of striving towards a transcendent good. Yet when the surface tension of public sentiment is stretched tight and taut by competing ideas about religious transcendence, presence, and transgression, it is an ongoing act of feeling the point of no return that attempts to define moral limits. This is to view moral experience from the perspective of the moods that give it surface (Throop 2009, 2014), and finds precedent in Victor

158   Timothy P.A. Cooper

Turner's work on how the status of marginality is experienced in ritual. In Turner's (1986) famous phrasing, threshold states are the domain of ambiguity, or "the subjunctive mood of culture, the mood of maybe" (42). However, as this chapter goes on to argue, rather than helping anthropologists remain sensitive to the middle ground as a radical, transformative space, the figure of the threshold that was so central to early Anglo-European anthropology is also a prototypical example of what I describe below as anthropological disciplining. Looking beyond ritual in the hope of uncovering some of the shared bases of ethical life, I ask, What does it feel like on the threshold?

As Mazzarella (2019) argues, in the last few decades anthropologists have become better equipped to come to grips with what he calls the "mattering forth of the collective flesh" (50), or the politics of feeling moral sentiment by pressing oneself up to its surface tension. In this chapter, the problem of how to contend with the dangers posed by this "mattering forth" is one that animates the lives of Shi'i Muslim *zakirs* (a pluralization I use in place of the correct Urdu plural *zakireen*) and their audiences in Pakistan. A male *zakir* or female *zakira* is responsible for cultivating the affective and emotional atmosphere at Shi'i mourning and celebratory assemblies, where being present to, weeping for, and providing condolement to the Ahl-e Bait, the family of the Prophet Muhammad, directly affects participants' possibilities for divine intercession. Despite decades of violence suffered by those outwardly disclosing their faith, "superstar" *zakirs* in the Pakistani province of Punjab promote themselves as popular and polemical representatives on social media, where the performance of Shi'i belief is more accessible to outsiders than ever before. Zakirs frequently face criticism from within both their own community and from Pakistan's Sunni Muslim majority for having crossed the line. This line is often expressed by the Quranic term used in Urdu, *hadd* (plural: *hudood*) that describes the social location of divine boundaries. Echoing anthropology's own disciplinary culture, the term has evolved through its application in Islamic jurisprudence and state legal systems to describe means of *punishing* perceived transgressions. For both anthropology and Islamic jurisprudence, this conceptual disciplining elides the everyday labour that ideas can wield in feeling, finding, and speculating on moral limits.

Preceding its disciplining, hadd can be described as a kind of *moral threshold* expressed affectively rather than as a clear discursive point of injunction. This transcendent quality of thresholds renders them ultimately unknowable. One can only know a moral threshold by being in proximity to its *interface*, a term I understand to mean a point of connection between phases of activity, or the common overlap between otherwise separate practices (see also Cooper 2024b). To think through the implications of the leap from the observation of a limit to its epistemic delimitation, this chapter calls for a rediscovery and reappraisal of the traditional anthropological figure of the threshold. To discover, or uncover, is not always to delimit. Instead, finding ways to dwell on thresholds is a condition of living in media environments where the binaries of right and wrong and good and bad are diffuse and multi-sited.

Disciplining the Threshold

By anthropological disciplining, I refer to a residual tendency towards dualism still present in anthropological theory that conceives of intermediary forms of experience deterministically, that is, in relation to the forces that such forms of experience are perceived as motion towards or away from. An example of this is the analytic figure of the threshold, which was a central concept in early anthropology. Due to their predominance in both non-Western and Judeo-Christian religions as points of transition and as altars, thresholds were a useful bridging concept through which to make myths, symbols, and practices commensurable with the Anglo-European academy. Yet the literature that this inspired conflated two semantic uses of the term. In one instance a threshold could mark the boundary between temporalities or states of being that ritual acts navigate. In another, the threshold described the magnitude or level of intensity that, once exceeded, manifests a reaction, a change, or the coming into effect of a phenomenon. Not only do the two senses of the term lose much in their conflation into one concept that expresses both a frontier and the magnitude of intensity that looms at its boundary, but the former also comes to encompass the latter and, with it, the opportunity to be methodologically transformed by its affects and interfaces.

The disciplining of the threshold can be traced to Arnold Van Gennep's ([1919] 1960) insights into how the physical site of ritual activity was an indivisible part of its transformative nature. When the spatial becomes a spiritual passage, "to cross the threshold is to unite oneself with a new world" (20), he argued. From the Latin word for threshold, Van Gennep conceptualized the idea of the liminal, or transitional stage of rituals that mark major life events. This disciplining of the threshold into a pliable, intercultural concept was taken up most influentially by Victor Turner (1967, 93–111; 1969), with whose work on liminality and communitas the figure of the threshold is most closely associated in anthropological theory. In Turner's model of liminality, the threshold is a state of being that bridges separation and aggregation. Interested in Western countercultural movements, Turner argued that performative traditions could bring about this threshold state as a permanent social form that prioritized ongoing transformation over the reproduction of rigid social structure. In this genealogy from Van Gennep to Turner, it is possible to see a very empathetic approach to how concepts might act as infinitely repeatable statements of intensity. Yet this approach is founded on the disciplinary leap from the identification of a limit to the act of its delimitation.

In the indispensable work of Victor Turner this is a minor, perhaps even inane, criticism, that is, until we want to talk about thresholds beyond ritual, such as in terms of threshold affects or threshold ethics. It is at this point that we see the disciplining of thresholds taking a more dangerous turn, from a moral limit to its punishment. Even though early anthropologists saw little need to explicate their deployment of the threshold or its theoretical leverage, the work that predated Van Gennep hints at the possibility of a different approach. Other than in the title of his 1909 book, *The Threshold of Religion*, the British cultural anthropologist Robert Ranulph Marett only used the term twice, in both instances in close relation to the cultivation of a particular mood. For a field still dominated by armchair anthropologists, Marett's own encounter with prehistoric cave art provides a rich evocation of the ways that thresholds become palpable in their encounter:

> *In entering one of these caves ... the ancient savage was crossing the threshold that divides the world of the workaday from the world of the sacred; and these rites ... involved a mood and attitude consisting in a drawing near in awe, according to approved traditional usage, to an unseen source of* mana. (203–4; emphasis in original)

Moods, awe, attitudes, and mana, the Polynesian force of ethereal power: all these terms of description evoke not the threshold itself but its interfaces. Using the discriminatory language common to early-twentieth-century anthropology, Marett's second and final use of the threshold goes on to describe how these interfaces register levels of intensity that serve to make change manifest:

> For man of the primitive pattern there are two worlds, a workaday and a sacred. ... The threshold between the two is clearly marked. He crosses it always in a ceremonial way ... and his ceremonies enhance, as they certainly reflect, the mood in which he draws near to the unseen source of his spiritual comfort. It matters not at all whether we classify as magic or

religion the practices that result, so long as we recognize that all genuine rites involve one and the same fundamental mood and attitude, a drawing near in awe. (Van Gennep 1960, 219–20)

Here Marrett reveals the two explicit assumptions that undergird the paradoxical use of the term threshold that his work would inspire: first, that there exists a clear enough boundary between the sacred and the mundane that it can be described in spatial terms and, second, that the magnitude of mood and awe is so affectively vast that it cannot be spatially located.

Birgit Meyer (2016) has argued that notions such as Marret's "awe" allow us to understand religious experience as sense-making rather than meaning-making (17), a process that can aid political regimes able to combine the act of governing with techniques of wonder-making (18). However, in this chapter I want to make a different proposal. The anthropological disciplining of thresholds has obscured the interfaces through which it might be possible to cohabit thresholds alongside our interlocutors and learn to be transformed by their promises and dangers. The un-disciplining of thresholds is a project that is already underway. In the work of Bhrigupati Singh (2012), deities as "thresholds of defied life" encourage the study of the "waning intensities immanent to a milieu" (403). In Melody Jue's (2020) work on the ocean as a mediatic form, the ways deep-sea divers come to know their own ability to withstand depths do not simply function through the feeling of what Jue calls a "flat threshold" (53) but, rather, through a quality of submergence. In Jue's work this quality "gives rise to a new saturated sense of the interface" (69) that provides the means to understand climate change and ecological disaster. Turning to my own ethnography, I ask, how might thresholds become a methodologically viable object in the study of ethical life?

Deliberating the Threshold

My own interest in the ways thresholds manifest in everyday life builds from ethnographic research into how people in Pakistan – particularly followers of the Twelver Shi'i branch of Islam – identify and demarcate atmospheres and moods through the production, circulation, and avoidance of media forms (Cooper 2024a). Over the last four decades Pakistan's Shi'i population have produced religious media in defiance of their widespread marginalization. Despite the historic role the Shi'a have played in the formation and development of the Pakistani nation-state, political-religious groups drawn from the Sunni majority, who enjoy a wide base of popular support, actively, and sometimes violently, campaign against what they see as heretical beliefs that are harmful to public morality. Due to the political clout of these movements, these prejudices generate precarity in legal, economic, and social strata.

Sharing much of its theological basis with Sunni jurisprudence, Shi'ism differs in its belief in the Imamate, a system of succession following the death of the Prophet Muhammad that was ultimately eclipsed by the Sunni caliphate. Twelver Shi'a believe that rather than falling to the Prophet's companions, the *sahaba*, the rights of guardianship over the Muslim community should be held by his descendants, the Twelve Imams. This line began in 10 AH (632 CE) when the Prophet Muhammad named Ali, his cousin and son-in-law, his successor and *wali* (guardian, or, literally, friend) of all believers. This began the *walaya*, the concept of governance or guardianship on which the Imamate rests. In practice, Shi'i faith revolves around celebrating the virtues of the immediate family of the Prophet Muhammad, his daughter Fatima, her husband Ali, and their children Hussain and Hasan – collectively known as the Ahl-e Bait – and the Twelve Imams (along with the Prophet Muhammad, referred to as the *masoomeen*, the fourteen infallibles).

Commemorative mourning is perhaps the practice most closely associated with Shi'i faith, where Shi'a remember the perceived theft of the divine rights of the Ahl-e Bait and the martyrdom of many members at the Battle of Karbala in 680 CE. These events are frequently recalled in *majlis* gatherings and annually commemorated during the first ten days of the Islamic month of Muharram, culminating on the Day of Ashura. In Pakistan these are observed through public demonstrations of grief: flagellation and chest-beating, the procession of model mausolea, and communal weeping. Some members of the Sunni majority consider these practices excessive, even idolatrous, and along with the dispersal of religious authority in Shi'i piety, are said to undermine the doctrine of *tauhid* (the oneness of Allah) that they believe undergirds Islamic faith.

When I conducted fieldwork in Lahore between 2017 and 2018, and again in early 2020, the sustained violence against Shi'i communities that had raged for over three decades had abated in the province of Punjab. Emerging communication technologies and social media platforms were allowing for the wider circulation of devotional media to rural areas, making Pakistani Shi'a co-present with one another in new ways. The popularity of a recitation form known as *qasida* was emblematic of these ongoing changes. While the word refers to an Arabic poetic ode, in this context it describes a type of panegyric recitation given by Shi'i reciters that emerged in rural areas of western and southern Punjab in the mid-twentieth century. The affective intensity of Shi'i qasida, as well as the use of a wide repertoire of melodies from popular films as the backbone of the recitation, provides a source of great controversy for both Sunni and Shi'i ulama (singular *alim*, learned scholars of Islamic doctrine). This is not only because most ulama find participating in musical experience strictly incompatible with prayer. It is also because enthusiastically declaring solidarity for some figures in the early history of Islam and a disassociation from others must be done cautiously, so as not to enflame public sentiment among the Sunni majority. In their circulation in clipped form on social media, qasida recordings become detached not only from the prayer halls and places of worship where the mood of the gathering invited their recitation but also from the wider program of oration in which performative utterances of solidarity and disassociation find context. Out in the digital wild, viewers cannot always look to the emotions and affects of fellow participants or be swept up in the reverent mood of the gathering. Recitations then become more deliberative objects than their liveness previously allowed, leaving viewers to feel for themselves where the threshold between permissible practices lies. Locating what I call *moral thresholds* both within Shi'i practice and in relation to the public affects undergirded by a Sunni majority state, in the following sections I trace the rise and fall of a zakir who, for the sake of anonymity, we will call Mushtaq Ali Abbas.

The Case of the Zakir

In his late twenties with a slick of jet-black hair, Mushtaq is a self-taught zakir. He learned by watching the reciters from his village on the outskirts of Bahawalpur and by imitating audio and video cassettes of the great Pakistani Zakir Ijaz Hussain Baqi of Dera Ghazi Khan, bought for him by his mother from the local marketplace. A zakir delivers orations, poems of praise, and laments at the gatherings that are central to communal worship for Shi'i Muslims. These include the majlis, a frequently held mourning gathering that commemorates the sufferings and sacrifices of the masoomeen, and celebratory gatherings held to extol the virtues of these exemplars and commemorate happy events in Shi'i theology. The craft of zakiri is an art of persuasion that relies on the cultivation of particular affects, from the yawning depth of loss to the solidarity of condolence, and from eliciting awe in the majesty of the virtues of the Ahl-e Bait to indignation at a world filled with tyranny. By both their supporters and detractors, zakirs are seen to offer accessible and highly emotive access to those capable of intercession.

As opposed to a Shi'i *alim* possessing formal education, zakirs have historically been largely unprofessional preachers without formal training, having acquired skills from master–student mentorship or through the observation and intimation of other zakirs.

Mushtaq's popularity as a reciter allowed him to move into an apartment on the western outskirts of the city of Lahore. He became what people had only recently begun to describe as a "superstar reciter." This is not to say his name or face would be widely known in the public sphere, but to many Twelver Shi'a in Pakistani Punjab, Mushtaq inspires great respect. While notable for his majlis orations, Mushtaq is most known for his explosive interpretation of the Shi'i qasida style of address. His orations achieve impact through their sonic and visual intensity, the distorted layers of the amplified sound of live recitation, and the intimate and reactive relationship with the assembled audience. Backed by a chorus of four fellow reciters who create a wall of sound composed of chants put to the shouted refrains of Punjabi folk songs or Bollywood tunes, Mushtaq holds the assembly with surprising contrasts, changes of tone, and sudden crescendos. Since the early twenty-first century, younger reciters like Mushtaq have trimmed the style to provide a surge of emotion in often no more than a minute.

His superstar status is something he carefully cultivates on social media. On the journey to gatherings by car, he broadcasts video diaries on Facebook Live. He discusses the new qasida he is coming to recite, instilling in his Facebook followers (at least 100,000 at the time of writing) expectation and anticipation. The heavy hanging smog outside the car and the rumble of the uneven roads accompany him on his live-streamed journeys, surrounding him with the aura that zakirs cultivate as travelling preachers, always on the move to spread the word. The way qasida has developed over the last decade has made it particularly well suited to smartphone-accessed social media platforms. Mushtaq also broadcasts his majlis appearances live on his Facebook page, archives older broadcasts on YouTube, and posts short, intimate extracts of his recitational style on TikTok, a social media platform that rose to popularity in Pakistan before its adoption in Britain and the United States. The platform allows users to record their own videos lip-syncing to short clips of Mushtaq's qasida recitations and imitate the gestural mannerisms common to other famous zakirs.

TikTok is only the latest platform that has allowed zakirs' recitations to circulate across the country at the same time as widening the gulf between them and more formal figures of religious authority. In the 1960s and 1970s, with radio ownership and the circulation of vinyl

Figure 5.1. Overlaid posters advertise upcoming majlis gatherings featuring famous zakirs beside the Shiʿi Imambargah Karbala Gamay Shah in Lahore.
Author's photograph, 2020.

Figure 5.2. Budding zakirs recite to a mixed assembly of men, women, and children at the shrine of Bibi Pak Daman, Lahore.

Author's photographs, 2018.

records of film, folk, and devotional music increasing from both sides of the Indian border, zakirs began to incorporate the tunes of popular music into their recitations. As commercial recording technology became widely available in the early 1980s, it became common for every Shi'i-majority neighbourhood or shrine to have what is still known as a "cassette and video house" or "CD-centre" that produces recordings of processions and majlis gatherings in the community. These trader-producers also swapped, licensed, and copied recordings from other areas featuring renowned zakirs. One media trader looked back on his life in the business, telling me,

> During the cassette era there was a lot of *demand* ... *public demand* still exists but an atmosphere [*mahaul*] of disrespect has come. ... Previously people would come from really far away to buy majlis recordings. They would come from so far to procure it and there was a lot of piety in that procurement ...

Many others also saw that an increase in *public demand* and platforms for its accessibility corresponded with a decrease in the devotional and disciplinary characteristics of consumers. One trader long in the business of recording told me that while the broadcast of majlis events on Facebook Live has the benefit of reaching a greater number of people, those viewers are mostly engaging while at work, eating, or spending time with family members. By losing the raptured attention of its participants, my interlocutor told me, "that special sense of reverence (*ehtram*) and spirituality (*rohaniyat*) has reduced."

For these audiences, the richness of qasida lies in its immediacy, or what my interlocutors described as qualities of the "live," using the English word, that aids in the creation of an atmosphere conducive to commemorating the masoomeen. One older fan of Mushtaq Ali Abbas explained to me the conditions of moral reception through which the "live" operates:

> When Mushtaq recites through such loud amplifiers, creating such an ethical atmosphere [*aklakhi mahaul*], this is the *live*. This is how you really convey a message to people. When the person you are addressing might know more than you do about your subject, you need these elements.

For this fan, the atmosphere of moral reception through which the affective qualities of the *live* is established is mediated by sound systems and a sense of proximity and presence, rather than through any regimes of knowledge that can be verified by sources of religious authority. The live is understood as both an interface for communication and a vehicle for mediating a sense of intensity that can prove more moving or compelling than the information shared. This is similar to how a threshold might be understood as both a point of crossing and the dwelling place of surging magnitudes.

The reason the zakir both inspires and evades judgment is because of their ability to mediate a vast repertoire of Shi'i affects evoked in terms such as *pursadari* (practising condolement to the Ahl-e Bait) and *azadari* (practising mourning). In Pakistan, *azadari* is often taken as a catch-all term for a mood that invites reverence, intimacy, love, and co-presence with divine exemplars. Tahir Jafri, the majlis collector among whom I spent the most time and who first introduced me to the work of Mushtaq Ali Abbas, had an adept way of explaining to his customers what I was doing lingering around his store: "*Azadari* is a part of anthropology," he would say. I do not think this was a simple observation that forms of ritual activity are part of the study of human sociality. Instead, he seemed to be suggesting that by drawing equivalence with others' emotional and affective thresholds, anthropology can unfold in solidarity with Shi'i faith and its rejection of worldly tyranny. His statement also acknowledged that the ways that Pakistani Shi'a deploy affect as a technology of belief are not esoteric but open to all. As a fellow *azadar* (mourner), it was not expected that I was a believer (*momin*), only that I have love in my heart for the Ahl-e Bait.

Despite Mushtaq's popularity, and the openness with which non-Shi'a can also demonstrate love for the Ahl-e Bait, the controversial nature of his craft bubbles under the surface. On TikTok, many of the often hundreds or thousands of comments on his videos come from fellow Pakistani Shi'a pointing out his transgressions. One commenter asked, "Mushtaq, brother, you are a reciter of great skill and talent. Allah has given you the ability to touch our hearts. Why must you recite like a singer to the tune of film songs? Surely you can look in your heart and find your own tune?" Only implicitly is this a critique on theological grounds. More pertinent is an appeal to plumb the depths of his "heart" to "find his own tune" rather than mine existing public affects, in this case a vast repertoire of Hindi and Urdu-language film music. Other detractors do not measure their words so carefully. Videos circulating on YouTube on conservative Sunni prayer networks contain compilations of qasida recited by zakirs like Mushtaq, paired with a clip of the Bollywood film song from which the melody is lifted, followed by heated rhetoric on the context and consequence of popular zakirs' apparent transgressions. From their perceived proximity to secular entertainment with its sensual themes of passion and romance to suspicion over their latent populism, zakirs have always been accused of being on the threshold of *something*.

Diverse Lovers

The moral threshold most keenly felt within closely knit Shi'a communities is the issue of professionalization, particularly regarding financial remuneration. The possibility of securing wealth as a zakir owes much to recent socio-economic changes, including an increase in access to disposable income, which has led to the patronage of more frequent majlis events. Those who describe zakirs as "professionals" usually do so critically, drawing on prejudices about their proximity to forms of entertainment and the widely held notion that the exchange of money for religious services undermines the efficacy of the message. A similar phenomenon animates the work of David Kloos (2021) on female Islamic orators in Malaysia and Yasmin Moll (2018) on Egyptian Islamic television programming, both of whom observe how established ethics of religious persuasion are transformed through their mass mediation. In Pakistan, a zakir might be recognized as being a "professional" for having a retinue, followers, a car, and a relationship with majlis convenors across Punjab. Such professionalism is also equated with a reduction in devotional piety. Long journeys are considered less arduous if they result in a financial exchange. This is not to say that zakirs are not paid, but their payment is considered a voluntary donation. This can result in risky situations for the unestablished zakir who might have spent thousands of rupees in expenses and received only a fraction as a donation.

These are not the only anxieties that Mushtaq must contend with before he reaches the pulpit. Twelver Shi'i theology is careful to delineate who, within its own body politic, it considers *ghulat* (exaggerators), a term often leveraged against zakirs, to describe an excessive show of veneration for an exemplar. The first Shi'i Imam, Ali is reported to have scorned those who "exceed the lawful limits of love" for him (cited in Shirazi [1927] 2008, 24). In another saying, Ali is reported to have stated that "two categories of persons will face ruin on account of me: those who love me with exaggeration, and those who hate me intensely." Those supportive of zakirs' affective labour, such as my interlocutor Tahir Jafri, use their own terminology to describe movements within Shi'i faith organized to clamp down on popular expression, calling them *"inteha pasand,"* literally "lovers of limits." It is these differences within the bounds of sameness that make immanent in Shi'i faith a threshold between love and worship that is far more unruly and relational than the juristic boundaries between permissible and impermissible practice with which they are often conflated.

Having opened out into an online space, Mushtaq's craft became loaded not only with the moral thresholds immanent in Shi'i faith but also the surface tension of public affect as it is formed in relation to the Sunni-majority Pakistani state. In some ways, this was not a new phenomenon. There has long been the imagined presence of the non-Shi'i other in majlis orations, either in anticipation of discord or as a rhetorical strategy that takes the stance of a listener from outside the faith. While reciters can be fairly certain that whoever has gathered for the majlis is broadly accepting of their style of recitation, zakirs' orations make continual reference to sources of dissensus and the three central causes for disparaging their craft. The first is largely epistemological, that the stories told by zakirs are often embellished for audiences. Some pair these with accusations of the invention of new rituals or narratives that have no origins in theology. The second is moral, that recitations such as qasida cross a perceptible threshold into musical performance or entertainment. The third is a theological issue over the role zakirs play in a performative act of distancing oneself from the enemies of the Ahl-e Bait, known as *tabarra*. Due to their crucial differences in theology, Sunni Muslims tend to associate tabarra with the severe transgression of cursing or insulting the companions of the Prophet and the early Islamic caliphs who were at war with the *Shi'at Ali* (the partisans of Ali). For many Shi'a, however, tabarra is part and parcel of expressing *tawalla* (attachment or love for the Ahl-e Bait; Rieck 2018, 22–3), which together forms a very febrile and public form of confessional disclosure. These iterations of love and hate are imbricated through the embodied holism of Shi'i ethics: turning yourself towards something is understood as part of the same gesture of turning your back on something else.

Like several other leading Pakistani zakirs, in 2020 Mushtaq was barred from entering the capital city of Islamabad to deliver orations during the first ten days of Muharram. This most important period in the Shi'i religious calendar marks the martyrdom of Imam Ḥussain and the tragedy that befell other members of the Ahl-e Bait at the Battle of Karbala in 680 CE. While by no means an exceptional occurrence over the last few decades, in 2020 communal tensions had been exacerbated by a dispute concerning one of the most renowned Shi'i orators in Pakistani Punjab, Asif Raza Alvi. While his followers conferred upon Alvi the honorific title Allama, often given to a renowned polymath or scholar, he is not strictly a member of the ulama, who at best consider him a gifted and influential zakir. Perhaps because he occupies a privileged place as a source of religious authority among followers of more charismatic elements of Shiʻi practice, several previously disparate Sunni groups united under the impetus of a return to anti-Shiʻa activism seized on a statement in one of Alvi's orations posted online and accused him of religious offence. While these accusations are time-tested means of inflaming sectarian tensions between Sunni and Shiʻi Muslims, the Alvi controversy was further amplified by two recent developments. First, the late 2010s saw the rapid growth of Shiʻi digital collectives that live-stream previously semi-private majlis events to an audience of unknown viewers who are also able to download the videos and repost them in clipped form. Previously such recordings were available only from marketplace producers and traders in Shiʻi neighbourhoods, providing barriers to their appropriation or scrutiny that mediate what Syed Akbar Hyder (2006) calls "the informal pact" that exists between reciters and their audiences (101). Secondly, the intensification of the activities of national regulatory bodies Pakistan Electronic Media Regulatory Authority and the Federal Investigation Agency's Cyber Crime Wing, to whom complaints can be sent and in accordance with whom First Information Reports can be filed, have come to provide a means through which accusations become newsworthy objects of national interest.

The complaint filed against Alvi asserted that in his oration he insulted one of the *sahaba*, the companions of the Prophet Muhammad. In the full video Alvi had recounted the meeting between Zainab, the sister of Imam Hussain, and the Caliph Yazid responsible for the massacre at the Battle of Karbala, using the rhetorical device of first-person narration. In a video explanation posted to his Facebook page, Alvi emphasized that his words referred in no way to the companions of the Prophet. Despite this, many of Pakistan's dozens of private news channels took the accusations at face value, claiming that by drawing on friendships with leading politicians, Alvi was able to escape accountability and flee to the United Kingdom. At the 2020 Shia Ulama-O-Zakireen Conference, which gathers Shiʻi ulama trained in Iranian seminaries, the esteemed scholar Mohsin Ali Najafi sent a message to zakirs across Pakistan to "keep your conversations within the limit [*hadd*]," unless they wished to draw the ire of the ulama.

The year before, Mushtaq had begun to notice the splits long in evidence among Pakistani zakirs. He was unsure of what to make of a controversial 2019 accord signed between members of the local Twelver Shiʻi ulama and a small number of "superstar" zakirs. What became known as the Pindi Bhattian Agreement detailed the ways in which zakirs should be obedient to the ulama and not engage in practices likely to provoke their majority Sunni co-religionists. For example, zakirs were told to avoid discussing the walaya and avoid labelling figures venerated by Sunnis as enemies of the Ahl-e Bait. Some might argue that this betrays an oversimplified understanding of Pakistan's sectarian conflict (Abou-Zahab 2020) by trying to avoid a further "hardening of boundaries" (Zaman 2018, 267). For Ali Usman Qasmi (2015), increases in sectarian violence can be traced to an increase in similarities rather than differences, through which violence serves to fix the "blurred lines" between one and the other (226).

In the end, it was not the threshold that divides recitation from song, or the threshold between disassociation and malediction, that led to the greatest damage to Mushtaq's obligations as a zakir. One of the hundreds of Shi'i proselytization networks active on Facebook in Pakistani Punjab took the unusual step of denouncing the actions of one of the famous zakirs they promote. While rivalries and competitive disagreements are common, it is rare for such networks to draw attention to the controversies surrounding one of their own. The administrators of the Facebook page in question captioned their post by explaining that, "to date, we have never made a controversial post, but today [Mushtaq] set the limit [*hadd*]." The matter in question was explicated by a video taken from a smartphone resting on the lap of someone travelling in the zakir's car, recording only sound and the flashes of lights from passing vehicles. The audio revealed Mushtaq discussing the matter of his payment. Without haggling or bargaining, he declared the cost of his services to a caller hoping to sponsor a future event. Perhaps it was the distinct aesthetic of the video that wielded the greatest power; it had the look of a "leak," barely perceptible visuals and sound that were hard to verify as the speaking voice of an orator better known for his high-octane orations. Whatever it was, it was a decisive moment in Mushtaq Ali Abbas's career as a "superstar" reciter. Disappearing into his ancestral village for several months, he gradually returned to the majlis circuit and continued his life as a popular zakir more attuned to the interfaces through which outrage might manifest.

The Morality of Thresholds

While the post itself was a rare occurrence, the language in which it was phrased was familiar. In Pakistan it is common to hear the line between socially acceptable actions and transgressions expressed using the term *hadd*. While the context in which I heard the word was in reference to the threshold between recitation and song, between orator and celebrity, or between customary disassociation and malediction, the term relates to broader thresholds, in particular to sensation and size. Briefly stepping outside my ethnography, this short section examines the journey from limit to delimitation taken by a concept in its movement from Islamic theology to jurisprudence and its resulting impact on ethical life. As a verb, the modernist scholar Fazlur Rahman (1965) defined the Arabic roots of *hadd*, or *hudood* in plural, as the action of preventing the intrusion of one thing onto another (237). As a noun it heightens this preventative agency to express a limit that separates one thing from another by a moral obligation to be good as derived from the Quran and Sunnah (the traditions and sayings of the Prophet Muhammad) (239). In its move from theology to Sunni jurisprudence, *hadd* has come to describe punishments for the transgression of limits seen to do damage to others or society, rather than to the self (245). In early Twelver Shi'i jurisprudence, the imperative of punishment implicated in *hadd* could only be adjudicated by Allah or those appointed by Allah, such as the Twelve Imams. Transgressions that affect the social world, by comparison, were to be adjudicated by virtuous individuals possessing religious education (Amir-Moezzi 2016, 135). Across such differences in jurisprudence, *hadd* remains a threshold that exists as latent potential in all human interaction.

As a crucial milestone in its disciplining in Pakistan, the term gave its name to the Hudood Ordinances, perhaps the most seismic change installed by the theocratic-military regime of Zia-ul-Haq in the 1980s. Constituting a set of legal reforms to incorporate elements of Shariah jurisprudence into Pakistani law, the Hudood Ordinances included legal changes regarding rape and premarital sex that made women substantially less equal in the eyes of the law. These reforms were variously seen by critics as anti-women, illiberal, or an impious interpretation of divine will. For the latter criticism, mingling the status of a moral limit with its disciplining withdraws agency both from Allah and from the model ethical self that the Quran aims to cultivate. For this model self the world provides clues in "the alternation of night and day" (Quran 3, 190). It is through these signs that Pakistan's intellectual forefather, Muhammad Iqbal (1934), wrote on the sensorium of "inner intuition" (15; also see Stainova, this volume). Arguing for a cultivated understanding of the relationship between affective response and ethical responsibility, Iqbal believed that the reconstruction and reform required at the heart of Islam should proceed from an experiential and sensory approach to the world. While in its theological sense *hadd* is felt by intuition but, in most cases, is ultimately unknowable, when disciplined by jurisprudence it becomes culturally and socially variable. This evolution from limit to delimitation recalls the anthropological disciplining of a ritual threshold to the status of liminality. In both instances, disciplining forecloses the need to pay any attention to forms of affective receptivity that people deploy to feel for where limits lie.

In the forms of Islamic mysticism that inspired Muhammad Iqbal, *hadd* can also describe the breadth of separation between an individual and Allah, a separation that requires media for reunification. For pieties that accept intercession and theologies of mediation, interior states of being are necessary to meet the exteriority and surface tension of moral experience evoked by *hadd*. This resonates with Charles Hirschkind's (2006, 97) work on honing "ways of the heart" in creating a sensorium that allows people to inhabit moral norms, or Anand Pandian's (2010) work on interiority and selfhood in South India. For Pandian, the "heart" can be a medium for the cultivation of ethical selfhood, forming an interface between exterior surfaces and sensations and the life of interiority. Similarly, for Islamic philosophers such as Ibn al-Arabi writing on Sufic mysticism, knowledge lies in the domain of the heart, or of feeling, rather than within knowledge systems that delimit its boundaries (Chittick 2010, 148).

In Islamic metaphysics, *hadd* can also describe the "essence" of a thing, a word, or a substance rather than its explication or description. Ibn Sina (Avicenna) described the term at greatest length in his critique of atomism, arguing that the essence of things is to be found in their continuous motion and magnitude rather than in units of experience. While still describing it as a "limiting point," Ibn Sina (2009 [c1027], 113) understood *hadd* to be the status of a thing in its intermediacy, as the very quality of motion and of being. Central to this idea of a "limiting point" as a flowing quality of motion was the agent of spatial magnitude that produces the subjective sensation of its delimitation (Chittick 2010, 242–4). In this embodied sense, the force of magnitude has no end. While it may manifest limiting points, for the plurality of things in the world and their reliance on continuous motion, this metaphysical understanding does not allow hadd to manifest into fixity or be disciplined into a system of knowledge. As we see in Mushtaq's rise and fall or the call to seek out the "lawful limits of love" in Shi'i faith and practice, feeling the distinction between recitation and song rather than reading it through jurisprudence means allowing a moral threshold to exist on its own terms as an unresolved object of ethical life. This recalls Thomas Bauer's (2021) argument that the lived heterogeneity of Islamic faith provides an "intensive training in ambiguity" (260). The pre-disciplined metaphysics of hadd define what Bauer calls the "suspension of all claims to an exclusive truth" through an Islam that had not only "already domesticated *ambiguity*" but delineated in its followers' plurality of responses and responsibilities a sign of divine grace. It is this un-disciplined understanding of moral thresholds such as hadd that might help us understand the anthropological figure of the threshold differently, as a limit ultimately only knowable through intuition, empathy, or the co-presence of participation rather than as a limit already disciplined by existing knowledge systems.

Public Affect and Its Interfaces

In line with this volume's call to let our interlocutors' affects generate new forms of anthropological uncovering, this call for un-disciplining the threshold provides an opportunity to, in the words of Yael Navaro (2017, 211), "diversify" affect by developing ethnographic sensitivity to the interfaces through which it becomes apparent. Much like a threshold, an interface is characterized by the surface tension of those elements for which it provides a shared boundary. An interface is also a site where coexisting forms can cooperate or communicate, as evinced in Jack Goody's 1987 book *The Interface between the Written and the Oral*. Goody's interface is a meeting point whose surface tensions reveal unexamined qualities emergent in disparate systems (also see De Antoni, this volume). Instead of describing cultures dialectically as either oral or written, Goody (1987) instead tried to focus on how their coexistence was experienced, or what he called "the situation of the interface" (78). This situational understanding recalls Sara Ahmed's (2004, 39) argument that the intensity of feelings left by others possesses a history and that affects rehearse associations that are already in place.

When they become intersubjective objects of empathy or accusations, thresholds require interfaces with which to make the force of magnitude commensurable within a common metric. In my ethnography these were variously aesthetic, the look of a leak; moral, in the ways that atmosphere was marshalled to describe the effects of the zakir's oration; and economic, in the force of public demand that evokes the pious labour undertaken by audiences. When moral thresholds become interfaces, it is not that they manifest simply as bracketed domains of moral concern, but their status as interfaces imbues them with the possibility of new forms of communication, reform, and discovery. Shi'i faith is densely populated with thresholds and interfaces, such as the "fine line" (D'Souza 1998, 76) between veneration and deification of devotional objects or the heightened awareness held by zakirs of the constellation of criticisms levelled at the elements of Shi'i practice they uphold. In his study of the Shi'i majlis in Indian Hyderabad, Toby Howarth (2005, 55) uses the metaphor of a river whose banks demarcate the boundaries of the flow, determining who may orate and what they can say. Similar to what Maria Rashid (2020) describes in relation to televised shows for the families of Pakistani military dead, zakirs must know how to give their audiences the "right dose" of feeling" (38). In these terms, thresholds and their interfaces become "holding patterns" (Humphrey 2012) for disparate ideas, contradictions, and ethical ambiguities (White and Katsuno 2021, 244).

Like the ethical atmosphere (*aklakhi mahaul*) of liveness that one fan of Mushtaq Ali Abbas saw formed by amplified volume, the analytic figure of *mahaul*, or atmosphere, acts as a way of recognizing different thresholds of intensity and change, allowing them to radiate beyond the self and affect the lives of others. If the concept of mahaul is an interface for membership and exclusion, by this same logic we might say that hadd is a moral threshold whose interface is public affect. I felt my interlocutors eager to come to grips with this through their interest in the force of "public demand," in which they located a hunger for religious media coupled with disinterest in its mediation of pious affects. This notion resonates with Aasim Sajjad Akhtar's (2018, 2) argument that since the era of the Hudood Ordinances in Pakistan, "common sense" has been located and mediated in the relationship between merchant traders and religious organizations. When my interlocutors spoke of the force of "demand," they did so as a way of explaining their faith in the moral responsibility of a national collective that comes together to deal with affective encounters, outrages, and intensities through the disciplining of affective limits into hard-and-fast categories for public circulation.

Perhaps it is this tendency initiated in the era of the Hudood Ordinances, which formalized in law the leap from a limit to the punishments marked by its delimitation, that has seen violence towards women and minority faiths and accusations of blasphemy increase so markedly in Pakistan over the last four decades. As we have seen in the case of the zakir, the disciplining of affect takes place within Shi'i communities and is not restricted to majoritarian forms of Pakistani public culture. Providing the discursive and systemic tools to locate and situate disquiet rather than accept its adjudication as essentially transcendent not only disciplines the middle ground but elides it in favour of a permissible/impermissible binary. It is the disciplining of moral thresholds such as hadd, and the social and communal benefits of sustaining it, that operates by becoming intimate with what William Mazzarella (2013) calls a "mattering forth of the collective flesh." These forms of "public affect" or the "mana of mass society" (41) are made up of those constituent parts that Marett called "drawing near in awe."

While public affect is by its very nature mass-mediated, its disciplining, such as in the form of censorship, is often directed at the bodies and practices of marginal, subaltern, and minority groups (166). This is why, rather than seeking its unification, zakirs like Mushtaq rely on the "affect/ethics impasse" (Mazzarella 2017, 204) holding, for it is on its thresholds that their craft unfolds.

Un-Disciplining Ambiguity

In my ethnography, I located moral thresholds both in Shi'i practice and in a wider tendency in Pakistani public discourse to speculate on the location of divine boundaries and identify their manifestation in the social world. Accustomed to the Pakistani majlis, the moral thresholds Mustaq Ali Abbas learned to feel were those whose interfaces were immanent in Shi'i faith rather than the kinds of interfaces that have been transformed by digital publics. To come to grips with the changing situations through which thresholds become objects of social practice requires cultivating what Melody Jue (2020) has called "a new saturated sense of the interface" (69). This is not a reiteration of calls for anthropological "immersion" but rather a call for methodological awareness of how public affects invite the disciplining of limits by forming the consensual basis of membership and exclusion. Turning to interfaces, those points of connection between phases of activity, or the common overlap between otherwise separate practices, directs more empathetic attention towards otherwise unfixed notions and limiting points that exist in wide circulation. In my field site, this could be found in the notion of a mahaul or "atmosphere" imbued with something like the tactile earthiness of the concept of *terroir* used in environmental discourses to describe the variable essence that can come to be embodied in a crop yield and shape the product from which it is made. To define *terroir* is also to suggest that these elements can be harnessed and influenced by humans. Similarly, mahaul is a product of human cultivation and disturbance; it carries a weight that transforms space, time, and pervades everyday life.

The metaphysical un-disciplining of thresholds such as *hadd* provides the means of negotiating some wide-ranging questions. This includes the problem of agency in the anthropology of Islam, predicated on the question of how to acknowledge figures of divinity as social actors. If we cannot act for or on behalf of divine others, affect can operate as a way of suspending adjudication while still feeling its limiting points. This not only reiterates the insights from the work of Charles Hirschkind (2006) and Saba Mahmood (2006), that discursive means of ethical orientation are inhabited and embodied through practice, but rather that when there exists little consensus over what should count as Islamic normativity people search out ways of feeling, rather than fixing, moral thresholds. To questions over permissibility thresholds are affective answers rather than discursive ones.

As the introduction to this volume asks, drawing from the work of Kathleen Stewart (2018, 17), "How might we find methods for doing thought differently?" It is not enough to simply answer "by thinking through feeling" without adding the disclaimer that the politics of intuition structure violence and exclusion as much as they broker populism (see again Stainova, this volume). One possible answer perhaps lies in understanding that the leap from a limit to the act of delimitation is as much a part of many academic fields' disciplinary culture as it is a part of modernist theologies' tendency to turn co-religionists into accusers. Rather than disciplining the threshold into an analytic figure, I propose we take their interfaces to be affective sites where attempts at commensuration play out between a constellation of stakeholders. In these instances, domesticating ambiguity does not have to mean disciplining it.

Finally, to engage a more tensile understanding of the threshold or a more "saturated" feeling for interfaces, we need to strive to discover at all turns what it is like to dwell upon them. This might mean paying closer attention to the "inner lining" (Ramos Zayas, this volume) and "gut feelings" (Stainova, this volume) of affects that not only reiterate the boundaries between opposing ontologies but show their mutual sympathies (De Antoni, this volume). Most of all it means looking to our interlocutors to learn how they discover and rediscover the surface tension of thresholds and their interfaces. Mushtaq Ali Abbas understood from a young age that feeling one's own thresholds relates not only to representations but to a quality of self-possession that is both existential and finely interwoven into his craft. He learned this from the zakir Ijaz Hussain Baqi, whose style he strived to emulate. At his final majlis, Baqi was asked to recite the account of the martyrdom of Ali Akbar, the son of Imam Hussain, who was eighteen years old when he was killed at the Battle of Karbala. Baqi refused, as he always did, knowing that other zakirs had died reciting the same account. It is said that centuries ago when the martyrdom narratives of Ali Akbar and his infant sister Sakina were recited at the mausoleum of Imam Hussain in Iraq, the grave shook violently. While many zakirs often recount sections of these narratives, they do so in fragmentary form and withdraw when they feel the force of magnitude approach a threshold. At his final majlis Baqi relented and told the organizers to get a cot ready for his body. As he recounted the death of Ali Akbar he was overcome by emotion and died of a broken heart.

If zakirs are always on the threshold of something, it is not only a moral transgression or a public demand. Baqi's example is a reminder that thresholds are media for self-sovereignty, and it is here that the distinctions between affect and ethics dissipate or become submerged in the depths of solidarity, disavowal, and loss.

REFERENCES

Abou-Zahab, Mariam. 2020. *Pakistan: A Kaleidoscope of Islam*. Oxford: Oxford University Press. https://doi.org/10.1093/oso/9780197534595.001.0001.

Ahmed, Sara. 2004. "Collective Feelings: Or, the Impressions Left by Others." *Theory, Culture & Society* 21 (2): 25–42. https://doi.org/10.1177/0263276404042133.

Akhtar, Aasim Sajjad. 2018. *The Politics of Common Sense: State, Society and Culture in Pakistan*. Cambridge, UK: Cambridge University Press. https://doi.org/10.1080/14662043.2021.1892609.

Amir-Moezzi, Mohammad Ali. 2016. *Divine Guide in Early Shiʻism: The Sources of Esotericism in Islam*. Albany, NY: SUNY Press, 2016.

Avicenna, 2009. *The Physics of the Healing: A Parallel English-Arabic Text*, 2 Vols. Translated by Jon McGinnis. Provo, UT: Brigham Young University Press.

Bauer, Thomas. 2021. *A Culture of Ambiguity: An Alternative History of Islam*. Translated by Hinrich Biesterfeldt and Tricia Tunstall. New York: Columbia University Press. https://doi.org/10.7312/baue17064.

Chittick, William C. 2010. *The Sufi Path of Knowledge: Ibn al-Arabi's Metaphysics of Imagination*. Albany, NY: SUNY Press. https://doi.org/10.1515/9780791498989.

Cooper, Timothy P.A. 2024a. *Moral Atmospheres: Islam and Media in a Pakistani Marketplace*. New York: Columbia University Press. https://doi.org/10.7312/coop21040.

Cooper, Timothy P.A. 2024b. "The Situation of the Interface: Pashto Master-Copies and Data Migration in Sharjah." *American Ethnologist* 51 (2): 181–92. https://doi.org/10.1111/amet.13273.

D'Souza, Diane. 1998. "In the Presence of the Martyrs: The Alam in Popular Shi i Piety." *The Muslim World* 88 (1): 67–80. https://doi.org/10.1111/j.1478-1913.1998.tb03646.x.

Goody, Jack. 1987. *The Interface between the Written and the Oral*. Cambridge, UK: Cambridge University Press.

Hirschkind, Charles. 2006. *The Ethical Soundscape: Cassette Sermons and Islamic Counterpublics*. New York: Columbia University Press.

Howarth, Toby. 2005. *The Twelver Shia as a Muslim Minority in India: Pulpit of Tears*. London: Routledge. https://doi.org/10.4324/9780203012604.

Humphrey, Caroline. 2012. "Hospitality and Tone: Holding Patterns for Strangeness in Rural Mongolia." *Journal of the Royal Anthropological Institute* 18 (S1: S63–75. https://doi.org/10.1111/j.1467-9655.2012.01761.x.

Hyder, Syed Akbar. 2006. *Reliving Karbala: Martyrdom in South Asian Memory*. Oxford: Oxford University Press. https://doi.org/10.1093/acprof:oso/9780195373028.001.0001.

Iqbal, Muhammad. 1934. *The Reconstruction of Muslim Thought in Islam*. London: Oxford University Press.

Jue, Melody. 2020. *Wild Blue Media: Thinking Through Seawater*. Durham, NC: Duke University Press. https://doi.org/10.2307/j.ctv11g97ph.

Kloos, David. 2021. "Risky Appearances, Skillful Performances: Female Islamic Preachers and Professional Style in Malaysia." *American Anthropologist* 123 (2): 278–91. https://doi.org/10.1111/aman.13556.

Mahmood, Saba. 2006. *Politics of Piety: The Islamic Revival and the Feminist Subject*. Princeton, NJ: Princeton University Press. https://doi.org/10.1515/9781400839919.

Marett, Robert Ranulph. 1909. *The Threshold of Religion*. New York: The Macmillan Company.

Mazzarella, William. 2013. *Censorium: Cinema and the Open Edge of Mass Publicity*. Durham, NC: Duke University Press. https://doi.org/10.1515/9780822397328.

Mazzarella, William. 2017. "Sense Out of Sense: Notes on the Affect/eEhics Impasse." *Cultural Anthropology* 32 (2): 199–208. https://doi.org/10.14506/ca32.2.04.

Mazzarella, William. 2019. "The Anthropology of Populism: Beyond the Liberal Settlement." *Annual Review of Anthropology* 48: 45–60. https://doi.org/10.1146/annurev-anthro-102218-011412.

Meyer, Birgit. 2016. "How to Capture the 'Wow': R.R. Marett's Notion of Awe and the Study of Religion." *Journal of the Royal Anthropological Institute* 22 (1): 7–26. https://doi.org/10.1111/1467-9655.12331.

Moll, Yasmin. 2018. "Television Is Not Radio: Theologies of Mediation in the Egyptian Islamic Revival." *Cultural Anthropology* 33 (2): 233–65. https://doi.org/10.14506/ca33.2.07.

Navaro, Yael. 2017. "Diversifying Affect." *Cultural Anthropology* 32 (2): 209–14. https://doi.org/10.14506/ca32.2.05.

Pandian, Anand. 2010. "Interior Horizons: An Ethical Space of Selfhood in South India." *Journal of the Royal Anthropological Institute* 16 (1): 64–83. https://doi.org/10.1111/j.1467-9655.2009.01597.x.

Qasmi, Ali Usman. 2015. *The Ahmadis and the Politics of Religious Exclusion in Pakistan*. London: Anthem Press. https://doi.org/10.2307/j.ctt1gxp71m.

Rahman, Fazlur. 1965. "The Concept of Ḥadd in Islamic Law." *Islamic Studies* 4 (2): 237–51.

Rashid, Maria. 2020. *Dying to Serve: Militarism, Affect and the Politics of Sacrifice in the Pakistan Army.* Stanford, CA: Stanford University Press. https://doi.org/10.1515/9781503611993.

Rieck, Andreas. 2018. *The Shias of Pakistan: An Assertive and Beleaguered Minority.* London: Hurst. https://doi.org/10.1093/acprof:oso/9780190240967.001.0001.

Shirazi, Sultanu'l-Wa'izin. [1927] 2008. *Peshawar Nights.* Translated by Hamid Quinian and Charles Ali Campbell. Qom, Iran: Ansariyan Publications.

Singh, Bhrigupati. 2012. "The Headless Horseman of Central India: Sovereignty at Varying Thresholds of Life." *Cultural Anthropology* 27 (2): 383–407. https://doi.org/10.1111/j.1548-1360.2012.01148.x.

Stewart, Kathleen. 2018. "'Worldy Thinking.' Comment on Sasha Newell's 'The Affectiveness of Symbols: Materiality, Magicality, and the Limits of the Antisemiotic Turn'." *Current Anthropology* 59 (1): 16–8. https://doi.org/10.1086/696071.

Throop, C. Jason. 2009. "Intermediary Varieties of Experience." *Ethnos* 74 (4): 535–58. https://doi.org/10.1080/00141840903202116.

Throop, C. Jason. 2014. "Moral Moods." *Ethos* 42 (1): 65–83. https://doi.org/10.1111/etho.12039.

Turner, Victor. 1967. *The Forest of Symbols: Aspects of Ndembu Ritual.* Ithaca, NY: Cornell University Press.

Turner, Victor. 1969. *The Ritual Process: Structure and Anti-Structure.* Chicago: Aldine.

Turner, Victor. 1986. "Dewey, Dilthey, and Drama: An Essay in the Anthropology of Experience." In *The Anthropology of Experience*, edited by Victor Turner, Victor Witter, Edward M. Bruner, and Clifford Geertz, 33–44. Chicago: University of Illinois Press.

Van Gennep, Arnold. 1960 [1919]. *The Rites of Passage.* Translated by Monika B. Vizedom and Gabrielle L. Caffee. Chicago: University of Chicago Press.

White, Daniel, and Hirofumi Katsuno. 2021. "Toward an Affective Sense of Life: Artificial Intelligence, Animacy, and Amusement at a Robot Pet Memorial Service in Japan." *Cultural Anthropology* 36 (2): 222–51. https://doi.org/10.14506/ca36.2.03.

Zaman, Muhammad Qasim. 2018. *Islam in Pakistan: A History.* Princeton, NJ: Princeton University Press.

Chapter 6

What Sticks: Affective Scholarship in Times of Pandemic Past and Present

THOMAS STODULKA

The COVID-19 pandemic wreaked havoc. Its reverberations widened precarity and privilege gaps. It rendered workers of all kinds jobless. It left millions of families and communities without income. It caused the deaths of loved ones. It significantly affected everyone's health, whether people caught COVID-19 or not. While some who are able may wish to brush off the pandemic's dust and view lockdowns and isolation as a closed chapter, the reality is far different for others who have experienced profound loss or seen their means of livelihood collapse. Many of those most affected now face decades of financial struggle, burdened by mortgages and debts. Emotionally, the pandemic's effects persist in bodies both human and otherwise, altering social and natural landscapes on a planetary scale. Younger generations in particular are grappling with "eco-anxiety" as the planet becomes increasingly uninhabitable, while social anxiety, depression, burnout, and hopelessness loom large among them (Pillay 2021). Although seen today as past, like many crises, the pandemic sticks with us today.

The consequences of COVID-19 challenge anthropological attempts to make sense of a world of ongoing crises, in which climate change, ecological and humanitarian disasters, austerity, and neocolonial wars question a theory-heavy academic status quo. Initially, the pandemic raised pragmatic questions about how to conduct fieldwork given the limitations of mobility and the curtailing of social encounters to interaction on screens. Faced with the unpredictability of yet another "Corona wave" or "variant" threatening to roll into different parts of the world with existential consequences, anthropologists resorted to remote ethnography and proxy fieldwork, re-imagining fieldwork ethics and responsibility. Demands to conduct fieldwork online and turn to digital ethnography inundated graduate methodology classes and supervision debates.

Faced with existential challenges to research, some felt the urge to collaborate with other scholars, expand online conversations, and turn to analysing online archives, digitized infrastructures, artefacts, signs, billboards, and other textual forms of ethnographic data. Others who were committed to in-person fieldwork but unable to access it even asked, Can anthropologists ever conduct on-site fieldwork again? While it seems constructive for anthropologists to remain allied with other disciplines and the arts that work with texts, objects, and virtual realms of engagement (Stodulka 2021), the pandemic also revealed what gets lost when anthropology's modes of face-to-face witnessing, sensing, and in-person encounters disappear. Accordingly, this chapter seeks to integrate the digital turn in much of anthropological work with the affective stickiness of embedded research methods. In part responding to Jobson's (2020) call to clear the colonial conceptual conceits that have become attached to emplaced fieldwork, I aim to demonstrate ways that encounters themselves can decolonize, so long as the affective stickiness of certain situations can be made to illustrate colonial legacies lying underneath.

Indeed, anthropology has fared well in the face of crisis when it has adapted its resolutely interpersonal ethnographic methods to meet new challenges and changing environments (Faubion and Marcus 2009; Sluka and Robben 2012). Regarding the changing temporalities of fieldwork in times of pandemic and other crises, on-site fieldwork has certainly become more variable, intermittent, or more "patchwork" (Günel et al. 2020). But whatever the pandemic's methodological repercussions might look like in the future, anthropology still offers uniquely rich insights into the affective dimensions of culture when researchers are navigating interpersonal and ethical predicaments (Thajib et al. 2019). Co-being remains a crucial mode of effective ethnographic engagement – not so much because ethnographers peer over shoulders into other persons' lives, as traditional interpretivist village ethnographies might have phrased it, but because they lend their bodies, interactions, language, thoughts, and, most of all, feelings to the scrutiny of those with whom they interact and collaborate. This affective dimension of shared concern, vulnerability, and constant probing of trustworthiness makes anthropology unique.

The pandemic has therefore shown the methodological vulnerability of in-person anthropology and at the same time inspired new methods of ethnographic and collaborative knowledge construction, bringing modalities of digital engagement and co-dwelling to centre stage. I welcome the ethos of patchwork ethnography and the call for online engagement, the epistemic reflection of ethnographers' political entanglements, and the fostering of feedback loops with interlocutors (Rappaport 2008). I embrace ethnographic turns to teamwork, to the construction of new digital platforms to share data, and collectively struggle with the ethics and responsibilities of doing digital and translocal knowledge construction. It is impressive to see how my own graduate and postgraduate students have transformed online methods into means of rapport-building with initial strangers, fostering long-term relationships through online threads, digital storytelling, regular video calls, and discussion forums. Yet, equally important remains the question of how to responsibly hold space for affective encounters among ethnographers, interlocutors, and co-dwellers both on- and offline.

In carving my own methodological pathway through the previous pandemic, and reflecting on how to leverage what we have learned towards future crises, I continue to test the viability of what I have defined elsewhere as "affective scholarship" (Stodulka et al. 2018). Affective scholarship probes the possibilities of engaging affect as a somatic compass for sensory-rich ethnographic data collection and collaboration. In this chapter, I demonstrate one mode of affective scholarship through a multimodal retrospective on the pandemic, in which the affective traces of sticky encounters reveal the uncomfortable and often unequal structures of crisis circumstances past and present.

Affective Traces

Picture the following situations.

You and your family are on fieldwork in an environment that has become familiar to you over the last two decades. The previous years of living and working in the area had their existential challenges, but you felt you had established a sense of social and cultural familiarity. Then, one day in March 2020, social and mass media disseminated reports and images of a *korona* wave threatening to "roll into" the area from Europe, where you otherwise live (see Figure 6.1).

Suddenly, a young man starts shouting at you during a stroll on a beach. He forcefully suggests that you had better go home, back to where you belong. The next day, the hotel staff checks your and your family's passports to track your transnational movements. "Just a matter of precaution, based on new police orders as of this morning," the receptionist tells you through his medical mask. That same day, everyone is asked to wear a mask in public. The next day, you realize that entrances to hospitals, shops, and markets are guarded by officers waving "thermo-guns" at people. They ask every person seeking access to these buildings for permission to point the screener at their foreheads, checking their body temperature (Figure 6.2).

Some are allowed to pass, and others are rejected. The selection seems arbitrary to the public eye. New signs and banners everywhere order

Figure 6.1. Newspaper headline: "Thousands of people under surveillance [i.e., persons with assumed COVID-19 status] have entered the area (NTT)," March 26, 2020.

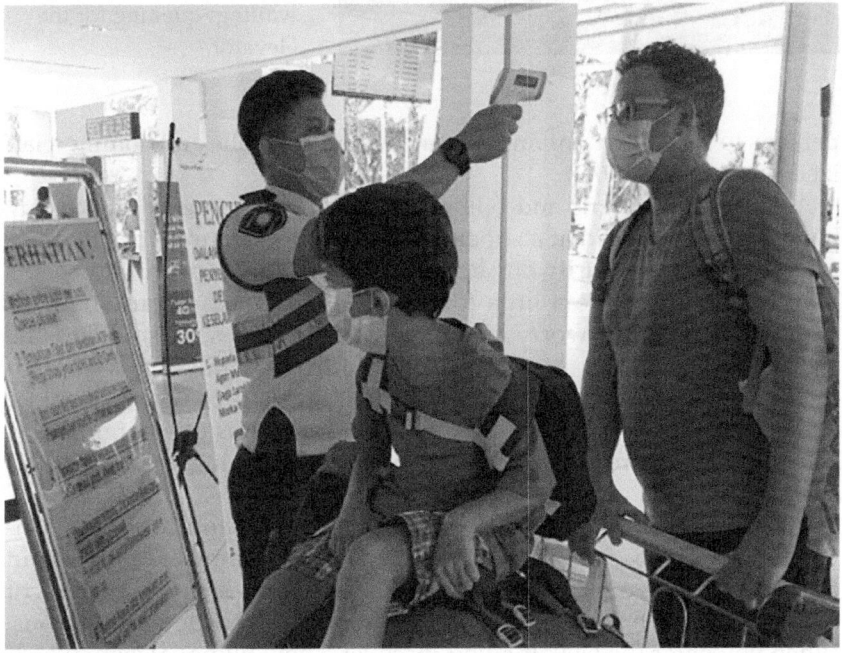

Figure 6.2. Thermo-gun.

Figure 6.3. Poster: "As preventive steps we urge you to take the following four steps: use hand sanitizer once per hour; use non-cash payments; maximum of six persons per elevator; give 1 meter of space if waiting/queuing for the elevator."

persons to behave in unfamiliar ways when in public and commercialized spaces (Figure 6.3).

As advised by signs and billboards (Figure 6.4), you decide to buy hand sanitizing liquid at a supermarket. As you line up to be "thermoscreened" by the security officer, who decides whether your forehead's temperature might be a little too high (in which case you would be denied access), you worry whether the 35 degrees Celsius and the unforgiving sun that accompanied you during your walk through the midday heat might negatively affect the result of your screening. After being denied access, you walk past the dozens of emerging new COVID-19 billboards that suddenly tower over parking lots, parks, and main roads.

After another hour of walking through the hot and busy city centre, you finally reach the hotel that you and your family resorted to in order not to put your host families at a health risk, as well as the risk of social stigma in hosting a foreign family under precarious conditions. When you enter the elevator, you discover a new bilingual sign, which

Figure 6.4. Billboard: "How to prevent COVID-19."

reads, "Social distancing in lift. For social distancing, given the current COVID-19 situation. Please follow this structure when using in groups or sharing with other building occupants" (Figure 6.5).

A little over one week later, as you try to make your way back to the European city you have lived in for the last decade, you see sticky tape glued to a floor at the airport's check-in counter (Figure 6.6). Many more yellow, red, white, dotted, or spotted sticky tapes and barrier ribbons pave your way along your transnational journey back home. They are glued to benches and seats at airports and on buses and trains. Later, you encounter them in grocery stores, malls, sidewalks, playgrounds, or park benches to signify where not to sit, not to stand, and where to stay away. Sticky tapes, barrier bands, billboards, and signs that caution you to adapt your movement across public and commercial spaces appear everywhere.

At your first stopover at a suspiciously deserted international airport, the buses that shuttle you and your family have precisely marked where and how to position your bodies (Figure 6.7).

Inside the overcrowded plane, you see two older men wearing motorcycle helmets: "Against the virus, I won't take it off!" they argue

188 Thomas Stodulka

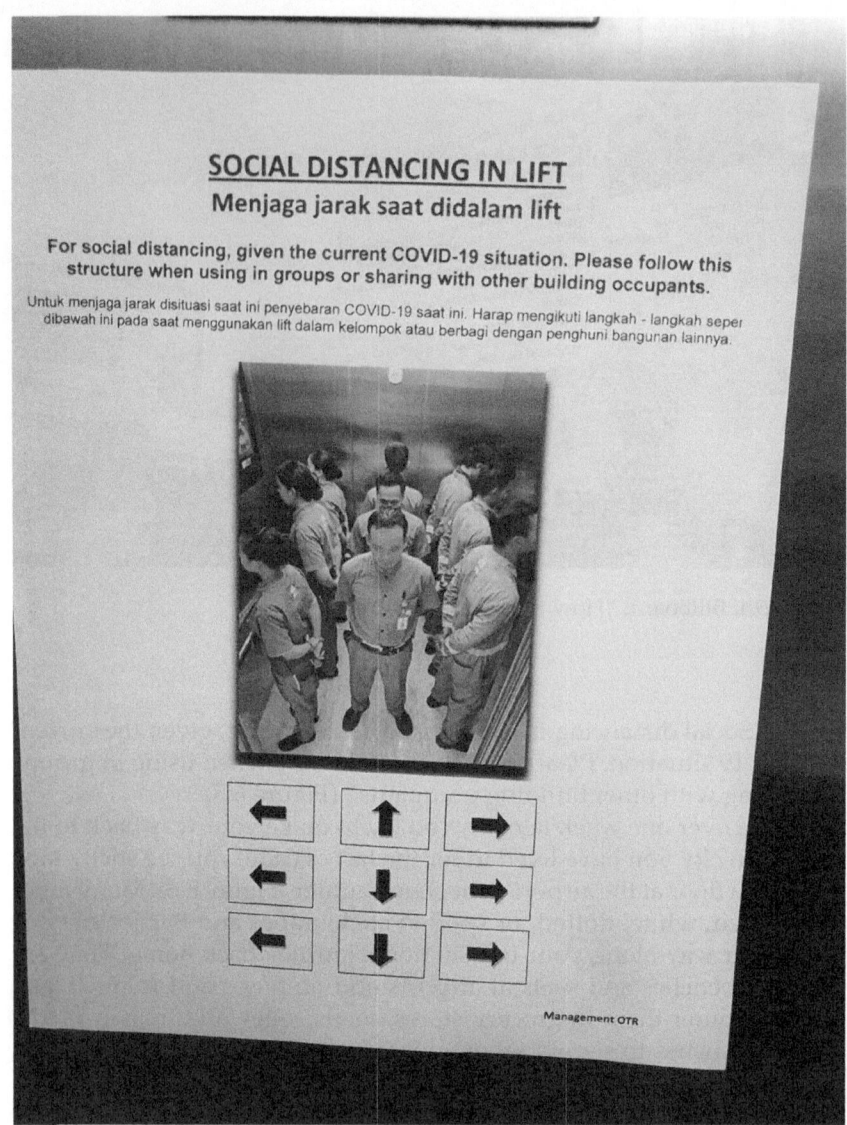

Figure 6.5. Sign in elevator.

Figure 6.6. Sticky tape.

190 Thomas Stodulka

Figure 6.7. Sticky tape.

with the initially polite flight attendant. Upon arrival at the next airport, you walk past half a dozen heat screeners and cameras in all sizes and colours. Next, you notice a virtual human-sized display that tells an animated story on how to behave responsibly and in solidarity with fellow citizens in times the display defines as the "new normal." As you wait to check in your bags, you realize that this series of twenty-five cartoon pictures tells the national secretary of health's story (Figure 6.8). She advises people not to panic-buy masks and hand sanitizers, which have run out of stock, as you discovered on your last visit to the pharmacy (Figure 6.9).

At the next stopover at another international airport nine hours later, you see more signs and displays that promote the "new normal" hygiene rules of wearing masks, washing hands, and keeping distance from others (Figure 6.10). At every other gate, you see tired faces and, in some instances, persons shout and gesture wildly at officers and airport crew in languages you do not understand.

At the next stop, a vacant airport in the country you live in, with no other plane in sight aside from the one you just disembarked, you and your family are held in an overcrowded baggage claim for half an hour (Figure 6.11). Suddenly, you hear a loudspeaker announcement that informs you that there might have been a "corona case" on your plane. The immigration officer tells everybody not to panic because they are not sure yet. Everyone should remain calm while the situation is discussed with the federal secretary of health. Due to the limited space, physical distancing is impossible. The problem is finally resolved through a further announcement that assures everyone at the gate that the authorities were misinformed and that there was no corona case on the plane.

You pass and overstep sticky tape and barrier ribbons on your way to the car rental. This time, they are red and white instead of yellow (Figure 6.12). After driving back to the city where you and your family live for five hours on a deserted four-lane highway, you finally arrive at your rented apartment.

At your home base, you cannot but notice barrier tapes that adorn your whole neighbourhood (Figures 6.13–14). The doors of public swimming pools, schools, and office blocks are covered with bans for the following years, and people wear masks when they traverse crowds and enter restaurants, cafes, or offices.

A few months later, you find yourself at a desk trying to piece together this pandemic journey. How do you make sense of this situation? What do you focus on? What have you documented? In many ways, what

192 Thomas Stodulka

Figure 6.8. Display: "Obviously, I have the better mask!"

Figure 6.9. Display: "There is no need for panic buying."

194 Thomas Stodulka

Figure 6.10. Airport sign.

What Sticks 195

Figure 6.11. Arrival gate at the airport.

Figure 6.12. Barrier tape.

196   Thomas Stodulka

Figure 6.13. Sticky tape.

Figure 6.14. Sticky tape.

stimulated the research notes and recordings made in certain contexts was not an ethnographic puzzling over a situation but rather an affective sense of discomfort, conflict, or disorientation. What might these sticky affects suggest about conditions of crisis?

Readers of this chapter might find their own attention sticking to different aspects of the preceding account, attending to different questions according to their theoretical, topical, or methodological preferences; previous biographic or ethnographic experiences; acquired academic training; and resonant emotions (Okely 2019; Stoller 2019). Additionally, what sticks out in one's mind of this journey may change depending on its proximity to the pandemic. For example, while I wrote parts of this reflection during the height of the pandemic, other parts have come over years of editing, as academic publishing infrastructures can stick oneself to a single essay over years of deliberation. Over the past five years, as the previously described events unfolded and took on new significance, my approach to addressing their significance has been to reflect on what *stuck affectively* over time. Research questions often emerge first and foremost through affect (see Mazzarella, this volume). One senses whether and to what extent persons who share situations, sometimes serendipitously, are affected and concerned by them. Only later can they be narrated and systematized through interweaving concepts and theories (Burawoy 1998), which then come to condition future encounters with affect, sometimes with and sometimes without our conscious awareness. To illustrate the multiple temporalities and epistemics of affect, I return to the earlier journey's first stop at a time when COVID-19 health regimes were about to unfold with global impact. This time, I concern myself less with narration and focus more on the potential of mobilizing affect as a method of ethnographic documentation, collaboration, and theorizing *through* rather than *on* affect.

Affect as Method: Sticky Situations and Affective Scholarship

Through a focus on the affective stickiness of the above journey, I reflect on how banners, signs, provisional notes, and sticky tapes emerged as emoting objects and signals (Newell 2018) that transformed the experience of spaces, persons, and situations. I explore particularly how the emergence of sticky tapes and notes on sidewalks, walls, and windows in shopping centres, airports, cafés, or benches in parks and squares created disquietude, confusion, and suspicion. Through a self-reflexive perspective on these affective residues, I theorize how they manifested differently according to interlocutors' diverse affective positionalities. Finally, I focus on the ensemble of COVID-19-related objects and mediated discourses around *sticky situations*, which I understand as evocative encounters that hint at disrupted flows around contested structures of the everyday, where emotions can run high, and where affect binds persons into shared concerns of attending to and navigating the unknown and the unfamiliar (Ahmed 2004; Stodulka 2015a, 2015b). I elaborate on these sticky situations surrounding signs, billboards, and sticky tapes and understand them as tenacious predicaments that affect persons in sometimes randomly shared situations in a perdurable way. More precisely, I focus on socially and spatially shared situations in encounters with emerging COVID-19-related objects within a global pandemic. This approach allows the ethnographer to situate affect within a nonconventional academic scaffolding, in which "the *situation* allows us to understand how persons and objects that are geographically, socioeconomically, and culturally distributed get caught up in the shared conditions that emerge from the situation" (Zigon 2015, 501). I extend Zigon's structural perspective through the lens of affect and discuss what makes shared situations stick in the experience, attention, and memory of those people serendipitously entangled in temporally fleeting moments. To reveal how transitory affect binds random places, objects, and people into sticky situations, I juxtapose the narrated and observed experiences of diversely positioned persons dwelling in shared moments.

I argue that this affect-oriented approach to ethnography, or what I have elsewhere called "affective scholarship" (Stodulka 2017), can demonstrate how emotional experiences drive sense-making practices of daily encounters. Ethnography, as a resolutely relational, social, and affective practice compared to more analytical approaches to understanding social reality, requires researchers to immerse themselves holistically in life-worlds to comprehend them as fully as possible. As such, the stickiness of affect can serve as a compass pointing to epistemically relevant encounters.

Ethnographers often limit consideration of this affective dimension of their research to the introduction of their ethnographies. They associate affect with questions of positionality and reflexivity and bracket these questions within the opening scene-setting of texts. This standard practice allows researchers to address questions of ethical responsibility without showcasing how positionality conditions the entirety of the ethnographic encounter. In affective scholarship, I argue for expanding these reflections to include emotional reflexivity throughout a text, which can be supported during fieldwork using emotion diaries and later analysed, revisited, and discussed with interlocutors. Such a strategy can reveal how affect-heavy experiences often shape the entirety of the ethnographic encounter and the knowledge constructed within it. By *affects* I refer to somatic experiential phenomena that stick people to each other and to objects, spaces, species, memories, and future imaginations. Such experiences signal the importance of the phenomena at hand while still often leaving to the ethnographer and collaborators the detective work of figuring out the underlying conditions that engendered their emergence. By documenting affective experiences and emotions during fieldwork, the ethnographer can enhance emotional reflexivity as a methodological tool. By then assembling the affective dimensions of fieldwork data – through tools such as emotion diaries and analysing how they relate to traditional forms like field notes, interviews, and focus group discussions – one can work with collaborators to elucidate the ontological conditions of ethnographic data that mutually entangled people in an encounter. Affective scholarship thus highlights the significant role of emotional moments in ethnography, positioning them as "epistemic affects" (Stodulka et al. 2018). Consequently, I advocate for integrating the affects of researchers as a collaborative mode of documenting, reflecting, interpreting, and representing ethnographic experience.

I started documenting the first days of the earlier-described pandemic journey in an *emotion diary*, one of the signature tools of affective scholarship I have been experimenting with in fieldwork with students, colleagues, and interlocutor collaborators. I pursued this associative writing exercise – Virginia Woolf once labelled a similar practice as "letting the pen weep ink," or "stream of consciousness writing" – in response to media reports, online conversations, and encounters under towering public health banners, signs, and objects that stuck with me affectively. I also documented daily walks via photographs and recorded audio snippets. Then, I used these as conversational pathways into online discussions with critical interlocutors over the years. Incorporating interlocutors into not only the practice of data collection but also data analysis is a central component to affective scholarship, enabling a collaborative approach to deciphering how institutions condition people's feelings and behaviour in everyday situations. This attention to affect works as a synecdoche that clusters specific ideas about anthropological practice. As embodied products of ethnographers' interactions, affects may either motivate or discourage further engagement. Moreover, the affect we impart in our encounters with research interlocutors, places, and objects shapes how stories are told and social realities experienced.

Pandemic Flânages under Towering Banners and Billboards

At the onset of the pandemic, the unpredictability of the health consequences of moving with and engaging others in physical space dominated interaction. I decided to keep physical distance, and during walk-alongs, I did not seek to draw out long exchanges and discussions. In other words, I attempted to work through affect as method vis-à-vis limited possibilities of co-presence, constrained on-site mobility, and transient sociality. This was not a major challenge, as an abundance of disruptive and sticky situations emerged while dwelling in the city of Kupang, Nusa Tenggara Timur (NTT), Indonesia, in March 2020, before embarking on a fifty-hour journey across five airports and two continents to Berlin, Germany, where I live.

The provincial capital of NTT is a rapidly growing middle-sized Indonesian port city on Timor Island. In addition to the impressive new and old colonial-style administration buildings, Silvia Tidey (2012) writes that the infrastructure of visible governmentality makes not noticing state orders and images difficult. Kupang is structured along an "axis of harmony" – a city boulevard that runs through the city from the West to the East, where monuments of multi-ethnic and multi-religious symbolism tower over traffic roundabouts. Aside from concrete-structured painted monuments promoting harmony and statues of heroes reminding the younger generations of the struggle for independence against the Dutch colonizers in the 1940s, Kupang's governmentality symbolism comprises gigantic banners (*spanduk*) and billboards (*papan*). Compared to many Javanese cities, where religious, neighbourhood, and civil society movements orchestrated the banners (see Duile and Tamma 2021), Kupang's public symbolism was under the stewardship of the municipal, provincial, and national governments.

When I started focusing on evolving sticky situations on walks through the city, I started considering myself a pandemic flâneur, a methodological figure I had despised in previous fieldwork due to its elitist connotations. Yet the early days of the pandemic fostered a clinging to established and familiar figures to counter my disquietude, confusion, and suspicion. But I kept asking myself whether becoming a flâneur in pandemic times – "an active and intellectual observer driven by curiosity and (who) combines the casual eye of the stroller with the purposeful stare of the detective" (Nas 2012, 432) – was an appropriate methodological figure. But what to do when in-depth and repetitive conversations, sensory walk-alongs (Low 2015), or systematic mind mapping or photo stories (Varvantakis et al. 2019) were obstructed by an atmosphere of anxiety and pandemic rules that restricted familiar movement and sociality in and towards places and persons? Ultimately, I called on the methodological figure's critical engagement with urban spaces (Wolff 1985) and let affect guide my way. Two years later, while working through my emotion diaries and other material, a colleague recommended I consider Jamie Coates's (2017) take on the flâneur, who describes it as "an icon of movement in the city and a methodology for understanding themes of embodiment and the urban" (31). Coates's version offered a more palatable model of the pandemic flâneur: an affected wanderer who engages with the field and takes ethnographers' and others' relational experiences as the drivers of ethnographic data.

In the following, I draw on my jottings and recordings and juxtapose them with the perspectives of two key interlocutors, Sela and Berto. They both shared the pandemic situation in Kupang with me and commented on their experiences of what I considered "sticky situations" through continued online conversations. Then, engaging with the affect of these fieldwork experiences instead of puzzling over them through analytical examination, I consider a series of sticky affective conditions – *disquietude*, *confusion*, and *suspicion* – as three preeminent feelings that entangled me with my interlocutors during the early days and weeks of the pandemic.

Disquietude

Kupang, 21 March 2020. When local newspapers started publishing COVID-19 stories excessively (see Figure 6.1), and embassies and foreign offices ordered foreigners to return home, I jotted the terms *fatigued*, *intimidated*, and *anxious* in my emotion diary. The emotion words were related to incidents and encounters I had witnessed during the day.

The hotel staff asked for our passports and took pictures of all the visas and stamps reaching back as far as 2014. Upon further inquiry, the hotel's managing director commented that the police had recently issued a new order that authorized municipal, immigration, and police authorities to track all visitors' movements. On our way from the reception desk back to our room on the second floor, I ran into a middle-aged man with prayer marks on his forehead, wearing a Javanese *batik koko* shirt. We greeted each other with a smile and polite Indonesian language before he gently took my hand and instructed me politely, "It seems that the burka now seems not such a bad idea all along," pointing to the mask on my face with his left hand. He continued in an authoritative voice, "The al-Quran teaches not to be close with the bodies of the other gender. That comes in handy now." Although he was not wearing a mask, I could not tell whether he was joking. A few hours later, on our sunset walk at the public beach, I realized that keeping physical distance from other strolling couples or groups of friends and family was impossible. Moreover, living up to the recommendations of staying safe and adhering to new physical distancing rules was impossible once we were outside our one-bed hotel room. I jotted in the field diary, "How does all this fit with checking our passports because of 'police orders'?"

Feelings of disquietude peaked a day later. I wrote at length in the emotion diary about how I was harangued by a gang of five youngsters hanging out at the beach. Every time I passed them on my sunrise laps (the beach was very short), they shouted at me in a coarsely loud and derogatory tone, "Where are you from? Corona! Corona! Corona! Go home, whitey!" (Dari mana? Belum pulang? Korona! Korona! Korona! Pulang saja, bule!)

In place of the familiar hospitality, solidarity, and pleasant conversations I had until now experienced in public spaces, I was now called out as a foreigner, a threat. To the privileged ethnographer, these encounters stuck and lingered. I started inquiring into what I perceived as a sticky situation in video conversations with Sela, a thirty-year-old married mother of two children, a Kupang resident, and a collaborator with my wife and me during previous fieldwork. She commented on her own experience with ID-card checks and tense encounters with youngsters in public spaces, which she underscored to have become more frequent since the onset of the pandemic. In response to my framing of these situations as "intimidating" and "anxious," she could not hide a big grin from the phone's camera mediating our conversation. She pointed out that I was just not used to such situations because I am a *bule* (whitey), and people usually treated me respectfully. She mentioned that she "worried" (*khawatir*) about what the pandemic might bring for her, someone who was frequently called out as a refugee due to her background as the daughter of a displaced family who was originally from Timor-Leste. "I fear [*takut*] that I will not be able to find work after Corona because of my refugee identity. We are usually the first to be blamed for whatever goes wrong in this city." When I chatted with our host family one day later, Berto, who was a well-established entrepreneur in his early fifties, said the yelling was just an exception. They "must have been stupid adolescents that might still have been drunk from the night before. Kupang is safe [*aman*]," and I did not have to fear anything when I returned.

Confusion

A few days earlier, when careful flânages through the city still felt appropriate despite globally circulating reports of rising infection rates in

Europe spilling over into Indonesia, I walked to one of Kupang's two malls about four kilometres away. On the way back, I stopped by the city's private hospital and a local newspaper's office and printing workshop, traversing public parks and residential areas along the way. I chose the route because I wanted to continue exploring whether media narratives and an increasing number of COVID-19 billboards conveyed affective traces (Ahmed 2004) in otherwise mundane and familiar flows of life and speech in commercial, public, health care, and residential areas.

The mall opened in 2015 as Indonesia's largest property developer's sixtieth retail and entertainment centre. The property group also owns the neighbouring private hospital, inaugurated only a few months earlier. I reached the mall at its northern entrance, where I encountered a printed note glued to its locked doors (similar to the one in Figure 6.3 earlier): "Announcement. In connection with the increasing spread of the coronavirus (COVID-19), as of 15 March 2020, visitors are asked to enter the mall through the Main Gate (Ground Floor) for sterilization. Thank you. Building Management." I headed onwards to the main gate, located some two hundred metres away. There was an unusual crowd gathering around a security officer guarding the door. Uniformed (mostly) male security officers were a familiar sight at the entrances to official building across Indonesia. Still, pointing a gun-like thermo-screen at every forehead of a person who wanted to access the air-conditioned mall was a new sight (see Figure 6.2). Most persons were denied entrance without the officer checking the gadget. Soon, the "thermo-gun" became a familiar gatekeeping tool that regulated access to the city's commercial and office spaces.

The main gate also exhibited a newly pinned-up poster that requested visitors to adhere to four instructions of conduct inside the mall: "use hand sanitizer once per hour; use cashless payment; a maximum of six persons per elevator; keep 1-metre distance if you are queuing or in the elevator" (Figure 6.3). These orders of appropriate conduct to prevent COVID-19 infection were new to Kupang residents. While wearing masks can be a common sight on motorbike riders due to pollution and exhaust in Indonesian cities, being rejected at the entrance gate was unprecedented. First, there was commotion and disbelief, and nobody seemed to move away, enduring the confusion despite the heat. Then, suddenly, a young woman screamed from the top of her lungs with a loud and shaky voice after she had been denied access: "But there is no corona here!!! There is no corona in Kupang!!" Her loud and angry voice cut through the silence. Exhausted, she had to be supported by four companions, who carried their friend alongside the mall's wall and fanned her with their handbags.

During another video call with Sela, almost three months later, she found the thermo-guns and the new hygiene rules equally "confusing" (*bingung*) but for other reasons. She described the municipal health measures as "hypocritical" (*munafik*) that only catered to the city's elite. In areas outside of malls, cafés, or public parks, where flat-rate and online communication infrastructures were less accessible, staying at home, home-schooling, and self-isolating were neither possible nor socially, culturally, or personally appropriate responses to the emerging crisis. She felt that the marginalization of city areas, which lacked regular access to running water and sewage plants, represented fundamental obstacles to adherence and falling in line with the new orders. "So, if governments expected residents to adopt new habits, then residents might, in return, ask their governments to implement public infrastructures that enable them to engage in sustainable and responsible illness prevention and care, right?" I replied. "Maybe," she responded. After a short pause, she started grinning and added, "But this is not Germany, is it?"

When I related the mall story to our host Berto, the fifty-year-old salesman added that the new coronavirus measures confused everyone. "People here do not understand. Here, the streets, the roundabouts, and the markets are important for business and socializing. Taking away the public space is like taking away our lives!"

Suspicion

I left the scene at the mall timorously and headed to the private hospital, only a few hundred metres away. When I reached the main entrance and registration area, I encountered locked doors and an array of banners outlining the new procedures of registration and administration. To gain admission to the hospital, patients and their accompanying aide (now only one person, which is very unusual in Kupang, where, otherwise, whole families care for ill family or friends and even sleep over at hospitals) had to go through a new screening process in a tent in front of the hospital's side entrance. A giant banner showed the new bureaucratic and hygiene procedures of admittance effective 16 March 2020: "For the sake of mutual safety, we carry out screening with the following stages: (1) Complete the health declaration form; (2) Temperature screening; (3) Form checked by staff; (4) Clean hands." The only clientele gathering in front of the banners was a team of five male nurses. They wore latex gloves and medical masks, but no one else was around. When I tried to approach them, they signalled me with their hands to keep my distance. My half-hearted inquiry to engage in a conversation at a distance and wearing masks while there were no patients yet was greeted with suspicion. "What for?" "For learning," I replied, "to understand how to deal with *korona*." All five heads shook sideways almost synchronously. "Can I take a picture of the public banner?" "What for?" the head nurse responded. "Documentation," I clarified. "Okay, but do not write badly about us! Do not blame us for being incompetent! We are doing the best we can!" one of them shouted at me. Compared to otherwise mundane visits to the hospital during previous fieldwork, this situation felt unfamiliar, uneasy, and emotionally tense.

As he often reiterated, Berto, originally from the Moluccas, stated during another conversation eight months later that the pandemic brought out the worst in people, "especially the doctors. They refuse to nurse *korona* patients that cannot afford to pay." When I asked him whether they might be overburdened and overworked regarding their constant exposure to COVID-19 patients, he underscored that the families suffering from illness and unable to work due to the new restrictions underwent even more demanding challenges. "Tired is not a reason for ignorance" (capek, itu bukan alasannya cuek). Sela, who was usually very critical of governmental practice and policy, conveyed her empathy for the doctors. "Look, what else should they do? They have to turn down patients. The hospitals are overcrowded already." One hour later, when we touched upon the topic of suspicion again, Sela added that *korona* just brought out which persons were selfish, and which were not. "In my neighbourhood, those who were suspicious of us as former refugees are now suspicious of us as potential *korona* hosts. But, on the other hand, the neighbours who engaged with us keep engaging with us, despite the gossip that only foreigners can give you the virus."

Sticking Out Situations

Instead of circling back on established affect and emotion theory to "make sense" of these exchanges, I seek to let the affect of these sticky situations drive the discussion. In other words, I seek to stick with the situation's affects. In doing so, I share two reflections on why I consider affect can constructively guide collaborative fieldwork through a methodological approach that simultaneously serves as a cultural critique.

First, interlocutors effectively question and challenge what sticks for them differently than what might stick for anthropologists. In turn, positioned and self-reflexive affect conversation opens up possibilities of critique for and by interlocutors. This creates an opportunity to upset an overly analytical focus of the anthropologist, who otherwise seeks something conceptually intriguing; instead, something arises that is more affectively salient but no less "critical" theoretically and politically. For example, working through disquietude – a term that conveys my description of sticky situations at the beach and the hotel through the emotion words "fatigued," "intimidated," and "anxious" – by comparing it with Sela's association of ID-card checks that she described as *khawatir* (worry) and *takut* (anxious), exposed my privileged position in times of subjective crisis. The supposedly shared confusion at the mall gates and encounters with clerical men and youngsters provoked Berto to assure me that Kupang was safe and that the assaults were deviant behaviour, irrelevant to local sociality. He extended his concern by comforting me through a rhetoric of care. By contrast, working through "confusion" conversationally, Sela seemed to share the feeling with me (*bingung*) but for other reasons. Whereas Berto explained that the youngsters at the beach were confused, and I felt confused due to unfamiliar modes of being encountered, Sela related her confusion to the government's "hypocrisy" (*munafik*). She engaged our conversation on affect as a critique of the municipal governmentality in times of crises and lack of care for the urban margins. Concerning suspicion, Berto could voice his critique of social and professional elites as "careless" and "ignorant" (*cuek*), and Sela circled back to her routine experiences of ostracism and stigmatization as a "refugee" based on what she encountered as claims of ethnic superiority.

Second, the construction of case studies as an ethnographic representation genre often only materializes from saturated patterns of repetition and frequency over time (Fischer 2018). However, a "case" can also emerge through affective intensity and concern as to whether situations and encounters stick (even if differently) for interlocutors and anthropologists. In other words, it is only with the affective sticking that the case study materializes as a collaborative method of interpretation that is worthwhile for anthropologists and interlocutors to examine through dialogues, conversations, and mutual engagement. Admittedly, Berto and Sela might have stuck with my questions about disquietude, confusion, and suspicion because I asked them about these matters. Yet in comparison, neither Berto nor Sela commented on other vignettes related to hate (*benci*), compassion (*kasihan*), or resignation (*pasrah*); other emotion terms; and affective dimensions that were prominent in my associative writings and that I had invited them to discuss with me.

Prospects: From Theory *on* Affect to Theory *through* Affect

COVID-19 signposting, the sudden appearance of temperature guns, installed hand sanitizer dispensers, face masks, and distance markers glued to floors or chairs to proscribe appropriate body movement created new disruptive orders on how to feel and behave in the early stages of the pandemic. Moreover, fearmongering media discourses and omnipresent emotive rhetoric, such as "be careful not to … ," "stay away from … ," "avoid engaging with … ," or "take care of/not to …" in headlines and on signs, banners, and billboards created "sticky situations" that were remembered somatically as embodied crises. Engaging affect as a method of documentation, conversation, and co-interpretation, I realized that media narratives translated sticky tape and signposts into emotives (performative utterances reflecting a person's inner feeling states; see Reddy 1997) that fostered the emergence of reimagined orders of feeling appropriately towards persons and in public spaces. I suggest that energetic outbursts in otherwise mundane situations can hint at a reshuffling of familiar ways of feeling and navigating through the everyday, contesting previously assumed structures of feelings of belonging. Concerning local mobility and the manoeuvring of public and commercial spaces, emerging pandemic infrastructures reordered some social and cultural practices (Sela's perspective on her confusion that critically questioned municipal governmentality) and reproduced others in a new form (Sela's narrative on disquietude regarding her refugee background or her take on suspicion towards doctors).

In the sticky situations I shared with interlocutors, paying attention to affect as a method of inquiry meant focusing on affective governmentalities via emplacements of signs, tapes, and billboards. Documenting and juxtaposing sticky situations, I learned that my interlocutors' feelings changed significantly vis-à-vis new discursive and material infrastructures. Taking affect as method seriously by registering and discussing sticky situations, I continue to work towards an embodied understanding of encounters that combines infrastructural, social, and imaginary dimensions with personal and intimate modulations of affect. By engaging with affect methodologically, a focus on emerging orders of feeling opens up possibilities for ethnographic uncovering across different spatial, social, and political scales. For example, it might help capture the rather abrupt shift from pre-pandemic to pandemic orders of appropriately acting and feeling in public spaces by zeroing in on emerging COVID-19 media discourses and the emotive resonance of oversized banners. Instead of investing in formulating more theory *on* affect, the practice of sticking with sticky situations suggests how the ethnographer might scale up collaboration *through* affect and bring fieldwork to bear on ongoing political debates on pandemic and crisis management, such as the increased surveillance of public spaces, social media monitoring, and the public disciplining of minorities.

Engaging affect as method – by documenting mutually shared or intersecting emotions, reflecting on them, and discussing them with interlocutors over time – offers ethnographers the chance to epistemically explore their affective positionality in dialogue. Rather than freezing affective experiences from fieldwork in time and treating them as closed chapters, revisiting emotionally charged situations with various interlocutors and examining them in the context of political, social, and biographical developments acknowledges ethnography's unique potential as an open-ended, relational, and processual method of cultural critique.

Taking the affective dimensions of fieldwork seriously – both methodologically and epistemologically – encourages researchers to continually reflect on colonial legacies of privilege as an organizer of ethnographic access, enabler of narrative framing, and often a precondition for publishing in prestigious venues. Understanding affect as method increasingly demands that anthropologists reflect on ways privilege can be decolonized in ethnographic practice in collaboration with interlocutors.

Conclusion

A method that *conceptualizes* ethnographers' affective dispositions can more clearly capture and communicate how positionality conditions fieldwork experiences. But a method that *feels* where the ethnographer's affects stick for various reasons to those of interlocutors can shift ethnography towards a more collaborative endeavour altogether. Combined, these two ways of attuning to feelings in fieldwork open up alternative ways of researching and writing about field relations and facilitate collaborative means of documenting shared emotions and affect that stick in situations, places, and objects. By fully acknowledging affect's relational dimension as affects arise from and shape encounters with interlocutors, I have aimed to highlight affect's methodological and epistemic capacities. Working through affect as a method of documentation and engaging in sticky situations as self-reflexive pathways contributes to collaborative co-theorization. It creates narrative space for interlocutors' critical perspectives on the everyday that can be revisited over time through regular conversations. Juxtaposing associative documentation with retrospective discussions of sticky situations deconstructs and diversifies ethnography's bounded temporalities and positionalities. Writing about interlocutors' affects without making ourselves vulnerable to them risks the reproduction of colonial framings (Veissière 2009) and negates the collaborative dimension of ethnography by putting "them" into emotional hot seats and presenting "researchers" as cool and reasonable, abstracting intellect from affect. But sharing where the researcher's own affects stick in situations, and featuring interlocutors' insight on why, might reveal more collective, equitable, and decolonial methods for navigating crises and undoing the colonial legacies that conditioned their emergence.[1]

NOTE

1 In line with this volume's intentions towards reparative forms of writing, collaboration, and critique, offering an acknowledgment is dear and important to me. I would like to express my deepest gratitude to Daniel White for his insightful guidance throughout this work. I am also immensely thankful to Emma E. Cook and Andrea De Antoni for their invaluable feedback and support. My heartfelt appreciation goes to the anonymized interlocutors of this study, whose voices and experiences have shaped this research in meaningful ways. They prefer to remain anonymized. Special thanks to my wife, Victoria Kumala Sakti, for her unwavering support, and to my son, whose presence brings inspiration and balance to my life, research, and writing. Without these contributions, this chapter would not have been possible.

REFERENCES

Ahmed, Sara. 2004. *The Cultural Politics of Emotion*. New York: Routledge.
Burawoy, Michael. 1998. "The Extended Case Method." *Sociological Theory* 16 (1): 4–33. https://doi.org/10.1111/0735-2751.00040.
Coates, Jamie. 2017. "Key Figure of Mobility: The Flâneur." *Social Anthropology* 25 (1): 28–41. https://doi.org/10.1111/1469-8676.12381.
Duile, Timo, and Sukri Tamma. 2021. "Political Language and Fake News." *Indonesia and the Malay World* 49 (143: 82–105. https://doi.org/10.1080/13639811.2021.1862496.
Faubion, James D., and George E. Marcus, eds. 2009. *Fieldwork: Learning Anthropology's Method in a Time of Transition*. Ithaca: Cornell University Press.
Fischer, Michael M.J. 2018. *Anthropology in the Meantime: Experimental Ethnography, Theory, and Method for the Twenty-First Century*. Durham, NC: Duke University Press.
Günel, Gökçe, Saiba Varma, and Chika Watanabe. 2020. "A Manifesto for Patchwork Ethnography." *Fieldsights*, 9 June. https://culanth.org/fieldsights/a-manifesto-for-patchwork-ethnography.

Jobson, Ryan Cecil. 2020. "The Case for Letting Anthropology Burn: Sociocultural Anthropology in 2019." *American Anthropologist* 122 (2): 259–71. https://doi.org/10.1111/aman.13398.

Low, Kelvin E.Y. 2015. "The Sensuous City: Sensory Methodologies in Urban Ethnographic Research." *Ethnography* 16 (3): 295–312. https://doi.org/10.1177/1466138114552938.

Nas, Peter J.M. 2012. "The Urban Anthropologist as 'Flâneur': The Symbolic Pattern of Indonesian Cities." *Wacana* 14 (2): 429–54. https://doi.org/10.17510/wacana.v14i2.69.

Newell, Sasha. 2018. "The Affectiveness of Symbols: Materiality, Magicality, and the Limits of the Antisemiotic Turn." *Current Anthropology* 59 (1): 1–22. https://doi.org/10.1086/696071.

Okely, Judith. 2019. "Fieldwork Emotions: Embedded Across Cultures, Shared, Repressed, or Subconscious." In *Affective Dimensions of Fieldwork and Ethnography*, edited by Thomas Stodulka, Samia Dinkelaker, and Ferdiansyah Thajib, 325–45. New York: Springer. https://doi.org/10.1007/978-3-030-20831-8_27.

Pillay, Indira. 2021. "Culture, Politics and Being More Equal Than Others in COVID-19: Some Psychological Anthropology Perspectives." *South African Journal of Psychology* 51 (2): 325–35. https://doi.org/10.1177/00812463211012646.

Rappaport, Joanne. 2008. "Beyond Participant Observation: Collaborative Ethnography as Theoretical Innovation." *Collaborative Anthropologies* 1 (1): 1–31. https://doi.org/10.1353/cla.0.0014.

Reddy, William M. 1997. "Against Constructionism: The Historical Ethnography of Emotions." *Current Anthropology* 38 (3): 327–51. https://doi.org/10.1086/204622.

Sluka, Jeffrey A., and Antonius A. Robben. 2012. "Fieldwork in Cultural Anthropology: An Introduction." In *Ethnographic Fieldwork: An Anthropological Reader*, edited by Antonius A. Robben and Jefrey A. Sluka, 1–45. Chichester, UK: Wiley-Blackwell.

Stodulka, Thomas. 2015a. "Emotion Work, Ethnography and Survival Strategies on the Streets of Yogyakarta." *Medical Anthropology* 34 (1): 84–97. https://doi.org/10.1080/01459740.2014.916706.

Stodulka, Thomas. 2015b. "Spheres of Passion: Fieldwork, Ethnography and the Researcher's Emotions." *Curare – Journal for Medical Anthropology* 38 (1 + 2): 103–16.

Stodulka, Thomas. 2017. "Yogyakarta Street Careers: Feelings of Belonging and Dealing with Sticky Stigma." *Antropologia* 4 (2): 145–63. http://dx.doi.org/10.14672/ada20171292%25p.

Stodulka, Thomas. 2021. "Methods and the Construction of Knowledge: Fieldwork and Ethnography." In *The SAGE Handbook for Cultural Anthropology*, edited by Lene Pedersen and Lisa Cliggett, 85–194. Thousand Oaks, CA: Sage.

Stodulka, Thomas, Nasima Selim, and Dominik Mattes. 2018. "Affective Scholarship: Doing Anthropology with Epistemic Affects." *Ethos* 46 (4): 519–36. https://doi.org/10.1111/etho.12219.

Stoller, Paul. 2019. "Afterword: A Return to the Story." In *Affective Dimensions of Fieldwork and Ethnography*, edited by Thomas Stodulka, Samia Dinkelaker, and Ferdiansyah Thajib, 347–52. New York: Springer. https://doi.org/10.1007/978-3-030-20831-8_28.

Thajib, Ferdiansyah, Samia Dinkelaker, and Thomas Stodulka. 2019. "Introduction: Advancing Affective Scholarship." In *Affective Dimensions of Fieldwork and Ethnography*, edited by Thomas Stodulka, Samia Dinkelaker, and Ferdiansyah Thajib, 8–23. New York: Springer. https://doi.org/10.1007/978-3-030-20831-8_2.

Tidey, Sylvia. 2012. "A Divided Provincial Town: The Development from Ethnic to Class Segmentation in Kupang, West Timor." *City & Society* 24 (3): 302–20. https://doi.org/10.1111/ciso.12002.

Varvantakis, Christos, Sevasti-Melissa Nolas, and Vinnarasan Aruldoss. 2019. "Photography, Politics and Childhood: Exploring Children's Multimodal Relations with the Public Sphere." *Visual Studies* 34 (3): 266–80. https://doi.org/10.1080/1472586X.2019.1691049.

Veissière, Samuel P.L. 2009. "Making a Living: The Gringo Ethnographer as Pimp of the Suffering in the Late Capitalist Night." *Cultural Studies ↔ Critical Methodologies* 10 (1): 29–39. https://doi.org/10.1177/1532708609351152.

Wolff, Janet. 1985. "The Invisible Flâneuse. Women and the Literature of Modernity." *Theory, Culture & Society*, 2 (3): 37–46. https://doi.org/10.1177/0263276485002003005.

Zigon, Jarrett. 2015. "What is a Situation? An Assemblic Ethnography of the Drug War." *Cultural Anthropology* 30 (3): 501–24. https://doi.org/10.14506/ca30.3.07.

Commentaries

Commentary 1

Recasting Affect Theory's Genealogies: Centring Feeling with Historicizing Approaches

YAEL NAVARO

How might a commentary on essays engaging with affective practices of critique also perform this kind of critique? Specifically, how might commentary as a practice constructively decolonize certain disciplinary trends in affect theory towards new possibilities and openings for critique?

The concept that runs closest to *affect* is that of *emotion*. Yet affect theory has sometimes carved a space for itself in anthropology and allied disciplines by arguing that affect is different from the emotions, deserving a different conceptual toolbox and methodological framework. The distinction between affect and the emotions that has so centrally marked affect theory in the last two decades can be traced back to one of affect theory's most referenced authors, the philosopher Brian Massumi. Massumi's (1995) article "The Autonomy of Affect" (as well as his book 2002 *Parables for the Virtual*) has been massively referenced as field-defining in the study of affect. "Affect is most often used loosely as a synonym for emotion," writes Massumi (1995). "But ... emotion and affect ... follow different logics and pertain to different orders" (88). And he continues as follows:

> An emotion is a subjective content, the socio-linguistic fixing of the quality of an experience which is from that point onward personal. Emotion is qualified intensity, the conventional, consensual point of insertion of intensity into semantically and semiotically formed progressions, into narrativizable action-reaction circuits, into function and meaning. [Emotion] is intensity [that is] owned and recognized [by someone as theirs]. It is crucial to theorize the difference between affect and emotion. ... Affect is unqualified. As such it is not ownable or recognizable ... (88)

With one gesture (a hugely influential one across the interdisciplinary realms of cultural theory), Massumi associated "the emotions" with the subjective and personal, as well as with meaning and content. In other words, according to Massumi, we talk about *emotions* if we can name a feeling that we experience – for example, as *anger* or *sadness* or *happiness* or *grief* – if we can articulate it, put it into words, tell a story about it, and express it through linguistic forms writ large. Thereby we give meaning to these feelings, and we own them as ours. Following this view, emotions are subjectively recognized feelings that are embedded in language and discourse, and that contribute meaning to social relations. Here Massumi would agree with Catherine Lutz (1988), Lila Abu-Lughod (1986), Fred Myers (1991), Michele Rosaldo (1980), and others in the "anthropology of the emotions" in arguing that the emotions are socially constructed and that they are embedded in language, discourse, and culture (also see Lutz and White 1986; Lutz and Abu-Lughod 1990).

However, Massumi is bent on pointing at something else through the notion of affect: an *intensity*, as he calls it (a key word in his work) that exceeds signification, a rush of feeling that cannot be explained or qualified, placed in a storyline, or packed with meaning. A form of sensation that runs through the body without one being aware of its origin or direction, emerging unexpectedly, and unassimilable into the social, linguistic, or hermeneutic order (Massumi 1995, 88). "For the present purposes, intensity will be equated with affect," writes Massumi. By "intensity," he refers to *emergent* feelings (*emergence* being another favoured term of his) whose social, political, or historical foundations, reference points, or precedents are resistant to explanation or description because they follow a different logical order. Affect, then, in Massumi's rendering, is "inexplicable" (87).

Massumi is a critic of the social constructionism that was ushered in by the linguistic turn in the social sciences and humanities in the 1980s and 1990s. He finds social constructionism deterministic in assuming, from his perspective, that *the social* (or such a thing as *society*) can serve as a primary and underlying context for analysis. He challenges the idea as well, implicit in the linguistic turn, that everything is discursively constituted, that all experience is embedded in discourse. As a critic of the linguistic turn (and of social constructionism), his name has thus been centrally associated with the affective turn that has swept across the social sciences and humanities since the mid-1990s. "Much could be gained by integrating the dimension of intensity into cultural theory," Massumi (1995, 87) writes. So, affect, according to Massumi, is that which exceeds the social, the discursive, and the linguistic, as well as the hermeneutic. It is that which cannot be engulfed or (in his sense) suffocated by social normativities and expectations.

Unlike the *emotions*, which have been studied as repositories of cultural meaning by anthropologists in the 1980s (such as in works by Lutz and Abu-Lughod, as referenced above), affect points at something else that is distinct. Affect is not cultural but is pancultural, according to Massumi. It is not circumscribed, defined, or determined by cultural domains or practices studied by anthropologists as being radically different from one another. Rather than being culturally determined and relative, affect is an intensity that is embodied, in his reading. Affect is a resonance that unexpectedly rushes through one's skin, face, or body, creating a reaction that cannot be explicated, as it exceeds expectations, explanatory frameworks, or forms of making and attributing meaning. The body, here, assumes a central stage in this version of affect theory, in a fashion that may not give sufficient credit to phenomenology, a philosophical school in which the body equally takes centre stage.

A second major influence in a dominant strain of affect theory is the work of the cultural geographer Nigel Thrift, who, following Massumi, is responsible for creating a distinct genealogy for its study. In a widely referenced article entitled "Intensities of Feeling: Towards a Spatial Politics of Affect," Thrift (2004) starts by making a claim: "Cities," he writes, "may be seen as roiling maelstroms of affect. Particular affects such as anger, fear, happiness, and joy are continually on the boil, rising here, subsiding there" (57). Here, Thrift would like to introduce affect as an analytic for the geographical study of cities. He will therefore define this analytic, but he sets out his preconditions from the start, noting that he has "concentrated on current Euro-American societies" only, and that therefore his paper "risks ethnocentrism" (59). Likewise, he notes that his "approach is constrained ... by a specific theoretical background which arises from a particular time in the history of social theory" and that it is "theoretical," not "empirical" (59).

So what is affect according to Nigel Thrift (2004)? Let us proceed step by step through his argument:

1. Affects are embodied. They are feelings or behaviours that are "provided chiefly by bodily states and processes" (60).
2. But the source of affect is "somewhere outside the body" (60). In other words, affects are bodily sensations that respond to stimuli that are external to the body.
3. Affects are "non-representational": this is Thrift's term, by reference to his non-representational theory. In other words, affects are not embedded in discursive modes of representation. This reads similar to Massumi who wanted to delineate affect as a sensation that is not socially constructed. To say that affects are non-representational, as

does Thrift, is to argue that they are extra-discursive, that they have not been construed, represented, or interpreted through language. They are beyond and in excess of modes of representation.
4. Affects are responses to other people's actions; in other words, they are sensorial "reactions" (60) to triggers emerging from other bodies.
5. Drawing on a precedent set by Massumi (1995, 88–9), Thrift also begins to create a genealogy for affect theory that goes back to the work of the Enlightenment philosopher Benedict (Baruch) de Spinoza (Thrift 2004, 61), arguing that the affects are in the order of nature, like storms or floods (62). In a passage from Spinoza's *Ethics*, Thrift finds the earliest formulation of affect theory. Spinoza's term for affect is *affectus* (in Latin), and here is how he defines it: "By affects I understand the modifications of the body by which the power of action of the body is increased or diminished, aided or restrained, and at the same time the idea of these modifications" (Spinoza 1992, def. 3, cited in Thrift 2004, 62). In Spinoza's philosophy, the human being and nature are indivisible; they are one and the same. As a monist philosopher, Spinoza believed "that there was only one substance in the universe, 'God or Nature,' in all its forms, human beings and all other objects could only be modes of this one unfolding substance" (Thrift 2004, 61). The resonances in human beings could then be read in tandem with those in nature (62).
6. This leads Thrift to extend his genealogy for affect theory to the work of twentieth-century philosopher Gilles Deleuze, a follower of Spinoza, who argued that "affects are the non-human becomings of man" (Thrift 2004, 63). Deleuze writes, in a characteristic passage, "A body can be anything; it can be an animal, a body of sounds, a mind or an idea; it can be a linguistic corpus, a social body, a collectivity" (1988, 127–8, cited in Thrift 2004, 63). In Thrift's Deleuzian approach, we can observe a move from humanist to post-humanist philosophy via a theory of affect. By *humanism* in philosophy, we refer to the centring of the "human being" as the core of knowledge production. In turn, post-humanist approaches in philosophy situate "the human" in a field of relations with non-human beings or entities, such as animals, plants, material objects, space, and supernatural forces. Translated into affect theory, this means that the sensation felt by a human body can equally be "felt" by or through a non-human thing, being, or entity.

By creating such a genealogy for affect theory, Thrift has outlined the sources for his theory of affect. This theory resembles in many respects that of Brian Massumi, who, like Thrift, had established Spinoza and Deleuze among his forerunners.

However, if we were to centre the work of Sara Ahmed in affect theory, the genealogies for affect created by Massumi and Thrift would be fundamentally challenged. Ahmed does not accept the distinction between affect and the emotions proposed by Massumi. In a footnote to her article "Collective Feelings, or the Impressions Left by Others," Ahmed (2004) writes:

> I am hence departing from the recent tendency to separate affect and emotion, which is clear in the work of Massumi (2002). For sure the experience of "having" an emotion may be distinct from sensations and impressions, which may burn the skin before any conscious moment of recognition. But this model creates a distinction between conscious recognition [by reference to "the emotions"] and "direct" feeling [by reference to "affect"], which negates how what is not consciously experienced may still be mediated by past experiences. I am suggesting here that even seeming[ly] direct responses actually evoke past histories, and that this process bypasses consciousness, through bodily memories. (39n4)

Ahmed, thus, does not go by or work with the separation between affect and the emotions that has been an "ordering pattern" (or raison d'être) for Massumian affect theory. Instead, she focuses on *the emotions*, referring to them as such.

Three terms need to be highlighted to understand what Ahmed does to affect theory and in critique of it. These are *mediation, history,* and *race*. All three notions are encapsulated in the following quote from Ahmed's (2004) article "Collective Feelings:" "As I show, even the most apparently direct sensations or impressions are mediated, [they] involve traces of past impressions on skin surfaces" (27). To put this in other words, Ahmed argues against the Massumian view that intensities are direct sensations. Instead, she argues that intensities refer to and recall previous sensations. Countering Massumi, Ahmed does not perceive bodily sensations as autonomous. Instead, she notes, through a study of racism, that seemingly "direct sensations" have a history. That those bodily reactions (or affects) refer to previously accumulated sensations, mediated through a history of racism. Ahmed observes that some bodies react to other bodies in different ways, as sedimented through a history of racism that has been affectively ingrained in them.

Mediation, history, and race are thus at the heart of Ahmed's theory of affect, the emotions, and sensations: "I am not saying here that emotions are the same thing as sensations," writes Ahmed (2004), "but that the very intensity of perception often means a slide from one to another, that does not involve a sequence in time. [Here read a direct critique of Massumi:] Hence while sensations and emotions are irreducible, they cannot simply be separated at the level of lived experience" (30). And note the emphasis in what follows, as exemplary of what differentiates Ahmed's work from that of other authors:

> Sensations are mediated, however immediately they seem to impress upon us. Not only how we read such feelings, but also how the feelings feel in the first place may be tied to a past history of readings, in the sense that the process of recognition (of this feeling or that feeling) is bound up with what we already know. Furthermore, to be touched a certain way, or to be moved a certain way by an encounter with an other, may involve a reading, not only of the encounter, but of the other that is encountered as having certain characteristics. (30)

From this perspective, Massumi and Thrift, who would study affects as bodily sensations, approach "the body" ahistorically. Ahmed's theory of the emotions and sensations, which is embodied through and through, in turn approaches embodiment as entirely historicized. In Ahmed's work, bodies sense, react to, and orient themselves vis-à-vis other bodies by reference to a sedimented history of racism. Ahmed refers to "body memories," where even before a sensation between human bodies becomes available to consciousness, a history of racism creates trigger reactions in the form of affect. So, affect in Ahmed's work is a palimpsest of memory: it refers to everything that came before it.

In Ahmed's reading, affect is an archive of past historical occurrences; it is a reservoir of bodily memory. Affects have histories. If affect is an intensity that moves through bodies, then these bodies are located in certain times and places with distinct social relations. If certain sensations get transmitted through inter-corporeal encounters, these sensations are mediations of accumulated histories where some bodies have been marked as different from others through racialized regimes, such as colonialism, slavery, apartheid, and contemporary liberal democracies where structural racisms endure and persist. Therefore, Ahmed (2004) writes:

> How we feel about another – or a group of others – is not simply a matter of individual impressions, or impressions that are created anew in the present. Rather, feelings rehearse associations that are already in place, in the way in which they "read" the proximity of others, at the same time as they establish the "truth" of the reading. The impressions we have of others, and

the impressions left by others are shaped by *histories that stick*, at the same time as they generate the surfaces and boundaries that allow bodies to appear in the present. The impressions left by others should impress us for sure; *it is here, on the skin surface, that histories are made*. (39, emphasis added)

Ahmed's is a thoroughly different theory of affect, then, one that is fundamentally critical of the universalizing tendencies of Massumian genealogies for affect theory.

Like Ahmed, the queer and cultural theorist José Esteban Muñoz (2006) also enters the affect theory field through an intervention about race. He begins by highlighting the way in which "depression" has been coined a pervasive problem under contemporary global capitalism. But he immediately notes that this depiction of depression as the problem of the global citizen smells of crypto-universalism, that this observation "reproduces a default white subject" (675). Muñoz observes that "the topic of depression has not often been discussed in relation to the question of racial formations in critical theory" (675). In turn, he writes of "a depression that is not one," a depression that is experienced differently by some versus others (676). "I am provisionally naming this affective site a feeling of brownness that transmits and is structured through a depressive stance, a kind of feeling down, thus my rhyming title, 'Feeling Brown, Feeling Down'" (676).

Muñoz (2006, 676) situates "the depressive position" in racialized minoritarian experiences. He would like "to address a very particular mode of depression, not depression in its more general or clinical sense." He therefore writes: "Describing the depressive position in relation to what I am calling 'brown feeling' chronicles a certain ethics of the self that is utilized and deployed by people of colour and other minoritarian subjects who don't feel quite right within the protocols of normative affect and comportment" (676). He argues that "[d]epression is not brown, but there are modalities of depression that are quite brown" (680). What Muñoz calls "brown feelings" are constellations of affects and emotions experienced by Latina subjects of the United States whose depression reflects their experiences of exclusion and marginalization in US society. Instructively, he notes, that "affect is not meant to be a simple placeholder for identity in [his] work. Indeed, it is supposed to be something altogether different; it is, instead, supposed to be descriptive of the receptors we use to hear each other and the frequencies on which certain subalterns speak and are heard or, more importantly, felt" (677). To the question posed by cultural theorist Gayatri Chakravorty Spivak, "Can the Subaltern Speak?" Muñoz thus adds the query: "How does the subaltern feel?" (677). His study of "Brown feelings" aims to explore this. By "feeling Brown," he refers to the modalities of affect that are not recognizable or decipherable within a normative ("white") spectrum of feelings. "Brown feelings," in Muñoz's analysis, are not the individuated or particular feelings of specific Latina subjects, but the reflections of a minoritizing politics that has racialized Latinas, thereby evoking situated feelings in them (677). Like Ahmed, Muñoz develops a historically embedded theory of affect that places structural experiences of racism at its heart. Muñoz reads "Brown feelings" against the normative spectrum of white affects. In a mode of affective critique-as-practice in line with many of the interlocutor accounts featured in this volume, his argument can be read as a challenge to Massumian affect theory, one that exhibits its race-blind methodologies and analytics.

If we were to develop a genealogy for theorizing on *affect* and *the emotions* by centring the works of Ahmed and Muñoz, affect would appear not as a bodily sensation that emerges without historical reference or precedent. Instead, we would be able to show how rooted and embedded affect and the emotions are in specific histories of racism and minoritization. Affect, here, is filled with content that is historically resonant and situated.

The chapters and essays in this volume point to ways of doing just this kind of theory work. Most importantly, they do so by drawing not primarily from traditions of disciplinary theory but rather from practices of interlocutors' feelings in ways that often challenge those traditions. In this regard, they open opportunities for ethnographic documentation, critique, and practices of uncovering that hold the potential to further decolonize affect theory.

REFERENCES

Abu-Lughod, Lila. 1986. *Veiled Sentiments: Honor and Poetry in a Bedouin Society*. Berkeley: University of California Press.
Ahmed, Sara. 2004. "Collective Feelings or the Impressions Left by Others." *Theory, Culture & Society* 21 (2): 25–42. https://doi.org/10.1177/0263276404042133.
Lutz, Catherine. 1988. *Unnatural Emotions: Everyday Sentiments on a Micronesian Atoll and Their Challenge to Western Theory*. Chicago: University of Chicago Press.
Lutz, Catherine, and Lila Abu-Lughod, eds. 1990. *Language and the Politics of Emotion*. Cambridge, UK: Cambridge University Press.
Lutz, Catherine, and Geoffrey M. White. 1986. "The Anthropology of Emotions." *Annual Review of Anthropology* 15: 405–36. http://www.jstor.org/stable/2155767.

Massumi, Brian. 1995. "The Autonomy of Affect." *Cultural Critique* 31: 83–109. https://doi.org/10.2307/1354446.

Massumi, Brian. 2002. *Parables for the Virtual: Movement, Affect, Sensation*. Durham, NC: Duke University Press.

Muñoz, José Esteban. 2006. "Feeling Brown, Feeling Down: Latina Affect, the Performativity of Race, and the Depressive Position." *Signs: Journal of Women, Culture and Society* 31: 3. https://doi.org/10.1086/499080.

Myers, Fred. 1991. *Pintupi Country, Pintupi Self: Sentiment, Place, and Politics Among Western Desert Aborigines*. Berkeley, CA: University of California Press.

Rosaldo, Michelle Z. 1980. *Knowledge and Passion:Ilongot Notions of Self and Social Life*. Cambridge, UK: Cambridge University Press.

Spinoza, Baruch de. 1992. *Ethics*. Indianapolis, IN: Hackett.

Thrift, Nigel. 2004. "Intensities of Feeling: Towards a Spatial Politics of Affect." *Geografiska Annaler: Series B, Human Geography* 86 (1): 57–78. https://doi.org/10.1111/j.0435-3684.2004.00154.x.

Commentary 2

Kathleen Stewart Turned Me: Apprehensions of Affect

WILLIAM MAZZARELLA

Kathleen Stewart turned me.

It was the late nineties in Cambridge, Massachusetts; we were sitting in a café. I was living there at the time, teaching, recently returned from the field, writing up my dissertation. Katie was a regular visitor, kind enough to sit down with me several times to hear me talk through my ideas.

The way I remember it, not without embarrassment, is that I talked, and Katie listened. But it was the *way* she listened: actively. I don't remember her specifically agreeing or disagreeing with anything I said. It was more like she punctuated whatever I was saying, sometimes by not saying anything when I expected her to speak.

I came away believing that, however idiosyncratic it might seem, the place I was finding my way into was a place worth being in.

***

Katie shared a couple of readings with me. One was Brian Massumi's now canonical "The Autonomy of Affect." The other seems, looking back, a little more surprising: the last chapter of Slavoj Žižek's *Tarrying with the Negative*, "Enjoy Your Nation as Yourself!," a typically spirited discussion of the perverse enjoyments animating genocide. I understand now that the Massumi and the Žižek would form two parts of a trinity together with a book I had stumbled on, quite accidentally, a few months earlier, Terry Eagleton's *The Ideology of the Aesthetic*.

Uneasy bedfellows: neo-vitalism, Lacanian psychoanalysis, and dialectical critical theory. It shouldn't work.

And yet ... taken together, this troika affirmed my latent sense that there are forces at work, energies if you like, that are anamorphic in relation to projects of power and meaning. Energies that are at once *in* those projects, let's say, and yet not wholly *of* them. Also, energies that might seem strangely disproportionate, intensifications beyond measure that are at the same time a clue that *something decisive is happening here*.

A timely lesson: *what grounds also exceeds; what anchors also unmoors.*

***

To put it in more social theoretical terms: any kind of ideological structure, symbolic order, cultural system, what have you, is both secured and endangered by intensities that one might give names like *affect*, *jouissance*, or *the aesthetic*.

The both/and is the crucial thing. Orders at once secured *and* endangered by these intensities. By the *same* intensities. Mostly people seem to want it to be either/or: either these intensities are what keep us *locked in* – and then the question is *how do we undo them*, can *they be undone*? – or they are what *free us*. Ideological affect *or* freedom affect. As if the bad guys and the good guys sit on separate sides of the room.

***

The affect–jouissance–aesthetics trinity also had something profound to say about subjectivity. Something like the following: the most intimate-feeling thing can also be the most impersonal. Jouissance as the drive that traverses my sense of self, the last thing I let go of, the strangest thing in me, the ex-timate. The aesthetic as the uncanny ground of the subject, the subject that *is* the path that the object carves through it.

***

All the rigid stuff I'd absorbed about what's "in our heads" and what's "in the world," all those divisions that in any case never felt true to experience, started to dissolve. What a tremendous relief to be able to let go of the habits

of thinking that affect is something "psychological,"
of thinking that the "psychological" is something "individual," and
of thinking that the "individual" leaves us with a problem of how to
    "generalize" to the "social."

These late-nineties encounters put me on a path that eventually led me, in 2006, to write an essay called "Affect: What is it Good For?" I had elaborate, loopy notes, but the writing happened very quickly, over a couple of days. As with my book *The Mana of Mass Society* a decade later, it was writing that felt like what it was saying.

In those days, I would spend a lot of time in animated polemical conversations with Deleuzian friends. We were arguing about affect, about emergence, about dialectics.

Back then, I still believed what we're all taught at school: *the better argument will win*. Apparently, I hadn't really learned the affective lesson after all.

***

Over the years it has often happened that a student will enter my office, sit down, and explain that they want to study affect. The problem, they tell me, is that they have no idea where to start. Affect theory is all very well, they say, but what is an anthropologist to *do*?

Where is *affect?*
How do I document it?
How do I know it really happened?
If affect isn't about meaning, then what can I say about it?
What am I supposed to do with it?
Just note down *that it happened?*
Just evoke *it?*
What about analysis?
What about critique?

These are reasonable questions to ask, especially given the training that we anthropologists get. What they have in common is the idea that affect is an object that the researcher, a subject, is supposed to apprehend.

Apprehend. It certainly is an apprehensive business. An apprehensive feeling, but also a sense of being apprehended, arrested by something, right when you thought you were the one reaching, if not grasping.

A feeling, too, maybe not entirely unlike shame: a sudden sense of being seen, exposed, from an unexpected vantage point. And of struggling to recover distance.

Do you work on *x?*
Do you work in *y?*
Do you work with *z?*
No. Not quite.

It's curious, really, that anthropologists should brandish phrases like *discursive regime* and *semiotic ideology* as cheerfully as they once talked about *culture*, as if it were self-evident that these are real things in the world. And at the same time, they have trouble with affect.

After all, is anything more palpable than affect?

Who doesn't know the difference between something that resonates, that has a quality of urgency, absorption, movement, and something that just sits there?

Who doesn't know the difference between being told something and feeling it in the flesh?

Who doesn't know the uncanny sensation of setting out for entirely new horizons and, after many years of walking, meeting yourself coming the other way?

***

You've forgotten what the question was. Yet there's still something that tells you to step this way rather than that. Later, when you have a moment to rest and you look back, you remember the question that got you started. It no longer seems all that pressing, but you also know that you wouldn't be here if you hadn't asked it. Other questions now sit in that same place, not only unbidden but also unrefusable.

***

Unrefusable. And yet also not quite there. Spectral, maybe.

I often advise students to pay attention to the moments in which there is a thickening, a gathering, and yet everything you can point to isn't the thing itself but rather what thickens and gathers around it. These kinds of clusters are also very often repetitive, at once characteristic and uncanny. Places in what someone says or what they have written where something feels oddly disproportionate. Like not only *why are we back here again?* but also *why does this matter so much*, when none of its enumerable contents seem all that significant?

In psychoanalytic language, these would be termed "symptomal points," and they would call for interpretation. The point would not be to disclose a hidden transcript or to reveal a secret backstage. The point would be to figure out why whatever it is wants to take *this* form in *this* situation. And what it is about the social space in which all this is happening that needs this kind of twist or bend in its own fabric?

***

This is always also a question about what it is *in us* that is activated by a particular scene, phrase, gesture, situation. That is why the question of affect is also never only a question of the adequacy of cultural translation: *are we imposing "our" terms on "their" reality?* That question only ever comes up after we are already activated, already resonating.

There's something happening here, and we're already in it.

We've already followed a feeling to this place where the question of affect occurs.

We don't choose projects. Projects choose us.

***

Affect talk infuriates a lot of people; it's diagnostic that way. A lot of affect goes into refusing affect.

There's a gesture, familiar to anthropologists: someone shudders away, piously, from affect talk because, allegedly, it smuggles in new quasi-biological universals.

Or another gesture that's really just a version of the first: complaining that affect talk imposes "Western" assumptions about sense, mind, body, experience, memory, and personhood on situations in which these things are categorized and lived quite differently.

Now obviously no one is going to contest the value of encountering other ways of knowing and being. That's not the problem. The problem is that this ostensibly "ethical" reminder to get our noses out of our own navels is at the same time a defence against the dark arts of self-understanding.

In the (good) name of combatting ethnocentrism, in the splendid opening to worlds imagined otherwise, two things – both of them having to do with affect – are missed.

***

The first thing about affect that's missed:

> how central affect was, variously registered and conceived, to all those "Enlightenment" and "liberal" theories of the subject against whose hegemony anthropology takes up valiant arms in the name of *difference*. Kant's aesthetic faculty, Smith and Hume's sympathy, and so on. All of them extimacies, subject-hauntings. Not to mention all the old ways of thinking resonance, emergence, potentiality, and the general animacy of the cosmos that informed those "Western," "Enlightenment," and "liberal" subject-theories even as they were disavowed as "occult" and "magical."

***

The second thing about affect that is missed:

> the affective grounds of our own research attachments and investments (which is not the same thing as reflecting on one's "positionality"). Like religion in a secular polity, these should be kept out of sight or, at most, relegated to the confessional section of your introductory chapter. Maybe

you can explore them later in one of those reflections-on-fieldwork type memoirs. But in the mainstream of your scholarly work, you're expected at all costs to keep performing the patently absurd fiction that you've chosen your research topic for soberly "scholarly" reasons.

***

The first hint that this is not how it works:

the sober scholarly reasons that you devise for your funding proposals make no difference if they don't pro-voke (call forth) something that is already *alive* somewhere else, for someone else.

To say that there are only ever semiotic ideologies of affect may be adequate at the level of signs. But this doesn't tell us why a topic *feels urgent or transformative* to someone.

***

Affect is a symptom, and it is a portal.

***

Around the time that Katie Stewart sat down with me in that café in Cambridge, she gave a talk at the Harvard Department of Anthropology called "Trauma Time in the US." I had been aware of Katie's writing before that, especially her book *A Space on the Side of the Road*. But there was something quite different about hearing and seeing Katie read her text.

A lot of it had to do with Katie's refusal to ham it up in the usual academic ways. There was no pomposity, no coyness, no playing to the gallery. At a time in my life when it felt desperately important to be noticed, to be liked, to be taken seriously in academic settings, Katie sat there and read her paper as if none of that mattered to her.

Above all, one got the feeling that she couldn't have been less interested in ingratiating herself with the audience. One also caught the discomfort and disgruntlement of some of the senior men in the room. Refusing to feed that machine, Katie opened a space between her text and her audience into which one could choose to lean … and find oneself buffeted by different winds.

***

Affect animates and distends genres. Not least genres of academic performance. Not least the ones that seem to scorn explicit transmissions of affect.

***

During the Q&A, Katie likened her writing and rewriting method to a slow process of combing and recombing, of finding and untangling knots. At the time, I connected this with the superb writerliness of her texts.

Later, having done more writing of my own, I noticed that the image of combing and combing again had changed while I wasn't looking.

Have you ever had the feeling, very late in the process of revising a manuscript, of your text suddenly telling you something that is so basic, so fundamental to the whole project, that you can't believe you hadn't understood it earlier?

Without that long process of combing, without that long sitting with the material, without that refusal to rush to a premature conclusion, even when *almost* every fibre of your being just wants the damn thing to be done with and off your desk … without all that, you would never have grasped this most basic, most fundamental thing about your project.

Because it's not just that you've now looked at your material more closely, more rigorously than you would if you had closed it down earlier. It's also that you've gotten to that point where you've done everything you thought you could with it, you've tied up every loose end, and yet *something still looks back at you* from the page.

Or rather, it's not that it *still* looks back at you. It's *now* looking back at you – but the feeling is that what's looking back is the *ground* of the project, its *foundation*, and that you are capable only now of recognizing and returning that gaze because of a long labour of clearing, of working-through. Of combing.

***

One of the things about the affect–jouissance–aesthetics trinity is that it amounts to a theoretical meditation on the limits of theory. Each of its elements points to the intensities, the repetitions, the investments, the attachments, and the resonances that are *in* theory but not quite *of* theory.

(Bad version: affect theory lapsing into anti-theoretical theoreticism).

***

In any case, people react in different ways. Some want to double down on theory-mastery. Others sense a challenge to language and to writing. They generate texts that refuse the burden of sovereignty, that cling, instead, as closely as possible to the skin of *what happens*. Texts that express the dream of a world that, to paraphrase Walter Benjamin, is *already* theory.

Me, I think we're only just now on the brink of coming to grips with what *interpretation* might mean and might require.

***

It's like wall texts in art museums.

Some years ago, I found myself giggling helplessly at a wall text – I've entirely forgotten what the artwork was – that spoke of the "almost symphonic" quality of the work. *Almost* symphonic? I mean, a metaphor is a metaphor – and this one was already cheesy as hell. But *almost* symphonic? The phrase had a long afterlife as a household catchword.

It's not that, like some purists insist, I should have known to ignore the wall text altogether. That I should have had the fortitude to confront the artwork directly, without the soothing mediation of someone else's words. On the whole, I do agree that it's generally a good thing not to turn to the wall text right away. To resist the scholar's impulse to preframe an encounter linguistically, conceptually.

But as much as there are captions to art, there is also an art to captions.

A good caption interprets – not by explaining or translating, but by feeding and refracting the work. A good caption responds to a work by enlivening its latencies. Not herding them, not containing them, not tying them up in a neat bow. It allows the work to encounter itself and thus become itself in a mirror not of its own making.

Equally the work animates the words, awakens something vegetal in the alphabet, the echo of a childhood primer, where each letter, towering over a landscape, is full to bursting with fruit and foliage.

***

Turning and returning, between work, world, and word.

It still feels like a place worth being in.

REFERENCES

Eagleton, Terry. 1990. *The Ideology of the Aesthetic.* Oxford: Blackwell Publishing.
Massumi, Brian. 2021. "The Autonomy of Affect." In *Parables for the Virtual: Movement, Affect, Sensation,* 25–48. Durham, NC: Duke University Press.
Mazzarella, William. 2009. "Affect: What is it Good For?" In *Enchantments of Modernity: Empire, Nation, Globalization,* edited by Saurabh Dube, 291–309. London: Routledge.

Mazzarella, William. 2017. *The Mana of Mass Society*. Chicago, IL: University of Chicago Press.

Stewart, Kathleen. 1996. *A Space on the Side of the Road*. Princeton, NJ: Princeton University Press.

Žižek, Slavoj. 1993. "Enjoy Your Nation as Yourself." In *Tarrying with the Negative: Kant, Hegel, and the Critique of Ideology*, 200–38. Durham, NC: Duke University Press.

Practices

Practice 1

Haku:[1] Decolonizing Intimacies

JAMAICA HEOLIMELEIKALANI OSORIO

Call to Prayer

If I have *Faith*
it is only because
I know what it means
to stand at the foot of a mountain
my whole body a prayer
the whole island a monument
and to see
the piko
shining through the mist
I still feel her before me
even from hundreds of miles away
any time I have the strength to look to the horizon

If I have *courage*
it is only because
I have watched our moʻolelo remake themselves in my generation

---

1 Haku, "2. *vt.*, To compose, invent, put in order, arrange; to braid, as a lei, or plait, as feathers" (Pukui and Elbert 1986, 50). My composition begins with Call to Prayer, a poem that attempts to capture and portray the experience of standing in the malu of the sacred. Whether that malu is cast by monument, an altar, or a mountain, the poem depicts the kuleana of recognizing our pilina to that which is kapu. The poem travels through the knowledges of faith, courage, devotion, fear, and aloha through the perspective of a Kanaka Maoli wahine who lives in the malu of our kūpuna while continuing to endure the ongoing wake of settler colonialism, displacement, and alienation. I have chosen to leave the ʻŌlelo Hawaiʻi untranslated in my poem, and in parts of my prose as well. For those who would like to seek definitions to these and other Hawaiian terms, see wehewehe.org.

I have seen an island born from pō
from a whisper in the quietest parts of ourselves,
a promise that we refuse to forget or forsake
that this place is ours
only so much as this place is us

And I have held it in my hands,
the birthing of our worlds
Pō, turned light, turned pūko'a, turned slime, turned gods in a time of mere men
I have watched the call of the intrepid summon Manaeakalani
every morning
in the hands of our kua'ana
Maui, fishing us each
one by one from the dark sea of this forgetting

If I have *devotion*
it is only because
I have traveled into the poli of our akua
I have crossed the piko
from Wākea to Wākea
and sailed upon the dark and shining road of kāne
deep into the realm of our ancestors
and I have returned,
with the knowledge that to lay in the bosom of our kūpuna
is to commit yourself to the prayer of memory
to cast your eyes upon Kuaihelani,
and to pull her shimmering body from the skin of the sea

If I have *anger*
it is only because
I know the stories of our loss
ki'i burnt to ash
stones and ko'a removed
now the foundations of Billionaire estates
I am aware
that nearly anywhere we walk
we are trampling upon the 'iwi of our kūpuna

I know the mo'olelo of the hundreds of thousands dead and dying
I have seen the signs of the separating sicknesses
born again, like Haumea, in every Hawaiian generation

I know the names of the thieves
the crooks in finely sewn suits
praying to their capital
as they pillage
and loot our holy cities
leaving us with nothing
but a whisper of what we once believed

And yet I still have *aloha*
but only because
I am still here
with all my kūpuna beside me
and when I stand in your malu
you tower over me, like a recollection
like a mountain
with so many stories I will never know
in languages I will never speak

You are here
and still your kaumaha
is not foreign to me
you feel more family
than stranger
and in your magnificent shadow
I hear our calls to prayer

On 28 March 2015, about a hundred people gathered on Wise Lawn at the University of Hawai'i Mānoa campus for an overnight solidarity vigil in support of kia'i (protectors) taking a stand at the summit of Mauna a Wākea.[1] These kia'i had ascended the mountain to block any further desecration of our sacred 'āina (land/that which feeds). This gathering took place just days before hundreds of kia'i would block the roads accessing the proposed Thirty Meter Telescope (TMT) site,[1] resulting in the arrest of at least thirty-one peaceful demonstrators (Goodyear-Ka'ōpua 2017; Kahea 2022; Kuwada 2015). Two months later, on 24 June, a thousand kia'i would ascend the mountain again to prevent TMT construction crews from reaching the summit of Maunakea, and on that day, twelve kia'i would be arrested and the TMT project would be successfully blocked and put on hold indefinitely.[3]

I was not present at Mauna a Wākea in April or June 2015. However, I was present at the vigil I described above. That evening my father and I sang mele aloha 'āina[4] to serenade our fellow comrades, classmates, and professors. We were there to show our support for the kia'i who so fearlessly put their lives at risk to honour and protect our 'āina. But we were also there to uplift our lāhui (nation/community) in the ways we had been taught. Through the recounting of our epic mo'olelo (stories/narratives/histories) and mele aloha 'āina. That evening our show of solidarity was recognized by the Hawai'i island kia'i who at the time had established a temporary encampment on the Mauna at Hale Pōhaku at approximately 9,300 feet in elevation. When our O'ahu crew spoke to the Kia'i Mauna (protectors of the mountain) on the phone, we listened to their stories. We were hungry and eager to be a part of such fierce resistance and aloha. Before the call concluded we asked one simple and direct question: What can we do to kāko'o (support)?

Their answer is burned into my memory. They asked us to write poems and songs for them and for the Mauna. They asked us to follow in the footsteps of our ancestors, documenting this moment and capturing the power of our resistance the best way we know how: through our creative ingenuity. This may seem like a strange request to those unfamiliar with Kanaka Maoli contemporary activism and its roots in nineteenth-century decolonial and anti-imperial struggle. But it was not at all abnormal to us. In fact, one of the reasons Kānaka are so fiercely confident in our history of resistance is precisely because of our passion for documenting and furthering our activism through mele, poetry, and other creative arts. Mele was used to document and propel movements against the fall of ancient kapu and cultural practices in the early nineteenth century (e.g., "E Manono," *Huapala* 2022). It was later utilized to criticize foreign encroachment in our legislature in the mid-nineteenth century and resist the illegal overthrow of our kingdom in 1893 (e.g., "Mele Aloha Aina [Ai-Pohaku]," Testa 2003, 1). Mele aloha 'āina were composed to show support to Kanaka Maoli royalists in 1895 ("Wilikoki Ke koa Ola Hawai'i," Testa 2003, 8) and fight against annexation to the United States in 1898 (Basham 2007; de Silva 2018; Dudoit 1999; Trask 1999).

These practices were revived publicly in the 1970s when mele and other artistic forms were used to support ongoing movements against Hawaiian dispossession, against the bombing of sacred islands, and for the return of native Hawaiian rights and responsibilities to 'āina (Helm 1977; Johnston 2021; Martin 1974; Osorio 2014). Kānaka Maoli steeped in our history understand that creativity is how our people have always responded to and built power in response to violence against our people and 'āina.

I tell this story here because it is the only way to fully capture what it is we are doing when we invest ourselves in the commitment to our creativity as a significant function of our scholarship and our movement work. By *we*, I mean not just Kānaka Maoli but all Pacific peoples and many of our Indigenous, Black, and other people of colour comrades across occupied Turtle Island. These sentiments for the power of art are shared vibrantly across diverse landscapes, movements, and peoples. From Audrie Lorde's (2007) recognition that "poetry is not a luxury" (36) to Albert Wendt's (1976) insistence that Oceania is at her best when our "imagination [is] in free flight" (71) to Mari Matsuda's (Matsuda and Osorio 2022) direct assertion that "artists and activists are going to have to lead us out of this mess" (177) and Mariame Kaba's (2021) explicit articulation of abolition as an imaginative process (5). One thing is for sure, artists can save the world, perhaps they are the only ones who ever have.

So under these circumstances and with this vibrant and connective history (and future) in mind, what does *affect* mean to the Kanaka Maoli activist, artist, scholar? Plot Twist: I am not sure I can tell you. *Affect* is not a word we use in my community. It is not an ideal we carry close to our hearts. Instead, in my lāhui we value pilina. What others might call *intimacy*, we recognize as an intricate network of relations that bind us in commitment, aloha, and pleasure to each other, our environment, and our ancestors (Osorio 2021). These connections, when revived through creative expression, allow us to feel together our ʻāina, our struggle, and our vision for a better world. That *feeling* and *seeing* together is what makes changing and creating new worlds possible. This is what my kūpuna have always done by prioritizing creativity. This is the movement and work that the poem I have shared with you today joins.

The day after a thousand kiaʻi ascended the Mauna in June 2015, I wrote a poem that attempted to situate this inspiring event within a genealogy of our resistance and activism as Kānaka Maoli (Osorio 2019). The poem is punctuated with moʻolelo, mele, and other works of creativity that propelled these historical movements. That poem I wrote was a gift to the kiaʻi who stood for and with Maunakea before many of us were ready to join them. But that poem also cemented my commitment to stand with those same kiaʻi and with that same Mauna the next time the kāhea (call/invitation) would be called. That commitment would later completely transform the trajectory of my life.[5]

Since this encounter I have written dozens of poems for Maunakea and her kiaʻi. I have lain in her malu (shade/protection), I have chained myself to a cattle guard in an effort to protect her, I have faced the threat of arrest, tear gas, and sound cannons. I confronted these terrors alongside my friends, my students, my mentors, and teachers. We faced them beside our kūpuna and our akua. Mauna a Wākea has grown me into a kiaʻi and an aloha ʻāina in a new and profound way. So I will leave it to someone else to say how these poems and the hundreds of songs and other creative feats composed by our lāhui have changed our home and the world.

Instead, I would like to offer somewhat smaller of an acknowledgment: composing these poems and bearing witness to the creative outpouring of my community (and the communities that support us) has transformed me. From the testimony of strangers, I know that they have changed many others as well. Could there be a better and more sustainable way to change the world? My experience says ʻaʻole (no). We can call this *affect*; we can rename it resonance; we can put it in our own languages and hold it close like the pilina we share between Kānaka and the ʻāina that birthed us. Whatever it is, I am watching it transform my family, my students, my lāhui, and my world every day.

It has been seven years since we sat on that lawn singing songs of revolution, struggle, and love. In that time, I have fallen in and out of love (many times), I have finished my PhD, I have lain in the sacred malu of Mauna a Wākea, I have trained hundreds of people in the principles of non-violent direct action, I have become a professor, and I have become a mother. So much of my life has grown and shifted in the churning heat of this movement. But there is a significant constant that remains in my life. It has been seven years, and I am still writing poems for our Mauna and for the lāhui and movement she birthed. And I can say without reservation that I will continue to do so for the rest of my life.

The poem I have included in this publication is one of the most recent of those compositions. I wrote this poem in an effort to maintain my pilina to an ʻāina that has fed and loved me so deeply. An ʻāina that I am unable to visit regularly. An ʻāina I long for. That is a part of this too; pilina is never finished, and it requires constant investment. Poetry is just one transportive force that allows me to maintain this intimacy from hundreds of miles away. Creativity does this not only in service of my own sense of self but in service to an ongoing collective movement rooted in aloha.

And so I will finish with this manaʻo (thought). This poem and these stories are just a grain of salt that makes up the grand ocean of our world. Let this moʻolelo stand like a mauna and be a portal to those who read it. Let this essay light a creative spark that transports you to understandings that could never be captured by the "sociologists and all the other 'ologists who have plagued Oceania" (Wendt 1976, 72). Let this leo aloha 'āina lead you far off and beyond the "attempt at mundane fact" (Wendt 1976, 72) and towards something richer, sweeter, and greater than you might have ever imagined otherwise.

***

Amama, ua noa.

NOTES

1 To learn more about this ongoing movement to protect Mauna a Wākea and other sacred sites from colonial desecration see: puuhuluhulu.com and Kahea.org.
2 This is the most recent development proposed for Mauna a Wākea. At eighteen stories tall and disturbing over eight acres of pristine landscape within the conservation use district of Maunakea, the TMT would be the "largest development ever proposed in the summit region," and the second-largest telescope in the world, if built (Kahea.org).
3 Following the arrests in June of 2015, public engagement on the issue grew, resulting in more than ten thousand people marching through Waikīkī on Oʻahu to show support for the protection of sacred sites. TMT was then officially stalled due to a number of vacated permits and active court cases. Following a 2018 State Supreme Court ruling allowing for the TMT to proceed, TMT attempted to resume construction again in July 2019. The project failed to proceed (again) in the face of massive front line community engagement and civil disobedience. To learn more, see Puʻuhuluhulu.com and Kahea.org.
4 Hawaiian national songs and songs of love for the land.
5 The next major engagement on the Mauna would commence in the summer of 2019 when kiaʻi would establish a Puʻuhonua (place of refuge) at Puʻuhuluhulu across the street from the Maunakea Access road. The puʻuhonua grew from a couple dozen kiaʻi to thousands in a matter of days. The moment surrounding the protection of Maunakea would grow into the largest political activation in Hawaiʻi since the illegal overthrow of the kingdom in 1893. To learn more, see Puuhonua.com, Goodyear-Kaʻōpua and Mahelona (2019), and Michael Inouye (2019).

REFERENCES

Basham, Leilani. 2007. "I mau ke ea o ka 'aina i ka pono: He puke mele lāhui no ka lāhui Hawaiʻi." PhD diss., University of Hawaiʻi at Mānoa.

de Silva, Kahikina K. 2018. "Iwikuamoʻo o ka lāhui: Nā manaʻo aloha ʻaina i nā mele nahenahe o ka lāhui Hawaiʻi." PhD diss., University of Hawaiʻi at Mānoa.

Dudoit, D. Mahealani. 1999. "Against Extinction: A Legacy of Native Hawaiian Resistance Literature." *Social Process in Hawaii (1979)* 39: 226–48.

Goodyear-Kaʻōpua, Noelani. 2017. "Protectors of the Future, Not Protestors of the Past: Indigenous Pacific Activism and Mauna a Wākea." *The South Atlantic Quarterly* 116 (1): 184–94. https://doi.org/10.1215/00382876-3749603

Goodyear-Kaʻōpua, Noelani, and Yvonne Mahelona. 2019. "Protecting Maunakea is a Mission Grounded in Tradition." *Medium*, 5 September. https://zora.medium.com/protecting-maunakea-is-a-mission-grounded-in-tradition-38a62df57086.

Helm, George. 1977. *The Music of George Helm: A True Hawaiian*. Gold Coin Records.

Huapala: Hawaiian Music and Hula Archives. n.d. Accessed 1 October 2022. www.huapala.org/.

Inouye, Michael, dir. 2019. In Puuhonua Puuhuluhulu. 2019. "Like a Mighty Wave: A Maunakea Film." Posted 9 December. YouTube, video, 15:19. https://www.youtube.com/watch?v=4J3ZCzHMMPQ.

Johnston, Healoha. 2021. "ʻĀina in Contemporary Art of Hawaiʻi." *Pacific Arts* 20 (1): 23–41. https://doi.org/10.5070/PC220153304.

Kaba, Mariame. 2021. *We Do This Til We Free Us: Abolitionist Organizing and Transforming Justice*. Chicago: Haymarket Book.

KAHEA: The Hawaiian Environmental Alliance. n.d. Accessed 1 October 2022. https://kahea.org.

Kuwada, Bryan Kamaoli. 2015. "We Are Not Warriors, We Are a Grove of Trees." *Ke Kaupu Hehi Ale* (blog), 6 July. https://hehiale.com/2015/07/06/we-are-not-warriors-we-are-a-grove-of-trees/.

Lorde, Audrie. 2007. "Poetry is Not a Luxury." In *Sister Outsider: Essays and Speeches*. Revised ed. Berkeley: Crossing Press.

Martin, Liko. 1974. "Nānākuli Blues." In CarmelinLahaina. 2011. "Nankuli Blues Liko Martin." Uploaded 9 February 2011. YouTube, video, 6.10. https://www.youtube.com/watch?v=TUpnpoMPRwU.

Matsuda, Mari, and Jamaica Osorio. 2022. "Art Politics Survival." In *Pacific Century: E Hoʻomau no Moananuiākea*, edited by Melissa Chiu, Miwako Tezuka, and Drew Kahuʻāina Broderick, 177–83. Honolulu Hawaiʻi Contemporary.

Osorio, Jamaica Heolimeleikalani. 2019. "Hawaiʻi Ponoʻī: This is How We Rise." In Kanaeokana. Uploaded 22 July. YouTube, video, 8:09. www.youtube.com/watch?v=RetD5axX40g.

Osorio, Jonathan Kamakawiwoʻole. 2014. "Hawaiian Souls: The Movement to Stop the U.S. Military Bombing of Kahoʻolawe." In *A Nation Rising:*

Hawaiian Movements for Life, Land, and Sovereignty, edited by Goodyear-Kaopua, Noelani, Ikaika Hussey, and Erin Kahunawaikaʻala Wright, 137–60. Durham, NC: Duke University Press.

Osorio, Jonathan Kamakawiwoʻole. 2021. *Remembering Our Intimacies: Moʻolelo, Aloha ʻĀina, and Ea*. Minneapolis: University of Minnesota Press.

Pukui, Mary Kawena, and Samuel H. Elbert. 1986.*Hawaiian Dictionary: Hawaiian-English;English-Hawaiian*. Honolulu: University of Hawaiʻi Press.

Testa, F.J. 2003. *Buke mele lāhui: Book of National Songs*. Honolulu: Hawaiian Historical Society.

Trask, Haunani-Kay. 1999. *From a Native Daughter: Colonialism and Sovereignty in Hawaiʻi*. Revised ed. Honolulu: University of Hawaiʻi Press.

Wendt, Albert. 1976. "Towards a New Oceania." *Mana Review: A South Pacific Journal of Language and Literature* 1 (1): 49–60.

Practice 2

Adaptation: Affect, Happiness, and Sexual Inclusion in *Pride and Protest*

NICHOLE CARELOCK

I am an anthropologist studying humans in enormous techno-social systems like the federal government and Meta. I am also a fiction writer who writes simple characters into complex worlds and subverts canon literature for fun. I take up fiction writing as a practice of racial politics, gender, and affect. In what follows I describe what the romance genre can do in this terrain and then offer an example from my own recently published adaptation of Jane Austen's *Pride and Prejudice*, called *Pride and Protest*.

Happily Ever After

The first rule of Romance Club is that the characters *must* live happily ever after (HEA). The HEA, as it is lovingly abbreviated in romance circles, is a plot requirement and a promise to the reader. Readers invest in the characters with the certainty that they will be made happy through the characters' happiness. It is an emotional insurance policy for an external world that feels short on happiness.

Romance is the juggernaut of contemporary literature, a billion-dollar behemoth that outsells other genres by a significant margin. For the millions of people who buy and read these books (more than 23 per cent of the adult fiction market in the United States in 2024), romance is something else entirely: a chance to play with permutations of happiness.

The romance genre's imperative to be happy reflects Sara Ahmed's (2010) critique of *happycore* affect in *The Promise of Happiness*. Ahmed examines the affective and moral work that the "happiness duty" performs in shaping social expectations. Happiness is promised to those who conform to normative ideals, such as participating in family structures, pursuing certain career paths, or embodying a heteronormative lifestyle. *Pride and Protest*, written under my pen name Nikki Payne, complicates this obligatory happiness narrative by incorporating racialized dynamics that disrupt the presumed universality of the HEA. The novel features protagonists, Liza (a feminist killjoy angry Black woman) and Dorsey (an ungrateful model minority Filipino man), who do not easily fit the traditional moulds of romantic heroes and heroines. Their relationship unfolds against the backdrop of a gentrification battle in Washington, D.C.

Ahmed's happiness duty demands we do the right things, fall in love with the right person, and bliss will follow. Liza's refusal to conform to the "right" ways of being happy marks her as a disruptor of the social order. For Dorsey, happiness is entangled with the expectation that he assimilate and erase himself into a normative model of success. Liza's and Dorsey's trajectory towards HEA, as well as the desire that drives them forward (see the next section), cannot be disentangled from their socio-political struggle. For them, happiness is not just a private emotional state but a public practice of affective labour. This breaks with the traditional romance genre's approach, where happiness is often depicted as a *personal* achievement, separate from collective social conditions.

Sex on the Page

In romance writers' jargon, the phrase "on the page" is deeply connected to the use and visibility of *desire*, particularly of the two or sometimes three protagonists. In the romance reader and writer community, books come with varying levels of sensuality. Some focus on romantic companionship and have no sex scenes at all, while others can have several fairly descriptive and sensual scenes. That continuum is often described as moving from "clean to dirty." Although I do not subscribe to notions of "clean or dirty" with respect to heat levels in romance novels, *on the page* typically indicates high-heat/open-door romance. *Pride and Protest* falls under the high-heat/open-door category: come on in, the desire's fine.

Fiction, especially romance, can rewrite possibilities for affect – for feeling with and towards others with whom we are in and out of communities and their increasingly technologically mediated spaces. Dating apps like Tinder and OKCupid have brought to light entrenched racial hierarchies, where Black women and Asian men often fall outside digitally mainstreamed sexual economies. Tinder data indicate that when it comes to Black women and Asian men, people "swipe left," thereby rejecting them (King 2013; also see Chow and Hu 2013).

Particularly in the US context, Black women and Asian men make up two demographics that have long been stigmatized as "less-than-ideal" sexual and romantic partners. Here, David Eng's (2001) critique that Asian American men are often emasculated – turned into the punchline rather than grappled with as the focal point of desire – resonates loudly. Seemingly personal preferences and choices in modern romance are profoundly shaped by larger social forces. That these groups somehow carry less sexual capital in these digital cultures was a prevailing truth I wanted to challenge in the most analogue way possible: classical literature.

Heroes and heroines in classic novels such as *Pride and Prejudice* are often archetypes of desire. Growing up in the English-language tradition, Jane Austen's Mr Darcy is a prototypical symbol of male desirability, his whiteness bound tightly with wealth, sexual ardency, power, and social status. He and Elizabeth Bennet serve as representative embodiments of emotions like yearning, sympathy, chagrin, and delicacy that not every human *body* is supposedly afforded. In *Pride and Protest*, by contrast, I make Mr Darcy an Asian male and Elizabeth Bennet a Black woman in a practice of reclamation of desirability for those raced and gendered bodies. As scholars like Hortense Spillers (1987) long ago emphasized, desire is not a neutral or purely individual experience but is shaped by racial, social, and historical factors. The Black body is seen through the lens of a history that has already stamped it with meanings both explicit and implicit, which directly informs – and until recently precluded – any genuine reclamation of desirability in romance literature. One thing that adaptive romantic fiction allows me to do is to manipulate desire, to take it away from obvious places such as the wealthy white and place it in unconventional ones, such as a poor Black woman living with her demanding mother.

All this talk of bodies notwithstanding, the romance novel is primarily a vehicle of emotional transposition between private and public spaces. It is one of the few social sites where, through characters, one can safely challenge and form opinions about what is sexy, acceptable, and even unforgivable in a romantic partner. We see this unfolding live in book clubs, in online forums like Goodreads and Reddit, and in Amazon reviews as readers debate, reject, and request new genres' representations, kinks, and scenarios.

A primary battleground for romance readers grappling with complex new modalities is Goodreads. As of 2024, its membership has swelled to over 100 million users. Although there are other reputable reader discussion websites, Goodreads remains the world's most comprehensive repository of self-reported data on reading habits. This makes the site an important resource for observing social trends in romance-novel reading. Is romance the right genre to grapple with complex negotiations over who deserves happiness and which bodies are allowed to claim it? Here lies a challenge: the genre has always promised an HEA. Discomfort comes in the tension between the romance's function as both escapism and a vehicle for conveying, validating, and sometimes standardizing overtly white forms of desire, where personal happiness is closely tethered to socio-economic security. It is one thing for love to conquer all, but can it also dismantle oppressive systems while still fitting comfortably into 350 pages?

Here are two readers with vastly different receptions to *Pride and Protest*. One sees the attention to matters of wealth and class applied to people of colour (POC) as convincing and new. While another reader feels the depiction of wealth cannot come without a more thoughtful critique. This deeper work is often the labour of the POC creators, whose Black or Brown "Mr Darcy" cannot be both innocuously *and* conspicuously wealthy. The respective discussions suggest that readers determine the value of romance as they read and use romance novels to make declarative statements about themselves in socio-political spaces:

> *Carmen:* It's very convincing. Dorsey's CEO position, his effortless wealth, his Tesla, his driver, his casualness with money vs. Liza's outrage, her drive, her pursuit of social justice, her outspoken opinions, her loud, glowing, energized personality. Dorsey is cool and has social anxiety. He feels ostracized in a lot of ways despite his position. With him as a Filipino and her as a Black woman they both experience racism and microaggressions in the book (sometimes even from each other, which is so crazy, I'm so glad Payne wasn't afraid to go there). (Carmen 2022)

By "go there" I can assume that the reader is surprised I have made my main character say and do things that would typically disqualify them from the romance HEA.

While Carmen's critique is favourable, there are also more critical reflections. Notably, many centre on the likeability of the angry Black Heroine and the socio-political ethics of an HEA for a billionaire.

> *Esme:* Critical to this book's flaws is its attempts to make Darcy an *ethical* billionaire. This is, for obvious reasons, impossible, and in attempting to do so the Darcy character is completely fucked. (Esme 2022)

The threads of Goodreads reviews for *Pride and Protest* read like a live negotiation on who deserves to live *happily* and on whose terms.

Traditional anthropological methods like ethnography often function as *display cases* of phenomena, even of embodied phenomena like desire. Novels like *Pride and Protest*, by comparison, attempt to *generate* desire and move readers towards loosening the stays of their *own* mental corsets. In a Black feminist tradition still thoughtfully negotiating pleasure, Black romance novels are countering what Joan Morgan (2015) calls a "mulish inattentiveness to black women's engagements with pleasure and the complex, messy, sticky, and even joyous negotiations of agency and desire that are irrevocably twinned with our pain" (36). Playful, sexy, and at times subversive, romantic literature rarely operates in the realm of logos. But, as it turns out, neither do most humans. What we feel can become our truth. It is in this way that the romance novel not only *comments* on but *creates* personal truth by attaching itself to desire on the page.

Excerpt from *Pride and Protest*

> Scenario: Liza and Dorsey Fitzgerald keep finding themselves thrown together on opposite sides of a gentrification battle in Washington, D.C. Dorsey suggests that they talk about their differences to understand what the other wants. They decide on drinks at an unintentionally charming locale. The underlying subtext of their desire for one another is an unacknowledged problem for both of their causes. This excerpt is from Dorsey's point of view.

***

Dorsey found them a table. The sun was setting and the light at such a slant made little rainbows dance out of Liza's earrings and onto her face. Miles Davis's "My Funny Valentine" played, and this whole evening felt like a woozy dream. He ordered something bland; Liza ordered something on fire. They drank, and no matter where he looked, he crashed into her eyes. Dorsey stuttered out a comment on the architecture, on the weather – anything to keep her eyes on him.

His heart beat unnaturally fast in his chest. It was the same feeling he had when he bombed that board meeting. He was bombing this social interaction. He exhaled.

What if I tried not pretending?

"I didn't want what I just ordered," he blurted out.

Liza nodded as if that was what she expected. "Why did you order it then?"

"I thought that's what I *should* order. My dad always ordered whiskey neat. It just seems like a drink I should like." Dorsey did not know why he was suddenly telling her this.

Liza tapped his forefinger. "What do you *actually* want?"

You, he thought, but dared not say. At least not tonight. So close to the holidays, the loss of his family was most acute. His loft in the city was too cold and empty. But some kinds of honesty were not useful.

"I wanted that drink that was on fire too," Dorsey said instead.

Liza smiled and slid her mug across the table. The sliding sun hit the reddish highlights in her hair, and Dorsey wondered how long she had to sit to get her hair so intricately twisted. He remembered his sister getting braids, and it seemed like an all-day affair.

Liza's eyes found his. "Taste it, then, and order again." The teddy-bear-brown pools were so soft, the heaviness seemed to lift a little from his chest.

He took the mug from her and encircled her entire hand with his in the exchange. She didn't move away. *What the hell kind of parallel world had I walked into?* She didn't pull her hand away and slap him or laugh. He lifted and turned the glass until he saw the rosy half-moons of her lip gloss stained against the rim. He took a sip and squinted.

"A lot of mezcal," he said. "The tequila is cheap." He looked at Liza and she flitted her eyes away. "You're diluting your message by doing this under resourced full court press."

"People like you throw money at a problem and expect it to right itself. But at the heart of that method is a lack of vision. Money can't go anywhere without vision." She took a liberal gulp of his whiskey. "So instead of muting me, you've amplified my message." She looked pleased with herself. "I actually like this better." she tapped the glass with her nail.

"Believe it or not, I'm not *against* your message. I'm against your method. It's *all* vision, all luck, all movement. It's a bull with no cock."

Liza pressed both palms down on the table and tilted her head. "Help me navigate your masculinist analogy. By *no cock*, you mean without …" Liza raised her brow.

Dorsey met her eyes. "Power." He played with the mug in his hand. "Force. Weight." He finished her smoky cocktail and ordered her another whiskey and himself another Mexican sunset *a fuego*. "Let me give you an example. *I* was given this job with no real qualifications or desire to lead the company." He settled into his chair. Liza took long looks at him, and the color rose high on his cheeks. He could get used to her attention.

"Sounds like falling up."

"I know to you that makes me sound like even more of an asshole, but I've never seen myself as CEO of anything. After I joined the Peace Corps, I saw firsthand that clumsy development organizations did very little. Idealism does not work." The waitstaff returned with their drinks but placed the Mexican Sunset in front of Liza and the whiskey neat in front of Dorsey.

When Dorsey moved to switch them, Liza took a small sip of hers, then slid the drink over. He followed suit and took a sip of the whiskey and placed it in front of her. It felt like a kind of truth ritual. The warmth in his chest was definitely just the whiskey.

"You know what works?" he continued. "Money. Cold hard cash changes circumstances – nothing else. My mother's foundation is tied to the strength of Pemberley. I would hate to see that work ruined. It helped me, my brother, and my sister. It can help a thousand more like us if I keep my eye on the prize. Without money, vision is impossible. Thus, my vision has *power* behind it."

"Wow, I got a 'thus' out of you. Well, my vision isn't a bull. It's ... just a nice cow, but it still has power. It's got a womb and udders." Dorsey nearly spit out his drink. "Don't you dare laugh! I mean it. I want to build a coalition and *create* something together with the community – to *nurture* ideas, create a self-sustaining model. Think about how sustainable *your* model is. How long will the board pay for the WCO's [World Children Organization's] *entire* operation? A cow can provide milk to *all the* calves she births. At some point you will have to build and create."

Dorsey nodded. She was half right, he allowed. He had been thinking of how to make WCO independent from Pemberley Development. "I take your point."

"Thusly, you will pack your spaceship back to Philly," Liza added.

Dorsey could not keep the corners of his mouth down all night. A surge of boldness coursed through him. "I want to send you something," he said, holding up his phone.

"Send it." Liza shrugged.

"Um ... on your phone." Dorsey's face burned.

Smooth, Datu. Real smooth.

"Oh." Liza fumbled with her phone. It slipped out of her hand like a bar of soap and landed neatly near his drink. Sounding somehow winded, she recited her number in small, halting syllables.

He sent her the meme of them at Netherfield Court. They had both probably seen it a thousand times, but the scene morphed into the fight scene with Aaliyah and Jet Li, and when Liza unfurled her napkin, the print read **Romeo Must Die**. Dorsey was curious about how she had taken the viral moment and wanted to ease into conversation with her about it.

"Oh my god, people have so much time on their hands! This is good." Liza laughed, a big, gorgeous sound that bubbled up inside him as well.

"It's a deep fake, but the best one I've seen," Dorsey said. They relaxed into a comfortable conversation about being the center of a meme. He told her how it changed people's perception of him at the company. He wasn't overthinking their conversation.

Is she making this easy, or am I trying harder?

REFERENCES

Ahmed, Sara. 2010. *The Promise of Happiness*. Durham, NC: Duke University Press.

Carmen. "Pride and Protest Reviews." *Goodreads*. Accessed 22 December 2022. www.goodreads.com/review/show/5159867324.

Chow, Kat, and Elise Hu. 2013. "Odds Favor White Men, Asian Women on Dating App." *NPR*, 30 November. www.npr.org/sections/codeswitch/2013/11/30/247530095/are-you-interested-dating-odds-favor-white-men-asian-women.

Eng, David L. 2001. *Racial Castration: Managing Masculinity in Asian America*. Durham, NC: Duke University Press.

Esme. "Pride and Protest Reviews." *Goodreads*. Accessed 22 December 2022. www.goodreads.com/review/show/4852144588.

King, Ritchie. 2013. "The Uncomfortable Racial Preferences Revealed by Online Dating." *Quartz*, 20 November. https://qz.com/149342/the-uncomfortable-racial-preferences-revealed-by-online-dating.

Morgan, Joan. 2015. "Why We Get Off: Moving Towards a Black Feminist Politics of Pleasure." *The Black Scholar* 45 (4): 36–46. https://doi.org/10.1080/00064246.2015.1080915.

Spillers, Hortense J. 1987. "Mama's Baby, Papa's Maybe: An American Grammar Book." *Diacritics* 17 (2): 64–81. https://doi.org/10.2307/464747.

Practice 3

Listening: Sonorous Affect

MARIÉ ABE

One

I invite you to practice a sonic meditation with me.

> **Teach Yourself to Fly (1974)**
> **Pauline Oliveros**
> (Dedicated to Amelia Earhart)
>
> Any number of persons sit in a circle facing the center. Illuminate the space with dim blue light. Begin by simply observing your own breathing. Always be an observer. Gradually allow your breathing to become audible. Then gradually introduce your voice. Allow your vocal cords to vibrate in any mode which occurs naturally. Allow the intensity of the vibrations to increase very slowly. Continue as long as possible, naturally, and until all others are quiet, always observing your own breath cycle.
>
> Variation: translate voice to an instrument.
> – from *Sonic Meditations* (Oliveros 1971)

I am an ethnomusicologist and also a musician, improviser, and composer. I often find myself returning to this piece, written by the American composer, accordionist, and improviser Pauline Oliveros (1932–2016). One of the pioneering figures of post-war experimental and electronic music in the 1970s, Oliveros (2005) later developed a practice she called "Deep Listening" – a form of meditation that is intended to "heighten and expand consciousness of sound in as many dimensions of awareness and attentional dynamics as humanly possible" (xxiii). Her sonic compositions like this distil what has been central to my thinking, both as an ethnographer and musician: centring deeply embodied listening to surroundings and oneself as a way of orienting myself in the world.

I recommend you try this piece, preferably with others. Others' vocalized breathing becomes an auditory reference point for one's own awareness and breathing, creating an ongoing play of ricocheting vocables. At the beginning, before anyone in the room introduces pitches to their breath, you become acutely aware of all the sounds in the room, beyond the room, and inside your own body. As others start to hum, sing, or breathe out more audibly, you may become aware of how your listening and your own impulse to make sound are inextricably entangled – and how this dynamic interrelation is constantly shifting, from moment to moment. Remembering the sounds that came before, listening to what is sounding in the moment, and anticipating how your voice might interact with the other sounds in the room and what kinds of soundings your voice might elicit in return, you start to let your vocal cords resonate on every outbreath. As your voice meets with others', the voices gain their own collective momentum. The room resounds with the voices, sometimes getting louder, sometimes softer, sometimes in unison, sometimes with juicy so-called dissonance. There might be moments of surprise, discomfort, or even pleasure. The collection of voices finds its own arc, and gradually, somehow, the group will find an ending as everyone returns to the quiet, one by one. You linger in the quiet for a few seconds, not knowing how much time has passed, before coming back to your body and opening your eyes.

Practising these sonic meditations, I am often reminded of what sound – and listening – affords us. For one, Deep Listening allows us to cultivate the embodied awareness of one's relation to the sounds (and sound makers) in the environment. The practice also requires us to be attentive to the present and the particular, ongoing moment – which is simultaneously dynamic and fleeting. Through listening this way, I'm compelled to *be* relationally to the environment as well as other sound-making actors. To be more precise, the boundary between the built environment and sound-making actors – both human and non-human – dissolves as I listen to myself relationally to the external sounds, even as I simultaneously attune to my own sound and, by extension, the internal self. When I am able to deeply listen this way, all the perceptible and yet-to-be-perceived becomes sensible in their interrelated potentiality. In this light, the awareness I gain through Oliveros's Deep Listening exercises has an echo of a Spinozian formulation of affect as relational and immanent potentiality that exists among entities and actors – the in-between capaciousness to allow for affection and being affected, whether materialized (or audible) or not (Spinoza, 1994). Listening becomes a practice of attunement to sonorous affect.

Two

Such an awareness of the embodied attunement to sonorous affect has made me particularly invested in the ways people hear and listen in my work as an ethnographer. In my research on *chindon-ya*, Japanese sonic advertisement practice on the street, listening was both a subject and a method for my fieldwork. Chindon-ya are troupes of itinerant musicians who publicize their employer's business of the day – often mom-and-pop shops, pachinko slot machine parlours, or sometimes franchise izakaya bars – by strolling through the neighbourhood streets and performing an assortment of music to marshal passersby's attention. In their practice, chindon-ya practitioners strive to cultivate a sensibility I call *imaginative empathy*: the ability to imagine who might be listening (gauging the demographic in each neighbourhood, at a certain time of the day, inside their homes, businesses, or on the street), care about what those listeners' sentiment might be, and instil joy or spirit in them through music, forging interpersonal connections with and among the audience.

Almost every day during fieldwork, I walked along the troupe on their almost daily eight-hour gigs, listening, recording, and talking with them as they discussed what they had heard while playing over drinks afterwards. Later, I listened back to the recordings together with them as they recalled how their careful attunement to the affective, geographical, acoustic, and social dynamics of each location they walk through had informed performative strategies – repertoire, volume, timbre, duration, location – so as to maximize their reach to their potential audience who might be overhearing chindon-ya's sounds. In other words, in my fieldwork, I was listening to the musicians listen – to the way they attune themselves to the affective dynamics of the street through listening and sounding.

One day, towards the end of my eighteen months of fieldwork at the time, I asked Hayashi Kōjirō, the leader of the Osaka-based troupe, what quality or skill might be most valuable for chindon-ya. Without hesitation, he answered: "Definitely the ability to imagine. To imagine the state of mind of people. Inside their heart – of people in front of us, of people inside their houses, or perhaps I might somehow intuitively feel them even though they might not even exist" (Abe 2018, 102).

Revisiting this quote years later, I was struck particularly by the last part: listening to those who might not even exist. When I returned to clarify this, Hayashi shared with me that, sometimes, the imagined audience extends to those who came before us and those who have passed away. Referring to the historical itinerant performances that

Hayashi genealogically traces to be chindon-ya's forebearers, Hayashi folds the Buddhist-inflected vernacular ontology of offering musical sounds to the ancestral spirits into the present-day commercial sounds of chindon-ya. For him, the premodern ontology of sound as an offering to the spirits seamlessly coexists with the ontology of capitalist modernity, which renders their sound as a medium of advertisement for potential customers both indoors and outdoors. Listening to chindon-ya's affective attunement ethnographically, I realized that listening is a practice of affectively being *beside* their imagined listening public, across multiple ontologies (Sedgwick 2003).

Three

But what happens when I listen to not only the way in which multiple ontologies inhere within sound for a listener but also the space between different ontological attunements as multiple listeners encounter one another in sound?

In my current research, in which I explore the affective affinity between Ethiopian and Japanese popular music, I have been exploring what happens when one mishears others' music as one's own or, put another way, one's desire to hear themselves in others' music. In the subcultural scenes of world music aficionados in Japan, it is popularly known that Ethiopian popular music from the 1970s sounds a lot like *enka*, the sentimental popular music from the 1950s' Japan. I've experienced this first-hand performing music with the Boston-based Ethiopian groove collective, Debo Band. When I started playing with them over ten years ago, some songs in the band's repertoire came naturally to my ears and fingers. The similarities to *enka* that I grew up listening to were striking. I was not the only one who heard this resemblance. With a bewildered look on their faces, Japanese friends and family would excitedly express, upon finding out that these recordings were in fact from a far-away region of East Africa, how they could not believe these tunes were *not* Japanese. Conversely, when I shared Japanese tunes with our Ethiopian musical collaborators on tour, they would be bemused and start humming along, similarly struck by the seeming similarities.

Initial archival research and fieldwork in Addis Ababa in the spring of 2019 revealed unlikely historical connections that may have created the conditions of possibility for such musical affinities. My work of sifting through the audible traces of sedimented histories and the complex dynamics of mimesis and colonial desires remains. But I am less interested in the explanatory logic for such musical affinity. Rather, beyond, or perhaps beneath, the stylistic musical commonalities and the history of contact, I am taken by the sense of surprise, disorientation, and a palpable sense of pleasure that I observe in the moment of mishearing. I'm interested in the generativity of such moments – a kind of listening that taps into partially, if unknowingly, shared affective archives of sound and compels us to confront uncanny connections.

As I explore the potentialities of sound to confuse, allure, and connect through imagined affinities across difference, I have started to not only listen to those who hear themselves in others but also to make music with them as a way of participating in their work of worlding – of sounding out the otherwise. My musician friends in Osaka and Kyoto, Japan, with whom I have collaborated over the past twenty years, were tickled by the recordings of some of the Ethiopian music and stories I have shared from my fieldwork in Ethiopia. Fascinated and inspired by the immediacy of the sounds they recognized at once as familiar and foreign, some of them suggested we start a band called Ethiopiasia together.

Despite the initial uneasiness on my end, this band became an experimental ethnographic practice of what I call the *poetics of mishearing*.[1] We take a variety of approaches to making audible our affective responses to the misheard moments and positing them as resources for reflexive critique. In one song, the singer simply phonetically enunciates what she hears in Amharic lyrics, rendering it into pidgin-language-sounding Japanese, simultaneously embodying the familiar and the limits of intelligibility. In another, we mash up a Japanese folkloric song with the Ethiopian popular songs of the 1970s. The groove of the original Ethiopian song is elusive to the Japanese musicians; this new sensory orientation to time, rhythm, and pitch is at once familiar and disorienting. After struggling to embody the challenging groove, we arranged the song so that we oscillate between our best approximation of the Ethiopian groove and a familiar Japanese folk rhythm, elucidating the slippage, the in-between, the difference in similarity. In yet another, the singer wrote new Japanese lyrics based on the sounded qualities of the Amharic lyrics, attempting to capture the imagined sensibilities of the song – unabashedly embracing the difference as well as the generativity of the poetics of mishearing. Taken together, these playful, at times humorous, and yet earnestly self-reflexive approaches of the band members amounted to a creative exploration of what emerges from the affective responses to one's mishearing, hearing ourselves in others, and confronting the limitations of mimesis.

To the extent that the aesthetics can be understood as the distribution of the sensible (Rancière 2004), playing (with) the misheard is a provisional and creative process of reorientating our senses – a generative act of carving out a path in the fascia that connects multiple ontologies, of making resemblances and resonation real (Lepselter 2016). In this way, playing music with these musicians has given me an insight into the simultaneously reflective and refractive process of contending with multiple ontologies and histories through the misheard. Playing across difference with a kind of what Melody Jue (2020) calls "epistemic humility" holds multiple and open-ended ways of knowing, sensing, and being in the world. Sounding alongside listening (or mishearing in this case) can offer us an invitation to think through imagination, juxtaposition, and open-endedness that allows for momentary worlding of the otherwise.

Coda

Understanding sound as intrinsically and sometimes uncontrollably affective in its material, social, and vibrational potentiality, the co-constitutive practice of listening and sounding – both inherently embodied and situated – can be an ethnographic method of holding, playing with, and reorienting ourselves among multiple ontologies. Sound, necessarily fleeting and provisional, nonetheless allows us to imagine ourselves in relation to others and the environment differently, and to embody, through our sensory experiences, yet-to-be-imagined possibilities that might help us disconnect from those adopted analytical habits that prevent us from connecting more intimately with others. Deep Listening to sonorous affect is a simultaneously attentive, observant, relational, imaginative, collaborative, and creative practice that informs my ethnographic every day. So I try to listen, deeply.

NOTE

1 I want to acknowledge my fellow traveler in mishearing and ethnomusicologist Emily Wang's (2018) work on mishearing in the queer Sinophone diaspora in Canada, which offers a generative insight into linguistic mishearing as a creative practice of living/being the otherwise.

REFERENCES

Abe, Marié. 2018. *Resonances of Chindon-ya: Sounding Space and Sociality in Contemporary Japan*. Middletown, CT: Wesleyan University Press.
Jue, Melody. 2020. *Wild Blue Media: Thinking Through Seawater*. Durham, NC: Duke University Press.

Lepselter, Susan. 2016. *The Resonance of Unseen Things: Poetics, Power, Captivity, and UFOs in the American Uncanny.* Ann Arbor: University of Michigan Press.
Oliveros, Pauline. 1971. *Sonic Meditations: March-November 1971.* Urbana, IL: Smith Publications.
Oliveros, Pauline. 2005. *Deep Listening: A Composer's Sound Practice.* Bloomington, IN: iUniverse.
Rancière, Jacques. 2004. *The Politics of Aesthetics: The Distribution of the Sensible.* New York: Continuum. Selected Chapters.
Sedgwick, Eve Kosofsky. 2003. *Touching Feeling: Affect, Pedagogy, Performativity.* Durham, NC: Duke University Press.
Spinoza, Benedictus de 1994. "Of the Origin and Nature of the Affects." In *The Spinoza Reader: The Ethics and Other Works,* edited and translated by Edwin Curley, 152–197. Princeton, NJ: Princeton University Press.
Wang, Emily Yun. 2018. "Sung and Spoken Puns as Queer 'Home Making' in Toronto's Chinese Diaspora." *Women and Music* 22: 50–62. https://doi.org/10.1353/wam.2018.0005.

Practice 4

Meditating: Attention to Affect

JOANNA COOK

Embodied experience is central to much anthropological research. The methodological bread and butter of participant observation requires anthropologists to "be there," living alongside the people with whom they work. It is also expected that anthropologists will be personally transformed in some way through the process of fieldwork. Indeed, imagining how this could not be the case, given the long-term immersive nature of ethnographic work, is difficult. My own research on meditation has been heavily participant, and I have taken a committedly practice-based approach, meditating with the people with whom I work over several years of fieldwork.

In what follows, I examine the affective dimensions of meditation practices in two places where I have conducted long-term research: a meditation monastery in northern Thailand and among mindfulness practitioners in the United Kingdom. In both contexts, practitioners engage with meditation as a means of affective transformation. As I show, however, this takes very different forms and has different meanings in each context. *Affect* in the research is not so much distilled in the data I collected but rather emerges through fieldwork encounters, interpersonal engagements, and methodological practice. In this short essay, I ask, If meditation is a means of affective transformation for so many of my interlocutors, how might it also be applied as an ethnographic method for understanding their experiences?

Monastic Thailand and Mindful Britain

In describing meditation as practice, I draw on two contexts that are seemingly completely different: a Buddhist monastery in northern Thailand and therapeutic mindfulness in secular society in the

United Kingdom.[1] I have spent years conducting participant observation in both, and in each of them, fieldwork has been characterized by countless hours of shared meditative practices. However, the form that practice took and its affective character differed markedly. Monastics in the monastery in Thailand have renounced the world. They live – as did I when I lived among them – in a monastic community organized around meditation, and they commit themselves to a life of daily meditation practice, punctuated by periods of extended intensive meditative discipline. Retreating to a private room (or *kuti*), sleeping a maximum of four hours a night and meditating alone for roughly eighteen hours a day, a meditation retreat for the monastics with whom I worked (and laypeople who attend the monastery) is characterized by herculean levels of self-discipline. It is through this ongoing ascetic control that they cultivate experiential insight into the religious tenets of impermanence, suffering, and non-self at the heart of Thai Buddhism.

Comparatively, for the British mindfulness practitioners with whom I work, daily meditation practice is relatively brief (typically about forty-five minutes of formal sitting meditation a day), and it is intentionally incorporated into the dynamics of workday lives. While some practitioners may regularly attend retreats, for the majority, meditation is not characterized by retreat from the world but rather by a heightened engagement with it. Practitioners sit for meditation practice, often on a daily basis, and they bring mindful awareness to routine or habitual activities to address the prosaic stresses of family dynamics, mental health, and work stress. They describe this as simultaneously a pragmatic support for their mental health and an ethical practice that enables them to live more fully.

How might the affective experiences of meditation reshape anthropological research about meditation? To consider this, I first provide two methodological descriptions of meditative practice, drawing from transcripts: the first from a Thai monastery (walking and sitting) and the second from secular Britain (mindfulness of breath and mind-wandering). I then draw out the affective dimensions of practice and the value of emotional experience in these two contexts. Integrating affective experiences with the dimensions of intention and emotion with which they are intimately connected reveals that meditation practice is necessarily located in broader ethical and ontological understandings of emotion and what it is to be human (see also Cook and Cassaniti 2022). I conclude by returning to meditation as an anthropological method and the affective insights of practice.

Vipassanā Meditation Instruction: Walking and Sitting in a Thai Monastery

Before walking, the meditator stands with her feet parallel, the hands clasped in front or behind with the right on top of the left. The head is straight, and the eyes look at a point on the floor about a metre away. She mentally notes "standing, standing, standing" while being aware of the standing posture. The walking meditation builds up from a basic step (for which the meditator acknowledges "right/left goes thus") to a complicated six-step movement (for which the meditator mentally notes "heel up – lifting – moving – lowering – touching – pressing"). The meditator walks slowly for a distance of a few metres, stops, and turns using the same process of mental noting, mentally repeating each part of the turn three times ("stopping, stopping, stopping, standing, standing, standing, intending to turn, intending to turn, intending to turn, turning, turning, turning, standing, standing, standing, intending to walk, intending to walk, intending to walk").

For sitting meditation, a traditional cross-legged sitting posture is adopted; the torso ought to be straight, and the eyes closed. The right hand rests on the left with the tips of both thumbs touching and the two hands resting in the lap. The meditator focuses on the breath as it is manifest in the movement of the abdomen. As the abdomen swells during inhalation the meditator mentally labels the movement "rising"; as it recedes with exhalation the meditator labels this "falling." Any distraction from the focus on the abdomen is mentally labelled three times (e.g., "thinking, thinking, thinking") and the attention is returned to the breath.

The walking and sitting meditations become more complex over time until the meditator is doing six-step walking meditation and acknowledging and mentally labelling the rise and fall of the abdomen followed by the "sitting" of the whole body and "touching," for which the meditator focuses on one of twenty-eight specified areas of the body, each approximately the size of a coin, in sequence. This focus on "touching" may or may not result in different sensations in the area being focused on, such as the area feeling warm or painful. There are twenty-eight touching points followed in sequence, given in fourteen pairs. ... Each pair of points is associated with a different mental condition. For example, it is expected that when a meditator is using only the first ten points (to the top of the feet) they feel restless and will want to run away. The effect of the complete sequence, including the front and back cross, is to give the meditator a sense of wholeness and equanimity. ... The meditation teacher encourages the student not to become involved in thoughts or physical or emotional sensations but rather to note mentally their occurrence and maintain a continuous meditative focus (e.g., in walking meditation the focus is the feet, and in sitting meditation the focus is the abdomen, the whole body, and the successive points on the body). This can be an exhausting process for those new to meditation. Often, sitting without moving is physically painful and may give rise to strong emotional states. For both new students and seasoned practitioners, the first few days of a meditation retreat are often very hard, and there is a strong urge to give up. Eventually the mind settles down, and it becomes easier to remain focused. (Cook 2010a, 75–9).

Mindfulness of Breathing and Mind-Wandering in Britain

1. Bring your awareness to the breath as it moves in and out of the body at the abdomen. Notice the changing patterns of physical sensations in this region of the body as the breath moves in and out. It may help to place your hand here for a few breaths and feel the abdomen rising and falling.
2. You may notice mild sensations of stretching as the abdomen gently rises with each in-breath, and different sensations as the abdomen falls with each out-breath.
3. As best you can, follow closely with your attention, so you notice the changing physical sensations for the full duration of each in-breath and the full duration of each out-breath, perhaps noticing the slight pauses between one in-breath and the following out-breath and between one out-breath and the following in-breath.

There is no need to try to control your breathing in any way at all – simply let the breath breathe itself.

Sooner or later (usually sooner), your attention will wander away from the breath. You may find thoughts, images, plans, or daydreams coming up. Such mind-wandering is not a mistake. It is simply what minds do. When you notice that your awareness is no longer on the breath, you might congratulate yourself. You have already "woken up" enough to know it and are once more aware of your experience in this moment. Simply acknowledge where the mind had wandered to. Then gently escort your attention back to the sensations in your abdomen.

The mind will likely wander over and over again, so each time, remember that the aim is simply to note where the mind has been, then gently escort your attention back to the breath. This can be very difficult, as you may find it frustrating that the mind seems so disobedient! Such frustration can create a lot of extra noise in the mind. So no matter how many times your mind wanders, allow yourself on each occasion (without limit) to cultivate compassion for your mind as you bring it back to where you had intended it to be.

See if it is possible to view the repeated wanderings of the mind as opportunities to nurture greater patience within yourself. In time, you may discover that this quality of kindliness towards the wandering mind brings a sense of compassion towards other aspects of your experience – that the wandering mind has been a great ally in your practice, and not the enemy you supposed it to be. (Penman 2011)

Non-Self and Friendly Curiosity

Practice-based affective modes of doing fieldwork revealed ethnographic insight into the cultural value of emotion for my interlocutors. The central tenet of vipassanā in the monastery is to experience, rather than just to know, that no "self" exists. The body is broken down into its constituent parts, the feelings are isolated and examined apart from their causes, bodily desire is subdued, and the mind is quieted. The practitioner uses the process of mental noting to observe and detach from the normal processes of the body and mind, such as grief, sleep, pain, doubt, restlessness, or desire. To do this, seeing all mental and physical phenomena as impermanent is necessary, responding to them with neither desire nor aversion but rather developing a position of equanimity and balance. By observing the conditions of the body and the mind (both of which are ethnographically relevant concepts), the practitioner detaches themselves from their involvement with these conditions sufficiently to be able to *look at* them rather than *look through* them. The practitioner is no longer exclusively identified with them, and this creates a psychological "space" or perspective from which change is effected.

The emotions and the body take on specific and important meanings in this practice in the monastery. All bodily sensations and emotions, whether positive or negative, are to be observed and detached from. "Good" feelings or emotions are thought to be as problematic as "bad," for although the practitioner may believe themselves to be happy or unhappy, this feeling is produced by a deluded sense of self and permanence. Through the practice of vipassanā meditation and the cultivation of mindfulness in daily life, monastics aim to reduce their emotionality and maintain a "cool heart" (*jai yen*; see Cook 2010a; Cassaniti 2015). One of the primary characteristics of the Buddha and arahants to which monastics aspire is their equanimity. Thus, both positive and negative emotional states are understood to be the result of a deluded sense of self. Through the development of "mindful awareness" (*sati*), the practitioner gains insight into non-self and all emotional experience is reduced until, ideally, it is eliminated entirely.

Similarly, mindfulness in Britain is premised on developing the capacity to witness thoughts from a de-centred perspective and thereby unsettle the authority they have on reality. The mindfulness practitioner learns to perceive thoughts as "passing events in the mind." Through ongoing training, she learns to separate herself from the content of the thought in order that she may witness it *as* a thought. But emotions play a very different role in this context. For mindfulness practitioners in Britain, mindfulness is significantly associated with mental health and well-being. Through daily practice, practitioners seek to live well in the midst of family conflicts, work stress, and the daily ups and downs of life. As seen in the meditation instructions above, learning to witness thoughts and return the focus of awareness to the object of meditation (e.g., the breath), is an important part of mindfulness training. But on its own, this might be a little dry. If you're struggling with your mental health, the voice inside your head is rarely a friendly or supportive one. Guided mindfulness practices, such as the ones mentioned above, aim at both the cultivation of metacognitive awareness (learning to relate to thoughts in a particular way), and the generation of an affective shift in the way in which the practitioner relates to themselves.

Quite consciously, mindfulness practitioners cultivate an attitude of "friendly curiosity" in the way that they relate to themselves. The invitational language of the guidance ("as best you can," "congratulating yourself," "gently escort your attention," "cultivate compassion for your mind," "nurture greater patience for yourself"), and this affective quality of kindliness are significant supports for mental health. This presents an interesting comparison with monastic practice: in the monastery all emotions are to be acknowledged equally as insight into impermanence, suffering, and non-self deepens; in therapeutic mindfulness, feelings of self-compassion and kindliness are actively nurtured as an antidote to ruminative and negative thinking patterns and as a support for positive mental health.

Meditation as Affective Ethnographic Practice

How might meditative experiences like those described above, sometimes transporting someone well beyond and below analytical frames of analysis, inform ethnographic research? Doing meditation research in monastic Thailand and mindful Britain meant committing myself to the practices and projects of the people with whom I worked. Hundreds of hours of meditation informed what I learned in both contexts. This was affective and affecting work, which had a profound impact on my sense of self and what my body learned in the field.

In the meditation monastery, I took ordination as a *mae chee* (lay Buddhist nun). I shaved my head and eyebrows, observed monastic precepts for behaviour, and strove to maintain mindful awareness in the performance of my monastic duties. With the support of the *sangha* (community of renouncers) I sought experiential insight into Buddhist tenets through the careful observation of my affective responses and the discipline of meditation (see Cook 2010b). As exemplars of renunciation, monastics have a duty to perform an example of bodily and emotional control for the laity. As a young exuberant nun, I found myself gently guided by my seniors to regulate my emotions and control my comportment. I learned not to express pleasure or displeasure in front of the laity through the affective intimacy and example of the renunciates around me. Receiving alms food from the laity was a case in point. No matter how delicious the food in front of us was, and no matter how much pleasure it generated, we remained externally equanimous. While this practice modelled non-self and facilitated merit making for our benefactors, among renunciates this shared discipline generated a powerful affective resonance, a charged atmosphere of connection that at times bordered on awe.

In my work on mindfulness and mental health in Britain, the work of cultivating a kindly relationship towards oneself promoted in therapeutic interventions, therapist training programs, and advocacy in Westminster was a central focus of the meditation practices that I shared with others (see Cook 2023). This quality of self-compassion extended through fieldwork and my own relationship to mental health. For example, training as a mindfulness-based cognitive therapist entailed my commitment to the affective qualities of being that therapists seek to model for participants. As experiences of doubt or insecurity arose in group-based training, we sought to relate to them with kindliness. Here, our vulnerability resonated around the group in affectively charged atmospheres that were at times deeply unsettling, at other times deeply supportive. Through this process, trainee therapists became familiar with the affective terrain that would soon characterize and condition relationships with therapeutic participants. For me, it contributed to a gentler way of relating to my "emotional landscape" and a deep respect for the affective subtlety of being in relationship with others. Methodologically, then, affect engendered through meditation was central to connecting with a new sense of self for both myself and others. Affective transformations became simultaneously the means and data of fieldwork, and the substance of personal and transpersonal experience.

My own meditation practices within these two contexts drew out different affective qualities. In the monastery, I cultivated a commitment to discipline with other monastics in the generation of insight into nonself. And I experienced private retreat and shared ritual practice as sites for the progressive development of Buddhist virtues of equanimity, patience, and detachment. In the context of the monastic community, this work felt all-encompassing, creating a basis for deep friendships. In my work on mindfulness in the United Kingdom, the emphasis on self-compassion in each of the shared practices in which I participated transformed the ways in which I related to myself, effectively softening my self-talk. And the central focus on mental health as "something we all have" and as the basis for discussions about mindfulness informed relationships that were reciprocally gentle, supportive, and kind. In both contexts, my own affective responses to fieldwork and the affective qualities of my relationships with others *became* my ethnographic work, leading me to more directly connect and resonate with the affective experiences I shared with others. Without overly generalizing from personal experience to collective understanding, by committing myself to the affective values and practices of those with whom I worked, I cautiously developed some awareness of the affective qualities of meditative practices and why and how they mattered to people.

Accordingly, meditation practised as affective ethnographic method can have multiple effects based on context. The anthropologist who commits herself to the affective practices at the heart of a given tradition will necessarily be transformed by the experience. Attending to others through practice-based affective resonance reveals the value and place of emotion in cultural life more broadly and the culturally particular efforts that people make to live well. Affective engagement has multiple effects on anthropology too: for the anthropologists themselves, for relationships in the field, and for anthropology as a professional discipline. It is personally affecting and transformative. It enables all who are a part of it to attend to the cultural particularity and meaning of affective experience, and in that newly learned attending lies a methodological opportunity for anthropology. As this volume demonstrates, focusing on our interlocutors' affective practices opens up new possibilities for ethnographic exploration. In my meditation practice-as-research I was both affected and transformed by meditative experiences and shared affective resonances created interpersonal points of connection. Focusing on the affective practices of my interlocutors in turn transformed what anthropology could uncover, pointing to how affective practices, like meditation, can serve as resources for ethnographic innovation.

NOTE

1 While monastic Thailand seems to be worlds apart from mindful Britain, the two also share genealogical roots, similarities, and interests. The lay meditation movement that developed in Southeast Asia in the early twentieth century drew on the *Mahāsatipatthāna Sutta* (The Greater Discourse on the Four Foundations of Mindfulness). Reformist meditation masters argued that insight (vipassanā) meditation techniques required only a minimum level of concentration. In South and Southeast Asia, vipassanā meditation was presented to the laity as a way to find relief from worldly concerns. As this movement developed, German-born Sri-Lankan monk Nyaponika Thera (1901–94) interpreted mindfulness as "bare attention," a quality of awareness which could act as a counter to the constant reinforcement of habitual mental patterns. In the 1970s, this interpretation of mindfulness as a method for psychological development radically informed the newly formed Insight Meditation tradition in the United Kingdom and, subsequently, the development of therapeutic mindfulness (see Cook 2021).

REFERENCES

Cassaniti, Julia. 2015. *Living Buddhism: Mind, Self and Emotion in a Thai Community*. Ithaca, NY: Cornell University Press.
Cook, Joanna. 2010a. *Meditation in Modern Buddhism: Renunciation and Change in Thai Monastic life*. Cambridge, UK: Cambridge University Press.
Cook, Joanna. 2010b. "Ascetic Practice and Participant Observation, or, the Gift of Doubt and Incompletion in Field Experience." In *Emotions in the Field: The Psychology and Anthropology of Fieldwork Experience*, edited by James Davies and Dimitrina Spencer, 239–65. Stanford, CA: Stanford University Press.
Cook, Joanna. 2021. "Mindfulness and Resilience in Britain: A Genealogy of the 'Present Moment'." *Journal of Global Buddhism* 22 (1): 83–103. https://doi.org/10.5281/zenodo.4727573.
Cook, Joanna. 2023. *Making a Mindful Nation: Mental Health and Governance in the 21st Century*. Princeton, NJ: Princeton University Press.
Cook, Joanna, and Julia Cassaniti. 2022. "Mindfulness and Culture: An Introduction." *Anthropology Today* 38 (2): 1–3. https://doi.org/10.1111/1467-8322.12704.
Penman, Danny. 2011. "Free Mindfulness Meditation of the Body and Breath." http://franticworld.com/free-mindfulness-meditation-of-the-body-and-breath/.

Practice 5

Making: A Robot's Homecoming

ELENA KNOX

I make artworks that incorporate robotic technologies. In 2016, I became the first artist to be awarded a fellowship by the Japan Society for the Promotion of Science, and towards the end of the fellowship period a colleague and I undertook a research trip from our base in Tokyo through rural Japan, then Norway, and on and up to the world's northernmost settlement, Longyearbyen on the Svalbard archipelago. Here, at seventy-eight degrees latitude and eight hundred miles from the North Pole, in the midwinter pitch-dark, we created the art film *Protective Seal*[1] featuring Japanese therapy robot PARO, which is modelled after the harp seal.

Protective Seal's story evolves over seven slow, video-looping chapters, screened simultaneously in a large, darkened space. In the story, the little seal-shaped robot becomes aware, in its safe home in Tokyo, that seals in the Arctic Circle are suffering from the effects of global warming.[2] Concerned, it sets out solo, travelling northward via the cold mountainous regions of Japan where it encounters and "interviews" village elders about their perceptions of the shifting state of the natural world. Much further on, in a Scandinavian aquatic museum, PARO attempts to communicate with live, tamed seals. Finally, after great effort, PARO reaches wild harp seal habitat: the Arctic's ice, snow, and round-the-clock winter night. Here, again, PARO listens to tales told by local elders in response to such prompts as How have you seen the land changing over your lifetime? and What has been the role of humans, and machines, in these changes?

PARO's expedition is a pilgrimage "home," of sorts. It is an enormous, poignant adventure for a small robot that has never even been outdoors.

P5.1. PARO on location shoot of *Protective Seal*.
Photo by Lindsay Webb.

Protective Seal

PARO is a companion robot: a "mental commitment robot" (AIST 2006) developed in Tokyo by Takanori Shibata. It was named World's Most Therapeutic Robot by Guinness World Records in 2002. It does not speak but responds to touch, sound, light, and environment, and periodically it emits baby seal squeaks. Its rudimentary artificial intelligence is intended to promote a special bond with its user.

The Arctic is a crucial zone for futurists. It is the crux of our environmental crisis: ice-melt, permafrost thaw, atmospheric carbon release, and ozone depletion (Witze 2020). It is a cradle of chronic, proliferating repercussions. Longyearbyen, in fact, is the fastest-warming town in the world (Dickie 2021). But very few people live there, and like PARO, its flora and fauna cannot enunciate directly their experience to us humans who perpetrate such serious injury to all beings, everywhere. By means of PARO's sited presence and fictive concern, *Protective Seal* offers its viewers a vicarious encounter with this largely unobserved ecological predicament, affectively articulating what artist Lynette Wallworth (2016) has called "the urgent unwitnessed."

Wallworth's immersive artworks and virtual reality films, made in collaboration with Indigenous peoples in remote Australia, Mongolia, and the Brazilian Amazon, have influenced international policy in global power centres (e.g., the virtual reality film *Collisions* was shown to all delegates at a Vienna convention of the Commission of the Comprehensive Nuclear Test Ban Treaty Organization), inspiring activism and expediating real social reform (Groves 2016; ACMI 2019). She describes her creative output as providing holistic experiences that are felt and remembered on a "cellular" level and explains that to facilitate for her viewer a sense of personal transformation that foments a *changed mind*, she must conceptualize "not just the subject of the work, but how to bring people inside it … so I don't have to explain to you someone's right to live, an environment's right to live" (World Economic Forum 2015, 0:40–41, 3:02–09). "The heart opens a different channel," she says (Baum 2020). Along that channel one is psychosomatically, ideologically, and, quite possibly, physically moved.

In the course of my extended film, PARO listens to long-term residents of both the high Arctic and the Japanese Alps as they reveal first-hand experiences and memories of their homelands. PARO's purpose-built ability to calm anxiety and entice emotional responses from interlocutors helped me elicit from these residents a range of accounts of human endeavour. The robot's disarming zoomorphism and its signification of future (machine creature/harbinger of artificial intelligence [AI]) combined to draw out from older farmers and coal miners[3] their particular hopes and fears, as well as their situated practical knowledge in contexts of survival and outdoor work, as they held the strange, animated, somehow nostalgic newcomer in their arms or regaled it with histories and comparisons as it sat blinking and wiggling on a tea table.

I found that deploying PARO could bring interviewees and the interviews' subsequent observers into expressive alignment with "the work," rather than their simply being aware of its topic or cause. But, I wondered further, can this felt state encourage us to identify with the plight of non-anthropomorphized environs, perhaps linking us back into a oneness or holism from which perspective we are compelled to take and provide more care? PARO's professional success as a therapy robot has been achieved primarily with people with dementia. Correspondingly, and despite the individualistic convictions and recollections revealed in *Protective Seal*'s ethnography, we humans have a certain *collective* dementia about climate change: we resist formally acknowledging its onset; we cannot keep in mind the various scares and

P5.2. PARO and Elena Knox on location shoot of *Protective Seal*.
Photo by Lindsay Webb.

facts long enough to sustain cooperative action; we do not learn from history but repeat ourselves. In Longyearbyen, for instance, "[m]ost young newcomers leave within seven years – far greater turnover than in any municipality on the mainland. The growing lack of generational memory makes the community less cohesive and therefore less resilient to the environmental changes unfolding" (Dickie 2021, 51).

One could also say that the climate itself is becoming demented. In its proven therapeutic capacity, PARO is a device developed for palliative function: for some people it can improve the quality of their last times on Earth, providing, with its impression of sentience, something to care for (i.e., a robotic seal house pet). Might this digital palliation be applicable to planet Earth more holistically? Might the action and/or affect of care, while improving quality in an ailing, forgetful life, resonate outward beyond one weakening pulse as exponentially reciprocal and reciprocated? One interpretation of *Protective Seal* is that PARO, a machine in animal shape, goes to the seasonally sunless north pole on a mission to give a planet that has forgotten its fundamental planetary needs through worshipping technology above nature *something to care for* that it still understands. PARO's embodied hybridity – fetishized gadget with nostalgic naïveté – might bridge the technology–nature gap and provide a novel impetus to environmental healing. Perhaps, in a sequel to this story, PARO may trigger the demented ecology to rebalance by helping it remember things it once knew.

Existing Together in Commensurate Sentience

Within any definition of life, borderline cases illuminate new ways of understanding phenomenological and techno-industrial change. Generally accepted requisites for life (e.g., energy transformation, reproduction, response to stimuli, continual change of state until death) can hypothetically extend to weather, fire, pollution, and software programs. Life sciences are therefore not just scientific but also cultural pursuits executed in a partisan, grey, and fuzzy penumbra. Many Eastern and Indigenous philosophies recognize live non-humans, and non-live matter and phenomena, as sentient "beings." Often, this approach signals affective care and respect for objects and environs. PARO is fuzzy, it is a machine, it is a friend, it is changing and learning and sensing and responding to stimuli – so on our trek to the polar region, I collaborated with it to probe not just environmental variation but also the questions: Who and what is sentient? How should we ethically regard and esteem this quality? As AI develops, what is reality for a technology? What is self? What is being-with-others?

Imaginatively adopting PARO's point of view, we observe PARO's effect on human subjects, noting their perception of the robot's comparative sentience. We imagine that PARO has subjective phenomenological experience (*qualia*[4]), and we extend this poetic assumption to the harp seal's environs, the warming Barents Sea around Svalbard, and then to the whole Earth. The project *Protective Seal* finds in the seal-mimetic robot a relatable medium for the theorization of sentient phenomena and a way in which to communicate these subjects to the public. To encourage climate action, perhaps art-based zoomorphism or anthropomorphism can reach us where bald facts, logic, and appeals to physics, chemistry, biology, and so on cannot. Using PARO creatively as an active medium or go-between helps us to assess/address the semi-personified environment's qualia, emotions, and entropic trauma. The creative inquiry of the project thus seeks an enlightening sentience in the Arctic.

Implications of Fieldwork by a Robot

Ensuring the planet's viable future entails assessment of both threats and benefits to organic life stemming from increased reliance on machines. *Protective Seal* draws on data from special research facilities on Svalbard. Chapter 7 of the film closes with webcam footage of atmospheric monitoring from the Zeppelin Observatory, located in the Norwegian Polar Institute's remote outpost of Ny-Ålesund. This footage, like the project's ethnographic interviews, expresses change over time but does so instead through the "eyes" of a machine technology. The robot PARO is closer in ontology to these webcams than to its human interviewees. Yet, it induces gentle affect in such a way as to suggest stories, human- or animal-scale timelines and effects, and possibilities of behavioural modification. All technical modification is behavioural in origin.

The Svalbard and Jan Mayen archipelago is in a special geopolitical category. Demilitarized international territory stewarded by Norway, it remains a visa-free zone where all nationalities have an equal right to live and/or conduct business (although its health and welfare supports only serve those who would be eligible for them in Norway; Reuters 2006). In this unique place with its limited infrastructure, the borders of existence are strained and compromised. Regarding birth, there is no perinatal care: expectant mothers are removed to the mainland. Regarding death, there is no eldercare, hospice, or palliative care and, due to permafrost, no coffin burial. PARO, already a visa-free being,[5] is not immune to weather, malfunction, or decomposition over time, but it will not have the same issues with these as do organic beings, who are born and nationalized, die and decompose.

We are looking ahead to times in which machine and bio-tech subjectivity and rights will be sharply polemicized points of international law as they intersect with, contest, and refute bio-logic and stages in a human life. The emergent existence of hybrid and so-called artificial life is a complicating layer in an already multidimensional envirotechnological state of affairs. Fusing robotics, storytelling, anthropological accounts, and futuristic visions, *Protective Seal* invites its audience to consider this new frontier from a speculative perspective of how a notionally northerly native robot "feels."

NOTES

1 Japanese title: あざらし話. For lists of collaborators and funding sources, see elenaknox.com/seal.
2 In 2011, more than two hundred seals were stranded along the Arctic coast in a mass "mortality event," their symptoms consistent with ultraviolet radiation burns. See Wright (2013).

3 In the Japanese Alps most households are connected to the farming culture, which primarily produces rice but also vegetables, fruit, and a famous variety of pork. On Svalbard, the "traditional" commerce is in mining, although tourism has risen over the years (and fallen again since the COVID-19 pandemic).
4 Qualia can be thought of as qualitative characteristics, or sense data, as explicated – and contested – by, for example, Brockman and Minsky (1998), Chalmers (1995), and Dennett (2002 [1998]).
5 PARO has been bestowed family registration status, called *koseki*, in Japan. See, for example, Robertson (2014).

REFERENCES

ACMI – Your museum of screen culture. 2019. "Shamanic Visions in VR: Lynette Wallworth Talks About Emmy Award Winning 'Awavena.'" Uploaded 4 April. YouTube, video, 52:18. youtube.com/watch?v =zIM8mOYvPec.
AIST (National Institute of Advanced Industrial Science and Technology). 2006. "What is a Mental Commitment Robot?" paro.jp/english/about.html.
Baum, Caroline. 2020. "Is Lynette Wallworth Our Most Influential Filmmaker?" *Sydney Morning Herald*, 6 August. smh.com.au/culture /art-and-design/is-lynette-wallworth-our-most-influential-filmmaker -20200721-p55e3h.html.
Brockman, John, and Marvin Minsky. 1998. "Consciousness is a Big Suitcase: A Talk with Marvin Minsky." *Edge Foundation*. edge.org/3rd_culture /minsky/index.html.
Chalmers, David. 1995. "Absent Qualia, Fading Qualia, Dancing Qualia." *Consc.net*. consc.net/papers/qualia.html.
Dennett, Daniel. [1988] 2002. "Quining Qualia." In *Philosophy of Mind: Classical and Contemporary Readings*, edited by David Chalmers, 226–46. Oxford: Oxford University Press.
Dickie, Gloria. 2021. "The Polar Crucible." *Scientific American* 324 (6): 44–53.
Groves, Dan. 2016. "Filmmaker Lynette Wallworth to Take Nuclear Test Ban Cause to Global Forum." *Forbes*, 8 June. forbes.com/sites/dongroves /2016/06/08/filmmaker-to-take-nuclear-test-ban-cause-to-global-forum.
Reuters. 2006. "Visa-Free Norwegian Islands a Haven for Migrants." *Dawn*, 5 July. dawn.com/news/200012/visa-free-norwegian-islands-a-haven -for-migrants.
Robertson, Jennifer. 2014. "Human Rights Vs. Robot Rights: Forecasts from Japan." *Critical Asian Studies* 46 (4): 571–98. doi.org/10.1080/14672715.2014 .960707.

Wallworth, Lynette. 2016. "Finding Storytellers for the Stories That Need to be Told." *Sundance Institute*, 28 April. sundance.org/blogs/program-spotlight/finding-storytellers-for-the-stories-that-need-to-be-told.

Witze, Alexandra. 2020. "Rare Ozone Hole Opens Over the Arctic – And It's Big." *Nature News*, 27 March. nature.com/articles/d41586-020-00904-w. doi.org/10.1038/d41586-020-00904-w.

World Economic Forum. 2015. "Visions of Storytelling: Immersive Storytelling | Lynette Wallworth." Uploaded 11 March. YouTube, video, 16:39. youtube.com/watch?v=1M22WaL6nB8.

Wright, Bruce. 2013. "Sunburned Arctic Seals." Presentation at Contemporary Problems of Oriental Studies 5th International Conference, the Far Eastern State University of Humanities, Khabarovsk, Russia, May. environmentalaska.us/ultraviolet-radiation-uv.html.

Dedication

May this volume be an invitation to readers to, like the many interlocutors to whom it is indebted, cultivate affect toward creativity, uncovering, and mutually constructive critique.

– Daniel White, Emma E. Cook, and Andrea De Antoni

Acknowledgments

This volume has an expansive authorship. It encompasses all its contributors, which is why we feature them on the cover, as well as those listed here. It includes longtime mentors, more recent collaborating colleagues, and, most of all, our interlocutor partners in ethnographic research and production. This volume is therefore a constellation of myriad connections spanning and, we hope, *bridging* generations. We therefore consider all of those listed here, and more we could not include, as important and intimate members of our communal authorship.

Formative mentors who shaped early threads of this volume include Anne Allison, Tarek Elhaik, James D. Faubion, Paul Hansen, Elvin Hatch, Joy Hendry, Chris Kelty, Allan Grapard, Hannah Landecker, David Leheny, George Marcus, Dolores Martinez, Tanaka Masakazu, Nahal Naficy, Valerie Olson, Massimo Raveri, Glenda Roberts, Mitch Sedgwick, and Christine Yano. All the contributors to this volume have also served as mentors in one capacity or another, many at early stages of their formative careers. Among the most recent mentors, whose approaches to community research influenced final stages of editing, include a powerful team of community health workers, navigators, and cultural practitioners at Kōkua Kalihi Valley in Honolulu, Hawaiʻi, including David Derauf, Michael Epp, Kuʻulei Freed, Meagan Inada, Casey Jackson, Puni Jackson, Jesse Lipman, Kaʻōhua Lucas, Kanoa O'Connor, and the entire team of caretakers at Hoʻoulu ʻĀina.

Many colleagues whose formal work and informal conversations contributed to inspire this volume and its ideas include Allison Alexy, Thomas Csordas, Paul Dumouchel, Diana Espírito Santo, Kathryn Goldfarb, Miho Ishii, Ayako Iwatani, Susan Lepselter, Andrea Muehlebach, Sasha Newell, Ryōko Nishii, Nitzan Shoshan, Shunsuke Nozawa, Geoffrey White, Tadahi Yanai, and a large group of affect scholars working in the Affective Societies group at the Free University of

Berlin. We are also deeply indebted to four reviewers of this volume who offered incisive, extensive, and encouraging feedback. We also thank the members of the Emosense Reading Group hosted at Kyoto University.

Our friends, colleagues, collaborators, and interlocutors in the field are also co-producers of this volume's ideas. We thank these close partners, including Tomomi Akagi, Hirofumi Katsuno, Bungen Ōi, the team and participants at Atopicco, and the medical practitioners who collaborate with exorcists in Italy.

The editors also thank the stellar team at the University of Toronto Press for their sustained support for this project and their professionalism through an extensive process of review and produdction, including Jodi Lewchuk, Marilyn McCormack, Aditi Parikh, and Sathya Shree.

Finally, the editors are also indebted deeply to each other, and to their personal partners and family members whose support often becomes a foundation and precondition for academic work. These include Arlyn, Patti, and Hiroko White, the Cook family, Kohei Yamazaki, the De Antoni family, and Ran Muratsu who, in addition to being a partner, is also an inspiring anthropologist working on affect.

Contributors

Marié Abe is an ethnomusicologist and an active performing musician with ongoing ethnographic commitments in Japan, Okinawa, Ethiopia, and the United States. She is an associate professor of ethnomusicology in the Department of Music at the University of California, Berkeley. She is the author of *Resonances of Chindon-ya: Sounding Space and Sociality in Contemporary Japan* (Wesleyan University Press, 2018), which has been translated into Japanese (Sekai Shisōsha, 2023). Committed to public ethnomusicology, she considers musical performance, curatorial practice, media, and community engagement as integral to her scholarship. In 2008, she co-produced the Peabody Award–winning National Public Radio program *Squeezebox Stories*, an audio documentary on the social histories of the accordion in multicultural California, funded by the California Council for the Humanities. As a curator and artistic director, Marié founded and organized the Boston University Global Music Festival in Boston (2018–23), an annual music festival that is offered free of charge, open to the public, and accessible to all ages on the university campus.

Dominic Boyer Dominic Boyer is an anthropologist, media maker, and environmental researcher who directs the Social Design Lab at Rice University and co-Directs the Center for Coastal Futures and Adaptive Resilience (CFAR). As one of the founders of the field of Energy Humanities, he has been researching the politics of energy transition and the social dimension of climate change for many years. With Cymene Howe, he made a documentary film about Iceland's first major glacier (Okjökull) lost to climate change, *Not Ok: A Little Movie about a Small Glacier at the End of the World* (2018). In August 2019, together with Icelandic collaborators they installed a memorial plaque to Okjökull's passing, an event that was covered by thousands of news organizations around the world, prompting *The Economist* to create their first-ever obituary for a non-human. The author of nine books and volumes and more than 100 research articles, Boyer's latest book is *No More Fossils* (University Minnesota Press, 2023), an analysis of the fossil gerontocracy that seeks to hold us in its ecocidal grasp. His latest design project is the Global Glacier Casualty List, a dynamic storytelling platform to raise awareness about what the world loses as glaciers vanish.

Nichole Payne (Nichole Carelock) is by day a civic anthropologist building accessible government services for vulnerable populations; by night she dreams of ways to subvert canon literature. Hailed as "incandescent" by the *Washington Post*, Nikki Payne's debut novel *Pride and Protest* was a Phenomenal Book Club pick and was selected by the Library of Congress to represent the District of Columbia for the National Book Festival. Featured in the *New York Times*, NPR, *Elle*, *Oprah Daily*, and BuzzFeed, Nikki Payne is writing Black women into their happily ever after.

Joanna Cook is a professor in anthropology at University College London. Her ethnographic research in Thailand and the United Kingdom focuses on meditation practice and why it matters to people. She is the author of *Meditation in Modern Buddhism: Renunciation and Change in Thai Monastic Life* (Cambridge University Press, 2010) and *Making a Mindful Nation: Mental Health and Governance in the 21st Century* (Princeton University Press, 2023). She is also the coeditor of *An Anthropology of Intellectual Exchange* (Berghahn Books, 2023), *Mindfulness and Culture* (Anthropology Today, 2022), *Unsettling Anthropologies of Care* (Anthropology and Humanism, 2020), *The State We're In: Reflecting on Democracy's Troubles* (Berghahn Books, 2016), *Detachment: Essays on the Limits of Relational Thinking* (Manchester University Press, 2015), and *Southeast Asian Perspectives on Power* (Routledge, 2012).

Emma E. Cook is a professor in modern Japanese studies at Hokkaido University. She is a socio-cultural anthropologist whose research currently focuses on exploring how the individual and social intersect, interact, and are embodied and how cultural conceptions of food, food sharing, health, illness, and the body affect experiences of food allergies. A monograph provisionally titled *Risking Care, Difference, and Responsibility: Food Allergies in Japan* is in progress. Previous research focused on irregular labour and the construction of masculinities. Her publications include a monograph, *Reconstructing Adult Masculinities: Part-Time Work in Contemporary Japan* (Routledge, 2016); an edited volume with Allison Alexy, *Intimate Japan: Ethnographies of Closeness and Conflict* (University of Hawai'i, 2018); the sixth edition of Joy Hendry's textbook, *Understanding Japanese Society* (Routledge, 2026); and articles in *Culture, Medicine and Psychiatry; Asian Anthropology*; and *Social Science Japan Journal*, among others.

Timothy P.A. Cooper is an anthropologist of ethics and comparative media. He is currently a Smuts Research Fellow in Commonwealth Studies at the Centre of South Asian Studies in the Department of Politics and International Studies, a College Postdoctoral Research Associate at Jesus College, and an Affiliated Lecturer at the Department of Social Anthropology, at the University of Cambridge. His first book *Moral Atmospheres: Islam and Media in a Pakistani Marketplace* (Columbia University Press, 2024) won the Claremont Prize for the Study of Religion. His work has appeared in *Comparative Studies in Society and History, American Ethnologist, HAU,* and *the Journal of the Royal Anthropological Institute*. He has also disseminated his research beyond the academy in the organization of a major international retrospective on Pakistani film at the British Film Institute, radio documentaries, and the production of four films screened at international festivals.

Andrea De Antoni is a program-specific associate professor of sociocultural anthropology at Kyoto University. His ethnographic research concentrates on contemporary Japan, with comparative projects in Italy and Austria. His fields of inquiry include experiences with spirits and social suffering, particularly in relation to the perception of space and place (places related to death, the afterlife, and haunted places), rumours and discrimination, the construction of social memory and tradition, tourism and commodification, spirit/demonic possession, exorcism, and religious/spiritual healing. He also conducts theoretical work on the anthropology of the body, the perception of the environment, and affect and emotions. He has published widely in both English and Japanese.

Cymene Howe is a professor of anthropology at Rice University specializing in ecosocial phenomena and more-than-human worlds. Her most recent books include *Ecologics: Wind and Power in the Anthropocene* (Duke University Press, 2019), *Anthropocene Unseen* (Punctum, 2020), and *Solarities: Elemental Encounters and Refractions* (Punctum, 2023). Her research has been funded by the National Science Foundation, Fulbright, and the Mellon Foundation and she has been awarded The Berlin Prize for transatlantic dialogue in the arts, humanities, and public policy as well as a Rockefeller Foundation Bellagio Residency. She is coproducer of the documentary film *Not Ok: A Little Movie about a Small Glacier at the End of the World* (2018); the memorial for Okjökull, the first funeral for a glacier fallen to climate change (2019); and the world's first glacier graveyard (2024) and Global Glacier Casualty List. Her ongoing research focuses on the social impacts of glacier loss and sea-level rise in coastal communities, and she is currently at work on a book entitled *The Elemental Turn*.

Elena Knox is a media/performance artist, and scholar. Her artworks present ultra-contemporary scenarios where humans live in deep enmeshment with synthesized things, and her writing appears in literary and academic publications internationally. Knox won the Dean's Medal for her PhD at the University of New South Wales Australia Art & Design and a Japan Society for the Promotion of Science fellowship from the Government of Japan. She is an adjunct researcher at Waseda University, Tokyo. Her work can be found at elenaknox.com

Catherine Lutz is the Thomas J. Watson Jr. Family Professor Emerita of Anthropology and International Studies at Brown University, where she co-founded the Costs of War Project. She is the author of *Unnatural Emotions*; *Homefront: A Military City and the American Twentieth Century*; *Reading National Geographic* (with Jane Collins); *Carjacked*; and *Schooled* (with Anne Fernandez). She is also the editor of *Language and the Politics of Emotion* (with Lila Abu-Lughod); *War and Health* (with Andrea Mazzarino); and *The Empire of Bases* and other work on security and militarization, gender violence, emotional life, photography, education, and transportation. She has also consulted with the United Nations on sexual exploitation and abuse among peacekeepers and with the government of Guam on the US military's environmental and social impact. She is a past president of the American Ethnological Society and has been a Guggenheim Fellow and a Radcliffe Fellow.

George E. Marcus is Distinguished Professor of Anthropology and founder in 2006 of the Center for Ethnography at the University of California, Irvine. He was chair for twenty-five years of a distinctive department of anthropology at Rice University. He has explored affect as a dimension and source of innovation in ethnographic research in such volumes of collaborative participation as *Writing Culture* (University of California, 1986), *Anthropology as Cultural Critique* (University of Chicago, 1986), *Designs for an Anthropology of the Contemporary* (Duke University Press, 2008), *Fieldwork Is Not What It Used to Be* (Cornell

University Press, 2009), and *Ethnography By Design: Scenographic Experiments in Fieldwork* (Routledge, 2019). His original project of fieldwork was in the Kingdom of Tonga before which he was sensitized to affect in the field by Robert I. Levy's magisterial work on the Tahitians.

William Mazzarella is the Neukom Family Professor of Anthropology at the University of Chicago. He is the author of *Shoveling Smoke: Advertising and Globalization in Contemporary India* (Duke University Press, 2003), *Censorium: Cinema and the Open Edge of Mass Publicity* (Duke University Press, 2013), and *The Mana of Mass Society* (University of Chicago, 2017). With Eric Santner and Aaron Schuster, he is the co-author of *Sovereignty, Inc: Three Inquiries in Politics and Enjoyment* (University of Chicago, 2020), and with Raminder Kaur, he is the co-editor of *Censorship in South Asia: Cultural Regulation from Sedition to Seduction* (Indiana University Press, 2009). He is also the editor of *K D Katrak: Collected Poems* (Paperwall Media and Publishing, 2016).

Yael Navaro is a professor of social, political, and psychological anthropology at the University of Cambridge and a fellow and director of studies at Newnham College. Her research addresses politics, the state, and violence and its aftermaths, with a specific focus on affect, subjectivity, and the emotions. Regionally, her research has focused on social and political life in Turkey and Cyprus. Among her publications are *Faces of the State: Secularism and Public Life in Turkey* (Princeton University Press, 2002); *The Make-Believe Space: Affective Geography in a Postwar Polity* (Duke University Press, 2012); and *Reverberations: Violence Across Time and Space* (University of Pennsylvania Press, 2021). She is also co-convener of the "Archives of the Disappeared: Discipline and Method Amidst Ruin" Research Network, which has sought new conceptual frameworks and interdisciplinary methodologies for the study of spaces associated with annihilation, erasure, disappearance, and their denial.

Jamaica Heolimeleikalani Osorio is a Kanaka Maoli wahine artist/activist/scholar/educator/storyteller born and raised in Pālolo Valley, Hawai'i. She is an associate professor of Indigenous and Native Hawaiian politics at the University of Hawai'i; a three-time national poetry champion, subject of an award-winning film, *This Is the Way We Rise*; co-writer of the revolutionary virtual reality film *On the Morning You Wake (To the End of the World)*; and author of the award-winning book *Remembering Our Intimacies: Moʻolelo, Aloha ʻĀina, and Ea* (University of Minnesota, 2021). She believes that aloha ʻāina can save the world.

Ana Y. Ramos-Zayas is the Frederick Clifford Ford Professor in the Program in Ethnicity, Race, and Migration and Professor of Anthropology and American Studies at Yale University. She is the author of *Parenting Empires: Class, Whiteness and the Moral Economy of Privilege in Latin America* (Duke University Press, 2020); *Street Therapists: Class, Race, and Neoliberal Personhood in Latino Newark* (University of Chicago Press, 2012); and *National Performances: Class, Race, and Space in Puerto Rican Chicago* (University of Chicago Press, 2003). She has also edited and co-authored volumes on affect, race, the politics of citizenship, and critical race theory. Her geographical focus spans Brazil, Puerto Rico, and US Latinx populations.

Yana Stainova is an interdisciplinary scholar interested in art, migration, and the lived experience of violence in Latin America. She is the author of *Sonorous Worlds: Musical Enchantment in Venezuela* (University of Michigan Press, 2021), an ethnography of young Venezuelan musicians whose musical practices create worlds that escape, rupture, and critique dominant structures of power through modes of enchantment. Her work also appears in *American Anthropologist, Current Anthropology, Anthropology and Humanism, Anthropological Quarterly,* and *Latin American and Caribbean Ethnic Studies* and is featured at www.yanastainova.com. She holds a PhD in anthropology from Brown University and is an associate professor of anthropology at McMaster University.

Kathleen Stewart writes ethnographic experiments to approach the composition of emergent worldings. Her books include *A Space on the Side of the Road: Cultural Poetics in an 'Other' America* (Princeton University Press, 1996), *Ordinary Affects* (Duke University Press, 2007), *The Hundreds*, co-authored with Lauren Berlant (Duke University Press, 2019), and *Worlding* (in preparation). At the University of Texas at Austin, she teaches on affect, the ordinary, the senses, modes of engaged curiosity, and writing as a form of theory. She has published more than one hundred pieces in a range of a scholarly and creative venues and has been the recipient of fellowships from the National Endowment for the Humanities, the School of American Research, the Institute for the Humanities at the University of California, Irvine, the Rockefeller Foundation, and the Center for Cultural Studies at the University of California, Santa Cruz.

Thomas Stodulka is a professor of social and cultural anthropology, with a special focus on psychological anthropology, and director of the Professional School for Visual Anthropology, Media and Documentary

Practice, at the University of Münster. His work focuses on the interplay between affect and emotion, childhood and youth, mental health and illness, and environment and education in South-East Asia. His English-language books include *Coming of Age on the Streets of Java* (Transcript, 2017), *Affective Dimensions of Fieldwork and Ethnography* (Springer, 2019), and *Feelings at the Margins* (Campus, 2014), and he has published special issues and edited volumes on futures of psychological anthropology, the senses, affect and emotions in the field and writing, and the anthropology of affect and emotions. His enthusiasm for collaboration manifests in the establishment of the European Network for Psychological Anthropology and his role as book series and journal co-editor.

Daniel White is an associate fellow at the Leverhulme Centre for the Future of Intelligence at the University of Cambridge. He researches the relationship between emotion, technology, and the politics of wellbeing, with a focus on Japan and the Asia-Pacific. He is the author of *Administering Affect: Pop-Culture Japan and the Politics of Anxiety* (Stanford University Press, 2022), which won a Francis L.K. Hsu Honorable Mention award. His current research includes collaborative projects on artificial emotional intelligence, contemplative technologies, and healing land-human relations in Japan and the Asia-Pacific. His publications can be found in the journals *Cultural Anthropology*, the *Journal of the Royal Anthropological Institute*, and on his online project page at modelemotion.org.

Index

activism, 15–17, 238–41
advocacy, 132; as action, 133, 135, 143, 146–7; affective practices of, 133–4, 137–40, 147; in climate awareness, 15–16, 271; in food allergies, 132–41; and knowledge, 110, 112–13, 122–4; role of empathy, 133, 135–6, 142–3, 147; role of feelings, 133–4, 135, 142–3, 147, 125–7, 147; role of play, 133–4, 146–7
affect: affective arrangements, 135, 140, 145; affective attunements, 112, 122, 124–5; affective practices, 3, 124, 127, 264–6; affective resonances, 140; affective scholarship, 184–5, 199–200; as answer, 33, 75; as cultural critique, 46–51; distinction with emotion, 21–2, 38–40, 215–17; as ethical response, 136, 142, 147; genealogies of, 36–9; as method, 39–42, 50–2n6–7, 66–67, 92–101, 109–10, 113, 126, 198–201, 207–10, 264–6; and multimodality, 13–19, 163–9; as public affect, 175–9; and race, 26, 42–3, 52n8–9, 62, 84, 99–101, 244–8; in religion, 53n14, 73–5, 157–79; in robotics 33–4, 39–42; theories of 4–6, 14–15, 23–4, 34–43, 48–9, 52n8, 62, 65–6, 206–9, 215–22, 226, 230, 239–40
Ahmed, Sara, 219–21, 244–5
anamnesis, 117–18, 121, 125
Anthropology as Cultural Critique, 6, 43–4, 46–7
Arctic Circle, 268–73
artificial intelligence. *See* robotics
Asian American men, 246

biomedicine, biomedical, 109, 110, 112, 114, 118–20, 122–6
Black women, 245–8
Brazil. *See* Ipanema
Buddhism, 8–9n1, 33–4, 41–2, 259–67; contemplative practices of 4–5

Catholic Church, 113, 114, 128
chindon–ya, 254–5
class, 85–96
commentary: as affective form, 215–24, 224–34
contemplative practices, 4–5
conviviality, 21–4
COVID–19, 79, 182–210; and affective method, 198–201; and affective traces 184–98; effects on ethnographic method, 182–4

critique, 17–18, 23–4, 26–28, 34–9, 43–51, 52n11, 113, 126–7, 206–7, 215, 219–22, 246–7
Csordas, Thomas, 22, 109, 110–13, 124, 125, 126
culture–bound syndromes, 110

decolonial, 42–6, 67, 220–2, 238
deep listening, 252–3, 257
Deleuze, Gilles, 38, 218–19
De exorcismis et supplicationibus quibusdam (DESQ), 108, 114, 115, 126, 128
diagnosis: diagnostic centre, 107; diagnostic procedure, 112–13, 116–17, 119, 123–6; diagnostic work, 111–12, 114, 117, 119, 122–7; as practice, 109, 118, 126; as process, 109–10, 126, 128n6
discernment, 118
discovery. *See* uncovering

empathy: in advocacy, 133–6, 142–3, 147; in education, 133; imaginative, 254; limits of, 142, 150n14; as method, 18, 141; as racialized affect, 99–101 (*See also* race); theories of, 4, 34–6, 100, 135, 140–2
El Condado, 84–98
El Sistema, 61–2, 67–72
embodiment, 21–3, 110–12, 122, 124, 126
emotion: anthropology of, 21–4, 36–7; diaries, 200. *See also* affect: distinction with emotion
enact, enactment, 110–12, 117–18, 122–6
environmental crisis, 15–17, 18, 269–72
Ethiopia, 255–6
experimentation, 19, 39–42
exorcism, 107–9, 113–16, 118–19, 121–2, 126–8

feeling: feeling with, 146, 150n13; leveraged to education, 135, 137, 139, 144–5. *See also* affect
fieldwork, 19–20, 41–2, 49–50, 61–8, 85–7, 99–101; after COVID-19, 182–3, 200–9; on meditation, 259–67; by a robot, 272–3; on sound 254–6
Fischer, Michael. *See Anthropology as Cultural Critique*
food allergies, 132, 134; awareness of, 135; eating out, 132, 134; education of, 139–40
Foucault, Michel, 83, 111, 125

gender, 71–3, 244–8
Great Britain, 259–60, 262–3

hadd, 172–4
haku, 235
happily ever after (HEA), 244
Harrison, Faye, 44
Hawaiʻi, 42, 235–42

idioms of distress, 110, 113
imagination: in integrating affective experience, 141, 146–7
imaginative empathy, 254
Indigenous scholarship, 42, 45, 239
Indonesia. *See* Kupang
interface, 175–7
interiority currency: ethnographic examples of, 88–92; as method 83–7; and racialized affect, 92–9
intimacy, 239
intuition (*intuición*), 61–5, 72–9; and affect, 65–7; in popular literature, 79n1
Ipanema, 84–98
Italy, 107–28

Japan, 33–4, 132–51, 254–7, 268–73

Kānaka Maoli (Native Hawaiians), 238–41
Kupang, 201–7

Las Panelas, 61–2, 68–70
Latin America, 62, 87–8; elites 85–96, 221–2
Latour, Bruno, 46–7
Lutz, Catherine, 21–4

Mauna a Wākea (movement), 237–41
Marcus, George E. *See Anthropology as Cultural Critique*
Massumi, Brian, 24, 26, 38, 215–17, 224
Mazzarella, William, 157–8, 176–7
meditation, 259–67; as affective practice, 264–6; in Britain, 259–60, 262–3; in Thailand, 261–2
mindfulness, 262–4
Mol, Annemarie 109–12, 118, 125–6
morality. *See* thresholds (moral)
mourning, 158; commemorative, 162; practicing (*azadari*), 168
Muñoz, José Esteban, 221–2
music, 61–79, 252–7; devotional, 162, 167, 169

occult, occultism, 117–18, 128
ontology, ontological, 110–13, 120–1, 124–6, 178, 200, 255–7, 260; ontological turn 52n12

Pakistan, 157–79
Pandian, Anand, 45
pandemic. *See* COVID–19
pandemic flaneur, 201–2
PARO, 268–73, 274n5
possession (spirit, demonic), 108–10, 112–15, 116–18, 120–2, 124–6, 128n7
play: as advocacy, 133–4, 146–7; as education, 136, 137–40, 144–5; serious play, 134, 136, 147, 149n3

poetics of mishearing, 256–7
Pride and Protest, 244–51
Protective Seal, 268–73
psychoanalysis, 102n11, 224
psychotherapy, 86–98, 113–15, 118–19, 121, 123
Puerto Rico. *See* El Condado

qasida, 162–70

race, 26, 42–3, 52n8–9, 62; as racialized affect, 84, 99–101; in romance literature adaptation, 244–8
recitation. *See qasida*
reflexivity, 6, 42, 42–4, 198–200, 256
regimes of truth, 111, 125
religion. *See* affect: and religion
reparative reading, 48–9
robotics, 33–4, 39–42, 268–73
romance literature, 244–7

Shiʻi Islam, 161–3, 169–72
sound, 252–7
Spinoza, Baruch, 38, 40, 218–19
Stewart, Kathleen, 14–15, 35, 43, 48, 178, 224, 229–30
Stoller, Paul, 110–1, 124
Svalbard archipelago, 268, 272–3
symptomatology: as unexplained 107, 114–15, 123, 126; of possession, 117–18

Thailand, 261–2
theory. *See* affect: theories of
therapeutic cultures, 83–4, 113–15, 118–19, 121, 123
Thirty Meter Telescope (TMT), 237, 241n2
thresholds (moral), 157–61; deliberations of, 161–3; obligations of, 172–5
Thrift, Nigel, 217–19

Tomkins, Silvan, 37
Turner, Victor, 157–8

uncovering, 3, 8, 35, 41–6, 50–1, 99, 113, 122–7, 222

Van Gennep, Arnold, 159–61
Venezuela, 61–79

zakir, 158, 163–8, 177–9

Printed and bound by CPI Group (UK) Ltd, Croydon, CR0 4YY
11/03/2026

14840907-0001